REMINISCENCES SERIES

Steam, Diesels and On-Track Machines

From Colwick to Derby via the East Coast Main Line

by
John Meredith

THE OAKWOOD PRESS

© Oakwood Press & John Meredith 2011

British Library Cataloguing in Publication Data
A Record for this book is available from the British Library
ISBN 978 0 85361 718 1

Typeset by Oakwood Graphics.
Repro by PKmediaworks, Cranborne, Dorset.
Printed by Information Press Ltd, Eynsham, Oxford.

All rights reserved. No part of this book may be reproduced or transmitted in any form or by any means, electronic or mechanical, including photocopying, recording or by any information storage and retrieval system, without permission from the Publisher in writing.

I call this photograph the 'First and the Last'. It shows ex-BR 'Britannia' class 4-6-2 No. 70013 *Oliver Cromwell* passing through Aslockton station on Sunday 10th May, 2009. Aslockton was the first station I travelled from as a child in the early 1940s and the last steam locomotive I ever saw working in BR service before the end in 1968 was *Oliver Cromwell* as it passed through Derby in July 1968 hauling a special. *Author*

Title page: This is a good example of the dangers of working on the railways especially with the civil engineer's on-track plant. The tamper is working on the down main line near Ratcliffe-on-Soar power station and on the up slow line is a passing London-bound passenger train, it could easily have been on the up main next to the machine then you would have to watch your step; although we had a lookout man you still had to keep a constant lookout when working on the machine. *Malcolm Stevenson*

Published by The Oakwood Press (Usk), P.O. Box 13, Usk, Mon., NP15 1YS.
E-mail: sales@oakwoodpress.co.uk
Website: www.oakwoodpress.co.uk

Contents

	Foreword *by Christopher James*	4
Chapter One	Starting a Life on the Lines	5
Chapter Two	Doncaster Works (The Plant)	33
Chapter Three	Back to Colwick	43
Chapter Four	Colwick and its Locomotives in the 1950s	49
Chapter Five	Travelling on a Free Pass	65
Chapter Six	Finsbury Park - The Learning Curve	87
Chapter Seven	Happy Days at Hitchin	93
Chapter Eight	Early Days at Derby	140
Chapter Nine	Working on the old C&HPR	145
Chapter Ten	Back to Derby	153
Chapter Eleven	A Few Characters	161
Chapter Twelve	Relief Work at Toton	165
Chapter Thirteen	Working on the CCE On-Track Plant	173
Chapter Fourteen	Living with a Tamping Machine	197
Chapter Fifteen	A Pioneer for Freightliners	213
Chapter Sixteen	Back to Happy Days at Derby	223
Chapter Seventeen	Working for the CM&EE	236
	Postscript	239
	Acknowledgements	240

Foreword

John Meredith was, in his own words, 'mad about railways' as a young boy so it was no surprise that when he left school at the age of 15 in 1954 he began a career on the railways with a six-year apprenticeship as a junior apprentice fitter at Colwick motive power depot, on the eastern outskirts of Nottingham.

The work at Colwick was physically hard and involved long hours in conditions which would not be allowed under today's Health & Safety regulations, but John thrived. Being the smallest and youngest at Colwick he was often sent to work in parts of the locomotives that the other fitters could not - or would not - reach, but luckily he did not suffer from claustrophobia. After his apprenticeship was completed in 1960, he was moved as a qualified fitter to a new diesel depot at Finsbury Park and then to Hitchin where he stayed for six years.

He then spent three years as a fitter in the Plant & Machinery Department at Derby which involved the maintenance of all the plant and machinery in the depot. He was sorry to miss the work on locomotives that he had enjoyed at Colwick but was pleased to find his responsibilities included the maintenance of three cranes, two of which were steam-operated.

In 1969 John was promoted to the job of shift supervisor at Beeston Freightliner terminal, but the work of the terminal was declining, and in 1971 he moved back to Derby with another promotion to the post of Nottingham Divisional on-track supervisor. Just over seven years later in June 1978 he made his last move on the railway to be statutory engineering inspector in the Chief Mechanical and Electrical Engineer's Department at Derby, but based at Nottingham.

In 1980 his 26 years as a railwayman came to an end when he was unexpectedly offered and, after some hesitation, accepted the post of head verger at Southwell Minster. He has described his 19 years in that role in his book, 'Verging on Work'.

In *Steam, Diesels and On-Track Machines* John describes the hard life that he led as a fitter, often working at night and at weekends but shining through it is his determination to get the job done as quickly as possible, often showing great resourcefulness and determination in undertaking difficult jobs himself on the spot, while others wanted to send for a breakdown crew. He also brings out the camaraderie and the good humour of his fellow workers, not to mention the practical jokes some of them liked to play on each other. After he was promoted to supervisory posts he missed the hands-on aspect of the job but knew that if he tried to get involved it would cause trouble with the unions.

As well as railways, John mentions his other interests including bellringing and church architecture, both of which he shares with his wife June.

John has an encyclopaedic knowledge of railways, especially steam locomotives and, since he stopped being a railwayman his interest has become even greater. He has travelled all over the British Isles and most of Europe seeking out and photographing trains, especially the remaining steam locomotives. He is in great demand as a speaker to clubs and societies, not just on railways, but on church architecture and bell-ringing as well.

Christopher James

Chapter One

Starting a Life on the Lines

Being a Nottinghamshire lad born and bred was bound to make me a fan of either the ex-London, Midland & Scottish (LMS) or London & North Eastern (LNER) railways and it was to the latter that I nailed my colours. I suppose living next to the old Great Northern Railway (GNR) line between Nottingham and Grantham had something to do with it.

I was introduced to the railway and its steam locomotives in the early 1940s, when at the tender age of three I was taken by train on a weekly basis from Aslockton to Nottingham Victoria, that cathedral-like station in the centre of the city - alas now just a memory, except for the old clock tower, standing amidst the ugly modern-day shops and blocks of flats. To me the locomotives appeared as large green and black snorting monsters of a bygone age, belching steam and smoke. I was to realise later that they were ex-GNR 4-4-0s and 0-6-0s, and even a 4-4-2 Atlantic thrown in for good measure.

In 1944 my family moved two stations down the line to Radcliffe-on-Trent. There my railway education began. In the early days I would lie in bed at night, and listen to the locomotives as they coasted down the bank from Saxondale Junction. The metallic sound of their side-rods carried far into the night air, especially on frosty evenings. We lived close to the line at a point where it crosses the River Trent by viaduct and bridge. In between trains, I would wait for the sound of the ex-GNR 'J52' saddle tanks as they pulled long lines of wagons out of the sidings on Spike Bank near Rectory Junction, and onto the viaduct for re-marshalling. Rectory Junction was named after the church rectory of Holme Pierrepont, just a short distance across the fields, and now the home of the National Water Sports Centre. The little locomotives would often stand waiting for several minutes, either for the road, or the passage of a train across the junction. And at times their safety valves would lift, letting out a mighty roar of steam. When we first heard it, my mother thought we had got a burst water pipe and was about to send for the plumber!

All these sounds were music to the ears of a young boy mad about railways. By the time I had reached the age of 10, I was making regular visits to the line side and the station. I was just in time to see the change over from LNER to British Railways (BR), although it was not noticeable at the time, and I well remember seeing the odd locomotive with LNER on its tender sides, even when I joined the railway in the mid-1950s.

At Radcliffe station, I soon got to know the staff: Stan with his cheery whistle and laugh, George in the booking office, and the men in the box. It was not long before I was invited in to the porters' cabin, then the booking office, where I would admire the rows of card tickets, to destinations I could only dream of ever travelling to. It was a privilege on occasions to be allowed by George to punch a ticket in the old Edmondson dating machine. All records of tickets sold, and receipts, were written down by hand in books, and kept in pigeonholes attached to the wall - all now lost in the mist of time.

Above left: The author aged three, by that time I had already taken several trips by train and it appears that I must have been quite keen on the time-keeping! *Author's Collection*

Above right: The joint Victoria station in Nottingham (GCR/GNR), opened in 1900 on Queen Victoria's birthday, with its fine facade and *porte-cochère* topped by the elegant clock tower, it's a pity that the shop had to be built in the front! Today only the clock tower remains after the station closed in the late 1960s, and the town planners developed the site into a shopping centre. *Author*

The author in 1950 with my father proudly showing off our prize Guernsey bull 'Monty'. My father was hoping that I would follow him onto the farm when I left school, but I had other ideas, you can see it in my face, which was a disappointment to him but he said he would not stand in my way. *Author's Collection*

This is where my interest in railways first began, at Aslockton station situated on the line between Grantham and Nottingham Victoria, when once a week I would be taken by my mother to Nottingham to visit my grandparents. When this photograph was taken in 1951 it was still a busy place, note the old GNR waiting room and crossing keeper's hut on the down platform, and the tall goods shed on the up side where the locomotive on the pick-up goods is seen shunting the yard, having left the rest of the train in the siding, behind the platform on the down side. *Author's Collection*

Aslockton station is still open today but very little of it is left, just a few buildings on the up platform in private use, and the GNR waiting room on the down side, the only one still in use on the line, where in the early 1940s my mother and I would wait for the train to Nottingham. Since I took this photograph in 2003 the waiting room has lost most of its glass to vandals. *Author*

A goods train hauled by Colwick-based 'K2' class 2-6-0 No. 61773 on 21st February, 1957 is on the four line section between Saxondale Junction and Radcliffe-on-Trent on the down slow road. It was these trains that I would hear when I lay in bed at night as a child wishing that I was standing on the station and taking down the numbers! *Author's Collection*

Radcliffe-on-Trent station looking east towards Grantham. Standing in the platform is an ex-LMS '2P' class 4-4-0 on a Northampton to Nottingham Victoria train in 1953. It was on these trains that we used to travel to Melton Mowbray North on market days, the service was withdrawn at the end of 1953. The old GNR waiting room is on the up platform and the station buildings on the down side, the tall building is the ticket office and beyond the rear of the train is the signal box, two places I frequented in the early 1950s. *Derek Thompson/GNR Society*

In the winter I would sit by the open coal fire, enjoying the warmth and dreaming of journeys I would make. If only I could afford it! It was strange that later in my railway career, I would work with George in the office near Nottingham Midland station. The final accolade came when I was granted permission to enter the signal box. From then on I spent many happy Saturdays watching the signalman going about his duties, helping him from time to time to pull a few levers. It was an extremely busy box, at the junction of a four-line section between Radcliffe and Saxondale. In between the many freight trains were local passengers, and in the summer months, the 'Seasiders' as we called them, to and from Skegness, Mablethorpe, Clacton, Yarmouth and Scarborough. These would sometimes have a class 'B16' 4-6-0 up front, and the others mostly hauled by 'B1' 4-6-0s, 'K2' and 'K3' 2-6-0s and interspersed by an odd 'J6' 0-6-0 or 'J39' 0-6-0.

Once a week on Saturday mornings, the local pick-up goods would call, bringing coal for the merchants and corn for the mill, a little further along the line from the station. This now gave me a chance for rides on the footplate, especially as I knew many of the drivers! Normal engines on these duties would be the ever faithful 'J52' 0-6-0STs or an ex-GNR 'J5' 0-6-0. I well remember Nos. 68768 and 65483. From time to time cattle specials would arrive, and when unloaded at the dock the cattle would be driven through the streets in the village to Trent Meadows - two or three hundred in a drove, bringing the place to a standstill.

In between all this local activity, I would make trips to Grantham to visit an uncle who worked at the locomotive sheds. Nearly always this resulted in a shed 'bash', to see as many 'A3s', 'A1s' and 'A4s' - and if lucky, a footplate ride from there to the station, on one of the locomotives changing over on an express. Southbound ones were best, as this made for a longer ride! On the occasional Tuesday in school holidays, my family and I would travel to Melton Mowbray North on market day. An LMS '2P' 4-4-0 up front made quite a change. This service finished in 1953.

My way home from school was always via the station, just in case there was anything different from the usual, maybe a Doncaster running-in turn. And to my surprise, one day I found No. 61997 *MacCailin Mor* passing through on a mixed goods. What a difference from the WD 'Austerities', 'J39s' and ex-Great Central Railway (GCR) 'O4' class. At that time the local passenger services were in the hands of the 'J6' 0-6-0s, 'K2' 2-6-0s, 'A5' 4-6-2Ts and the Grantham 'B12' 4-6-0s, which were always a joy to see. I was lucky enough to see the last of the GNR 4-4-0 'Bogies' in the shape of No. 62172.

With all this in mind, it was no wonder that when the time came for me to leave school, it was to the railway I would turn. My father had hoped that I would follow him and be a farmer, but when the careers officer paid me a visit I had already made up my mind that I wanted to work for the railway. In the summer of 1954, an interview was arranged for me with the locomotive superintendent at the motive power department at Colwick (38A). Of course like all young boys I wanted to be an engine driver! So I was sent to Peterborough for a medical, travelling on my first free pass. I set off from Radcliffe on the only through train from Nottingham Victoria to King's Cross, behind 'A5' class 4-6-2T No. 69807. At Grantham we joined up with through carriages from Lincoln, and the locomotive changed to 'A3' Pacific No. 60047

The long viaduct crossing over the Trent meadows at Radcliffe-on-Trent. On the left is the Clayton & Shuttleworth iron bridge over the river and the first three red brick arches constructed when the line opened in 1850, the rest of the viaduct is constructed in blue brick having been rebuilt from a wooden trestle type in the early 1900s. 'WD' class 2-8-0 No 90000 can be seen hauling a coal train to Peterborough on 6th July, 1955. In between trains the old GNR 'J52' class 0-6-0ST would draw their long trains off the Colwick yard Spike Bank on to the viaduct and then stand waiting for the road back into the yard, very often their safety valves would lift and it was this that my mother heard when we first moved to Radcliffe and thought that we'd got a water burst!
John Oxley/GNR Society

A peaceful scene in the centre of the village at Radcliffe-on-Trent in the early 1950s with the post office on the right. It's difficult to describe the same scene when the cattle were brought to the station in long cattle trains, unloaded and then driven through the streets to the Trent meadows to be fattened up through the winter months before being taken to the market in Nottingham. Then the shops were closed and the locals kept off the streets.
Author's Collection

Radcliffe-on-Trent station looking west toward Nottingham showing the details of the GNR foot-bridge and gas lamps, and on the left is the porters' cabin, another place I frequented quite a lot when trainspotting. *Ray Stephenson/GNR Society*

An East Coast express passing through Radcliffe-on-Trent hauled by Colwick-allocated 'B1' class 4-6-0 No. 61088 sometime in the 1950s. On the left can be clearly seen the GNR signal box. These trains were known to us as the 'sea-siders', or at least they were to the signalman and me! *T. Hepburn/Author's Collection*

The Grantham line pick-up goods running on to Spike Bank at Colwick hauled by 'J5' class 0-6-0 No 65483. In the background is Rectory Junction signal box. This locomotive was still in service when I joined the railway at Colwick in 1954 and was not scrapped until 1957, it was also one that I often rode on when it shunted the yard at Radcliffe. *Frank Berridge Collection*

Memories of trainspotting days at Grantham when I would visit my uncle, who worked at the engine shed, and if I was lucky I would sometimes get a cab ride on one of the engines doing a change over with a north- or south-bound express. Backing down on to the shed is 'A2/3' class 4-6-2 No. 60500 *Edward Thompson*. *Author*

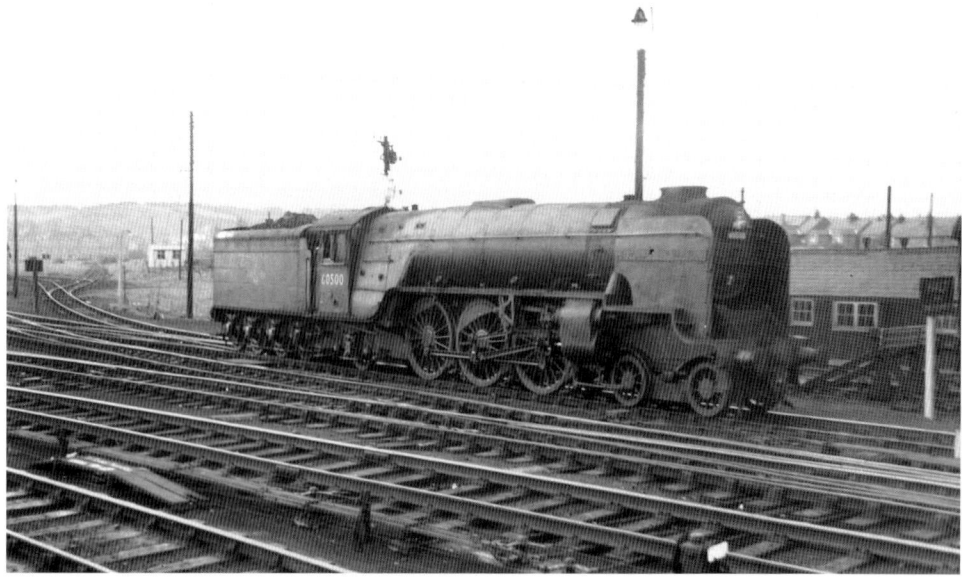

Donovan. Sitting back in my compartment, I had visions that one day it might be me up front, on the shovel, or even hands on the regulator. What dreams!

I went through the usual tests, was measured to see if I was tall enough, weighed, eyesight test, with the coloured dots in the book, to see if I could pick out certain numbers. Looking at lights on the wall, red, green, amber and white - it was obvious what that was for - plus knowing the difference between various coloured strands of wool. I passed with flying colours!

On my way home, I called off at Grantham to spend time at the platform end with my fellow trainspotters, proud of the fact that I was going to become a railwayman, and a footplate one at that. During all this excitement, I managed to lose my free pass. No doubt someone now has it as a souvenir! It took a bit of explaining when I alighted at Radcliffe, but at least they knew me.

My second interview was with the then well-known superintendent, Colonel John Blundell. He talked me out of the idea of the footplate and suggested that I become an apprentice fitter, 'More scope for you in later life, my boy'. I am not sure I agreed with him at the time. But my father made me change my mind. I joined British Railways in 1954 as junior apprentice fitter No. 1595. A railwayman at last!

Colwick motive power depot or 'The Loco', as it was known, was located inside a triangle of lines, approximately three miles east of Nottingham. To the south, the main Nottingham/Grantham Line, to the west the line to Derby via Gedling and Mapperley Tunnel. The third line ran north-west to south-east between Colwick North Junction and Rectory Junction. On this line was situated the marshalling yard, one of the largest in the region. The sheds which made up the Loco ran north to south, the open end facing north. I never could understand why GNR sheds were arranged this way. Colwick had been built by the GNR as a service and repair depot for its large fleet of locomotives, mainly used around the Nottinghamshire/Derbyshire coalfields. But later, between the wars, it had also absorbed those of the GCR as well. It is also worth noting that the London & North Western Railway (LNWR) built a shed at Colwick, a little to the east of the GNR one, for the use of its locomotives. These worked over the joint line of GNR/LNWR from the Northampton area. Mind you, its shed was constructed facing west. In later years this closed, and became a wagon repair shop, then a private engineering works.

Colwick Loco was made up of three sheds, the first one of four roads, known to us as 'Old Shed', built in 1875. To the south were the main offices, including 'Col John's'. On the east side the stores, first aid room, and at the north end the shed master's office - a place to be avoided! Above these the water tank which supplied the shed and water cranes around the yards. The water was supplied from an artesian well outside the east wall, approximately 15 ft across and 100 ft deep. A softening plant was not required. Also outside to the east was the iron store, an area for the storage of iron brake blocks, the joiner's shop, painter's shop, and a set of yard legs for lifting locomotives; this was powered by a gas engine. Later these were removed. The engine house became the maintenance fitters' workshop - a place in which I spent many happy hours.

In 1882 the Loco was further extended, with a new two-road erecting and repair shop, and an eight-road running shed, known as 'Big Shed'. The erecting shop also housed the machine bay to the south. It was here that I started my

After my interview at Colwick motive power depot I was sent to Peterborough for a medical examination where I passed with flying colours. On the way between Grantham and Peterborough the train was hauled by 'A3' class 4-6-2 No. 60047 *Donovan* and she is seen here hauling a London King's Cross-bound express and is approaching Grantham on what appears to be a special with the reporting number 646. *Author's Collection*

One of the many local trains that ran between Grantham and Nottingham with some running through to Derby Friargate via Basford North, this is one such train standing at Bingham on a Nottingham-bound local hauled by 'A5' class 4-6-2T No. 69814. *Author's Collection*

railway service. Further south came the blacksmith's shop and fitting shop, which contained the coppersmith benches and an open area for the metallers. Along the south side of the running shed were the time office and signing-on point, toilets and washing area and boilersmiths' shop.

The final extension came in 1897, when an extra four-road running shed, 'New Shed', was constructed on the west side of 'Big Shed', as well as a two-road wagon repair shop.

By the time I started in 1954, the wagon repair shop had been closed and transferred to another part of the yard. In its place was a departure board lobby, later incorporating the cleaners' foreman's office, oil stores, and more fitting shops with the mechanical foreman's office, mess rooms and boiler house. In 1912 a hot water washout system had been installed, making the boiler house quite extensive. Then came the tinsmith's shop and finally the book room. To complete the picture, outside to the west was a classroom, opened by Nigel Gresley in 1916, the sand house and running foreman's office, and in the locomotive yard were a set of wet ash pits (1923) and the coaling plant (1936), known to everyone locally as the 'Cenotaph'. There was also a 70 ft turntable and outside the erecting shop, and between the running lines of 'Big Shed', stood a wooden inspectors' office. This was to be a source of fun in later years!

The maintenance staff was upwards of 150 men, comprising fitters, mates, apprentices, boilersmiths, brick-arch men, washout men, coppersmiths, blacksmiths, white metallers, tubers, joiners, painters, tinsmiths and general labourers, plus two fitters allocated to shed maintenance. In 1954 Colwick had an allocation of 200 steam locomotives in 15 different classes.

It was this environment that I entered in fear and trepidation one cold morning in 1954, a daunting feeling to a young lad of 15, weighing 7½ stone, 5 ft tall and as thin as a rake! My first duty was to report to the assistant mechanical foreman Ken Pitts, in his office in 'New Shed'. At that moment, a six-years' apprenticeship seemed a very long time. It was not my first time in the shed, as I had been shown round at the time of my interviews. But on that morning it was big, cold, dark and very smoky. I was met by a member of the office staff and escorted to Mr Pitts' office, an overall under my arm.

It had been planned that I should spend at least six months training on each aspect of locomotive maintenance, plus six months in the main works at Doncaster and a further six with the depot maintenance gang. It did not always work out like that. Although I was still disappointed at not joining the footplate staff, I did get plenty of trips, as you will see later. After the usual filling-in of forms, I was taken away and introduced to the other apprentices, some twice my size. What had I let myself in for! Then I was placed in the machine shop, under the watchful eye of charge-hand turner, Morris Carnell. I was to work on a small lathe alongside two other apprentices, one like myself who had just started a few weeks earlier. He became a close friend and later was my best man at my wedding in 1961.

I doubt if the machine shop had changed much since the time of construction in 1882. Certainly a couple of the lathes dated from those days! Almost everything was powered by overhead line shafting, which extended through the wall to the blacksmith's and fitting shops. It was driven by a large electric motor standing in a corner, about the only modern thing at that time. The original power had been

The Colwick coaling plant constructed in 1936 and known to everyone as the 'Cenotaph', you can imagine what it was like when you had to climb to the top on a cold wet day in the winter to carry out a repair or change a dirty oily black wire rope! It was demolished in 1970. *Author's Collection*

Colwick motive power depot in 1954, the year I started there as apprentice fitter No. 1595. Looking down from the coaling plant area, on the left can just be seen the water tank above the old shed, next to it is the tall erecting shop and facing is 'Big Shed' and 'New Shed', a few railway cottages can be seen on the right. *Frank Berridge Collection*

A view inside the Colwick erecting shop in 1966: all manner of locomotive repairs could be carried out there, especially as it contained a 35 ton overhead crane, seen here above the diesel locomotives. The machine shop was at the far end beyond the locomotives and it was in there that I started my working life on the railway, and later in 1968 I was back in the shop again when I was called on to change over the engines in two of the '04' tamping machines, it was like coming home! *Frank Berridge Collection*

BRITISH TRANSPORT COMMISSION
BRITISH RAILWAYS

APPRENTICESHIP AGREEMENT

This Agreement made the Twentieth day of April 19 55. Between John Blundell District Motive Power Supervisor, Colwick on behalf of the BRITISH TRANSPORT COMMISSION (hereinafter called "the Commission") of 222 Marylebone Road, St. Marylebone in the County of London of the first part, and Walter Meredith of 3, The Green, Radcliffe-on-Trent in the County of Nottingham (hereinafter called "the Guardian") of the second part, and John Meredith of 3, The Green, Radcliffe-on-Trent in the County of Nottingham (hereinafter called "the Apprentice") of the third part.

WHEREAS :—

1. The Apprentice has completed a period of probation from the Twenty-ninth day of December 19 54 to the Eighteenth day of April 19 55 and has attained the age of 15 years.

2. The Commission are willing to accept the Apprentice to be taught and instructed in the craft of Locomotive Fitter.

3. The Guardian having enquired into the nature of the business conducted by the Commission desires that the Apprentice shall learn the craft of Locomotive Fitter in the service of the Commission.

Now it is hereby AGREED as follows :—

(1) The Apprentice, of his own free will and with the consent of the Guardian, hereby binds himself as Apprentice to the Commission in the craft of Locomotive Fitter on the conditions hereinafter appearing.

---

(2) The Commission hereby agrees with the Guardian and the Apprentice :—

(A) That the Commission will accept the Apprentice as an Apprentice of the Commission from the Twentieth day of April 19 55 to the Twenty second day of November 19 60.

(B) That the Commission will arrange, through its Officers and Assistants, during the said term, for the Apprentice to be taught and instructed in the craft of Locomotive Fitter.

(C) That the Commission will pay to the Apprentice, during the said term and so long as he shall be able to and does actually perform his service, wages at the rate prescribed from time to time for Apprentices in the service of the Commission.

(D) That the Commission will grant reasonable facilities to the Apprentice for attendance at classes in courses approved by them, subject always to satisfactory progress having been made by the Apprentice and providing his progress remains satisfactory.

(E) That the Commission will refund to the Apprentice fees for all classes attended with their approval, subject always to eighty per cent of possible attendances being made, to satisfactory conduct at all times by the Apprentice and to the taking of appropriate examinations.

(F) That on satisfactory completion of the apprenticeship the Certificate attached to this Agreement shall be completed by the Commission, and the Agreement shall then become the property of the Apprentice.

(3) The Guardian hereby agrees with the Commission :—

(A) That he will provide for the material needs of the Apprentice during the term of apprenticeship.

(B) That he will, to the best of his ability, restrain the Apprentice from all harmful influences during the said Apprenticeship.

(4) The Apprentice and the Guardian as surety for the Apprentice hereby jointly and severally agree with the Commission :—

(A) That the Apprentice shall during the whole of the said term honestly and faithfully serve the Commission and diligently apply himself to the learning of the craft aforesaid.

(B) That he shall keep the Commission's secrets and obey all lawful and reasonable commands and requirements of the Commission or its authorised representative.

(C) That he shall not absent himself during the usual working hours without the consent of the Commission.

(D) That the Apprentice shall not during the said apprenticeship engage in any other occupation or business whatsoever which might interfere with the successful carrying out of his apprenticeship.

(E) That the Apprentice shall attend and diligently study at such evening classes and day classes as may from time to time be approved by the Commission.

(F) That the Apprentice shall upon request of the Commission apply to the proper authority for and produce for inspection such certificates of attendance, reports or results of examinations, as may be required.

(5) If the Apprentice shall at any time be guilty of any breach or non-observance of any of the covenants herein provided or of any gross misconduct the Commission may forthwith discharge him and this Agreement shall thereupon be cancelled.

IN WITNESS whereof the said John Blundell on behalf of the Commission and the Guardian and the Apprentice have hereunto set their hands the day and year above written.

Signed by the above named } .... (Dist.Motive Power Supt.)
in the presence of .... (Father or Guardian)
.... (Apprentice)
.... (Witness)

steam and then a gas engine. Next to the motor were drilling and planing machines, plus the wheel lathe, used for profiling tyres and turning crank and axle journals. The rest of the machinery was scattered around in the shop in various positions. On the south wall there was an open coal fire, in the centre a GCR stove with a flat top and tall chimney reaching through the roof. It stood in a round cast-iron tray, which was filled with water to catch the hot ashes. At tea and lunch breaks, men would gather round this stove to boil water for their 'mash cans', toast bread, and in the winter try to get a bit of warmth. Long discussions would take place, putting the world to rights, anything from holidays to politics. Sometimes heated arguments would arise, but in the end everyone went off quite happily. In a corner stood a hydraulic pump used for raising and lowering the drop pit, situated on the other side of the wall in 'Old Shed'. When in operation, it made an appalling mechanical noise, water leaked from every pipe and piston gland. It was known as the two up and one down pit. Nevertheless it did the job.

The lathe I worked on first was used for the turning of piston gland packing. At the time we were turning iron packing for the cylinder glands of 'K2' class 2-6-0 No. 61777. A pair of callipers was used to take the measurements of the piston rods. She stood in the running shed amongst her sisters. (Steam engines were always referred to as 'she'.) It was a dark and gloomy place full of smoke. However, we soon got used to the atmosphere.

During my time in the machine shop, I covered a good selection of jobs, including the machining of axle boxes, on the ancient boring machine of 1882, tyre profiling, the turning of big end bearing and side-rod bushes - plus many other minor items, such as sharpening of lawn mower blades during lunch break! I did cause a bit of excitement at times, especially when I tried to screw myself into the lathe, when the turning handle of the saddle caught in my overalls. Mind you these were two sizes too big. It was a big knife job and a new pair of overalls!

At the end of six months I signed my apprenticeship papers, binding me to the trade for the next 5½ years, like it or not, plus six years of night school, at the local technical college.

My first chance to ride the footplate came in 1955, during the Associated Society of Locomotive Engineers & Firemen (ASLEF) drivers' strike. With the cancellation of most passenger trains, the National Union of Railwaymen (NUR) men were working goods. Getting to and from work meant walking from Radcliffe, or riding the first available freight. My ride came on a 'WD' class 2-8-0, working a Colwick-Peterborough coal train. Although it is only two miles to Radcliffe station, it took us a good 15 minutes. This started with a stiff climb out of the yard, past Rectory Junction and over the Trent viaduct. The 'WD' was in poor shape and ready for a works overhaul, with play in every bearing and box, she rolled and bucked most of the way. Was I glad to reach Radcliffe, feeling a little sick and well shaken. I jumped off. No slowing or stopping, you just did your best, but at 15 mph that is not much of a problem. Nevertheless it was an exciting experience.

As one of the junior and trusted apprentices, I was often called on to be the depot errand boy, or 'Gopher', for our district sub-sheds at Leicester (38C) or Woodford (38E). This was to be my first working knowledge of the GCR main line. I was mostly sent to take the special measuring instruments when

On my return from Peterborough I stopped off at Grantham to spend some time at the north end to spot and watch the expresses passing through. The north end of Grantham station in 1961 and running into the up platform is 'A1' class 4-6-2 No. 60146 *Peregrine* of York shed on a Newcastle to King's Cross express. On arrival at my home station I had lost my first free pass, it was a good job the staff knew me! *Author*

Standing on the wet ash pit is Colwick's star locomotive 'B1' class 4-6-0 No. 61111 on 13th May, 1956. The wet ash pits were installed in 1923.
J.F. Davies Copyright Rail Archive Stephenson (Photomatic) N7062

required. These were always kept at the parent depot - one set per district, not one per shed. I suppose it was a railway economy, even in those days. The instruments in question were the large micrometers, used for measuring the middle big end bearings of the Gresley three-cylinder locomotives, mostly of the 'A3' and 'V2' classes.

The journey was always via Nottingham Victoria, usually on the 10.35 am Marylebone express, normally worked by a 'B1' class 4-6-0. If I was lucky the ride would be on the footplate. At Leicester the walk to the shed was alongside the main line approximately 1½ miles away. I would report to the shed master's office and leave the instruments, have a good look round, eat my lunch, then prepare for the journey home. Instead of walking back to the station, I would take a ride on one of the engines preparing to change over on one of the expresses, usually the afternoon Bournemouth-Newcastle. It was on one such trip that I got my first go with the shovel, on 'V2' class 2-6-2 No. 60878; she was in a bit of a state, valves out of adjustment, and was being worked to Colwick for a motion overhaul, coming off at Victoria. Despite this, and the strange beat coming from the front end, she kept the express to time. I was handed the shovel by the fireman on leaving Leicester, 'Might as well earn your keep if you are travelling with us!' I was only too pleased to oblige. By Loughborough I had more coal on the floor than in the box! But by the time we reached Victoria I had really got into the swing of it. I think I would have made a good fireman!

I preferred the visits to Woodford though, the journey was longer and there was always a chance of seeing an ex-Great Western Railway (GWR) engine that had worked across from Banbury.

As well as being errand boy, I was also the smallest lad on shed. This was very handy when mistakes had been made. I would be called upon to perform all kinds of unusual tasks, such as putting my arm down the steam chest ports, when the blast pipe fitter had lost his chisel or spanners, or being put inside the top of boilers via the dome, in order to tighten the nuts on regulator 'J' pipe joints. It felt strange lying on top of rows of smoke and superheater tubes. It did not frighten me, but I suppose I was only too willing to try and complete these awkward jobs. Another favourite was sending me inside tenders and side tanks to clean out the water strainers. I remember going into the side tank of GNR 'N1' 0-6-2 tank No. 69451. She was in light steam; I came out a few pounds lighter, as though I had been in a Turkish bath! It is interesting to note that being so small the other fitters kept a check on how much I had grown each month. They put me with my back to a pillar, making a chalk mark for my height. By the time I left Colwick I had grown 10 inches and put on two stones! They really were interested in my welfare.

After my time in the machine shop, I went out into the big wide world of the running shed, working on live steam engines, in sections such as the injector gang, dealing with repair and servicing of water injectors, both simple and complicated exhaust types. Some of the older engines had combined live steam cocks, injectors and delivery valves (commonly known as the clack valve) mounted on the boiler front in the cab. These were known as the faceplate injectors. Most of the others had them fitted beneath the cab floor, especially ones with the exhaust type, or below the cab at the sides, making them easy to work

Climbing out of Colwick with a coal train for Peterborough and approaching Rectory Junction is 'WD' class 2-8-0 No. 90369 on 3rd September, 1954. On the left is Spike Bank, and it reminds me of my first real footplate ride during the footplate strike of 1955 when I rode a 'WD' from the yard to my home station at Radcliffe, at least it saved me walking across the viaduct.

John Oxley/GNR Society

Colwick-based 'K2' class 2-6-0 No. 61777 is standing in the siding behind the joiners shop, seen on the right, on 13th May, 1956. Behind the locomotive can be seen the roof of the erecting shop. This was the first engine I worked on, on my very first day of employment and it has always been one of my favourites, it's a pity that one was not saved for preservation.

J.F. Davies Copyright Rail Archive Stephenson (Photomatic) N8346

on. On most of these engines the live steam cock and clack valve were also combined together on the faceplate, except the 'WD' 2-8-0s - their clack valve boxes were mounted on top of the boiler. This meant climbing a ladder leant against the boiler and sitting on top, old sacking being kept for this purpose, in order to carry out the service. Up there you were inside the smoke stack of the shed roof. Not a pleasant job to look forward to, especially if the engine in steam standing next to yours had just had a few rounds of coal put on the fire by the steam raiser - it was like sitting in a London fog! And you could almost guarantee that a 'WD' needed its clack valve grinding in longer than any other locomotive.

It was whilst working with the gang that I almost met my maker, when renewing an exhaust injector on a 'K3' class 2-6-0 standing in the 'New Shed'. We had taken down the old one, and had the replacement ready on the pit side. Being the thinnest member of the team, I was reaching through between the driving wheels, with my chest resting on the rail holding the flange of the injector, whilst the fitter carried out a few minor adjustments, when without warning a driver bringing an engine into the shed on the same road gave us a rough shunt, pushing everything down the shed about 3 ft. I shot back into the pit and lay on the floor, shaking like a leaf, having visions of what I would say to my mother if I got home in two pieces! It is unrepeatable what my fitter said to the driver. We had 'Not to be moved' boards fitted, but that did not make much difference in those days.

Now followed a further period with the brake fitter, involved in the servicing of vacuum brake ejectors, steam brake valves and the overhaul of vacuum pan brake cylinders - mostly straightforward tasks until you came across the ones fitted beneath the cabs of the class 'K2s'. To remove these with ease meant the splitting of the engine from the tender, making the job twice as long as necessary. A great groan went round when the fitter returned from the foreman's office with a work card for vacuum pans on a 'K2'.

During my time with the gang, and much to my delight, I was involved in a footplate test run on the GCR – the locomotive in question No. 60102 *Sir Frederick Banbury*. Footplate riding came to an end when I was transferred to work on the drop pit, situated in the coldest part of the 'Old Shed', on No. 4 road. In the winter our only protection was an old wagon sheet hung from the roof, and a water crane brazier for a bit of warmth. We referred to this as 'Smoky Joe'. Not only was the work cold, but heavy going. Even in summer there always seemed to be a cold draught. You see what I meant about GNR sheds facing north.

The drop pit was used as a means of removing locomotive wheel sets for the repair of hot axle box bearings, also occasionally for wheel profiling. But then they were usually taken into the erecting shop. Otherwise it meant dragging the wheel sets from the shed, up the yard and down into the shop before they could be lifted into the lathe, the whole process being repeated after the work was done. The only problem with this method was that you needed a long rope, about a dozen men and someone walking at the side with a wooden wedge, just in case they tried to derail themselves. Nevertheless I saw this done on several occasions, when the erecting shop was full to capacity - mostly in the summer when engines were running longer distances with extra workings to the coast.

Every year on Good Friday we had a Fitters *v.* Apprentices challenge football match. This was my first match in 1955 and for the first time the apprentices won 3-1, the author is on the front row far left, I don't remember all the names of the rest of the apprentices, but the referee was Jack Gibson, the loco store keeper, and the trainer on the right Albert Grant, a fitter's mate.
Author's Collection

Nottingham Victoria station in 1953 where Colwick 'B1' class 4-6-0 No. 61111 is waiting to depart from the main line platform with a train to the east coast on 18th September, and in the bay platform is a Leicester (GC)-allocated 'V2' class 2-6-2 with a stopping train to Leicester. It was from the main line platform that I would depart south on my errand boy trips to Leicester and Woodford Halse engine sheds, usually on the 10.42 am from Nottingham, a Manchester to Marylebone express.
Charles Bayes/Author's Collection

Before the wheel sets could be dropped, most of the motion had to be removed, especially if it happened to be a driving set; after this came the springs and axle box stays, brake gear and any pipes that ran under the axles. All this involved double-handed work. The fitter I worked with at the time, Charlie Cross, used a 7 lb. hammer as a normal hammer. He was known to everyone as the 'Human 'Oss.' Charles was an excellent tradesman and extremely hard working. He became a friend of mine in later life, as we also both shared the art of bell-ringing. Before lowering the wheels, we had to make sure the pit was empty of water. Colwick being near the River Trent meant that the water table was quite high. Water would seep through the brick-lined walls of the pit and fill like a well. The water had to be pumped out before lowering could take place. Many a time I have seen wheels disappear below about 10 ft of water. Mind you, the old hydraulic pump did not help matters either, as water backed into the pit as fast as you could pump it out! It was a battle of wits. Once the wheel sets were down and the side rails brought into place, the locomotive could be towed away, and the sets returned to the surface, for the offending box to be removed and sent for remetalling and turning. It took ages for the wheels to rise with the 'two up one down' method. The boxes then had to be lifted off the axle by hand, or by wall crane if they were too heavy. An average box weighed around 3 cwt. You see what I meant about heavy work. After about five or six weeks of this, you were ready for a rest - no dashing about in the evenings living it up on the town!

Again, one class of locomotives we dreaded working on were our old friends the 'K2s'. Not only did you remove the motion, etc., but most of the pipe work too. I think Gresley designed these engines with the intention of routing everything beneath the rear axle. Despite all this they remained one of my favourite classes, and it is a great pity one was not saved for preservation.

During my time on the pit I carried out work on many different classes. I remember with pleasure three of the GCR 'Director' 4-4-0s, Nos. 62660 *Butler-Henderson*, 62663 *Prince Albert* and 62667 *Somme*. At that particular time they were working the Derby/Nottingham-Lincoln service. How they came to be at Colwick, I am not quite sure. Some of the Annesley '9F' class 2-10-0s working the 'Windcutters' came to the pit for removal of their pony wheels, owing to excessive wear on the right hand flange. I am not sure if they ever did solve this problem. Maybe it could have been the formation of the track bed. As far as I know, it didn't happen to others working in different areas. It will be interesting to see what happens to the one now employed on the present GCR. Maybe speeds will be too slow, and distance travelled too short to cause any major problems. It's a thought!

I was now transferred to the valves and pistons gang, carrying out No. 7 exams. This really meant an overhaul of the motion, and readjustment of the piston valves. Readjustment and setting of the piston valves on two-cylinder locomotives was fairly straightforward, but a different story when it came to the Gresley 3-cylinder classes, i.e. 'K3s', 'A4s', 'V2s' and 'A3s', especially as the inside piston valve was driven by the two outside ones. You could get the outside ones correct, and then the middle one would be out. Many times we have had to pinch-bar the engine up and down the road, sometimes almost for a day, before we could get it right. To pinch-bar, you needed a gang of fitters

The 'Master Cutler' arriving at London Marylebone hauled by 'A3' class 4-6-2 No. 60102 *Sir Frederick Banbury*. It was on this locomotive that I had a test run with one of the brake fitters when the train was experiencing a few braking problems.

Midland Railway Trust/Author's Collection

Departing Nottingham Midland station in 1957 is a Derby to Lincoln stopping train hauled by ex-GCR 'D11' class 4-4-0 No. 62667 *Somme*. It was one of the locomotives that worked these trains for a number of years in the mid-1950s before being transferred back to the old GCR main line, and I remember working on this particular engine at Colwick when it had failed on a Lincoln service with a hot box. In the background is '2P' class 4-4-0 No. 40454, the locomotive that hauled the RCTS special to Swindon in 1956. *Robin Sharman Collection*

and mates, especially if the engine stood on an uneven road. This did not go down too well! No wonder at times these locomotives had a strange beat. Again this was heavy work, removing con rods, side rods, cylinder and piston valve covers and crossheads. We had a marvellous gadget for parting the tapered end of the piston rod from the crosshead. It was in the form of a hydraulic gun. The small end pin and con rod would be removed, and then a false pin placed in the crosshead, to hold the gun; pressure would then be built up via a small pin on the end of the piston rod, this done by a ratchet screw. The gun contained grease, the more you screwed the greater the pressure became until something had to give, which of course was the piston rod parting company with the crosshead. When this happened, it went off like a cannon being fired! You always knew when a crosshead was being split, all the gang except the poor chap working the ratchet stood with their fingers in their ears!

At the time I worked in this gang, King's Cross was experiencing a shortage of fitters, so some of their Pacifics were sent to out stations for their exams. At Colwick we received a number of 'A3' and 'A4' class Pacifics and I remember working on No. 60007 *Sir Nigel Gresley*.

Time was drawing near for my main works training at Doncaster 'Plant'. But before then I was to do my six months with the depot maintenance fitters, who were responsible for the care of the coaling plant, turntable, water cranes and tanks, the hot water washout plant and the ash pit's 3-ton steam grab crane; also tanks, water cranes and turntables around the district. Linked with this training were breakdown duties as George Dawes, the chief fitter, was also responsible for maintaining the breakdown crane and dealing with call-outs to derailments. The Colwick crane was in great demand. Built by Cowans, Sheldon as a 45-tonner, with an extra long jib, it had been down-rated to 36 tons. This was very useful at weekends around the region for bridge replacements. Sometimes having travelled long distances it would return home with a hot axle brass. George soon carried out the necessary repair. Then came the normal test run, which usually meant a trip to Annesley: out via Mapperley tunnel and the Leen Valley, returning via the GCR main line, Nottingham Victoria and London Road High Level. On one such trip I was riding the footplate, instead of riding van. It turned out to be quite an eventful day. 'J11' class 0-6-0 No. 64388 was our engine, and when passing through Mapperley tunnel the track was in such poor condition that I thought we were running on the sleepers. No wonder the tunnel was closed down! At Annesley, No. 64388, whilst running round, almost derailed herself. And on the return journey, approaching Victoria, we were held at the peg (signal) inside the North tunnel. Leaving on the up road (let us not forget that the GCR was 'up' to Manchester and 'down' to London) was a clapped out 'B1' class 4-6-0 on an afternoon working. Owing to poor steaming, the fireman had banked up the fire whilst standing in the station. It passed us pouring out clouds of black smoke. Before the 'Bobby' pulled off the peg, the driver, fireman and I were on the floor choking our hearts out. I thought we were going to die.

Call-outs mostly involved derailed wagons at colliery or station sidings, either on the ex-GNR or GCR lines. It was on a call-out to Ruddington, that I came across the 'Windcutter' iron ore wagons. At times the speed seemed to be too high for the heavily laden wagons and they would run hot brasses. In this case it

Another locomotive that had failed with a hot box whilst working a special in the Nottingham area was King's Cross 'A4' class 4-6-2 No. 60029 *Woodcock*, here she is standing outside the 'Old Shed' on No. 1 road. Also on this road inside the shed was situated the wheel drop.

Sid Checkley/Author's Collection

Call-outs with the Colwick breakdown crane occasionally involved dealing with damaged wagon bearings which had run hot, especially those on the 'Windcutter' trains on the GCR main line. I attended one such breakdown at Ruddington station sidings. Annesley-based '9F' class 2-10-0 No. 92090 is working an empty coal train near Wilford south of Nottingham in 1959. *Author*

One of Colwick's more unusual call-outs, a derailed coach at Basford North station which almost finished up on the main road. It had been pushed over the buffer stops by a locomotive collecting its train in thick fog, for an early morning working, after the driver thought he was still on the main line. *Robin Sharman Collection*

Harby and Stathern on the LNW/GN joint line in the beautiful Vale of Belvoir. It was here that I was sent with the maintenance fitter to service the turntable, water cranes and tank. Standing in the up platform is '2P' class 4-4-0 No. 40464 on 1st December, 1953 working a stopping train from Nottingham Victoria to Northampton. The turntable was situated on the left behind the platform and that wonderful running board, and the water tank on the right behind the bay platform. *Charles Bayes/Author's Collection*

Another shot of the Colwick coaling plant where on the right can be seen the iron steps leading to the top and at the top the hoist beam for hauling up wire ropes and any spares etc as required. Changing a wire rope was one of the dirtiest jobs I helped to carry out during my apprenticeship. 'L1' class 2-6-2T No. 67756 was allocated to Colwick to help work the local passenger services around the Nottingham area. *Midland Railway Trust/Author's Collection*

In 1960 an engineering exhibition was held at Colwick and during that time a line up of guest locomotives was brought to the depot and put on display in front of the 'Old Shed'; from the left 'B1' class 4-6-0 No. 61227, 'A4' class 4-6-2 No. 60022 *Mallard*, a then-new Brush type '2' diesel and '9F' class 2-10-0 No. 92039. On the right is the erecting shop and above the 'B1' the depot water tank; the building with the tall chimney was the shed master's office.

D. Staton/Author's Collection

almost melted off the stub end of the axle. Luckily it was noticed before collapsing on the main line and was removed and placed in the station sidings. The crane was required to lift the wagon on to a low loader for transportation to the repair shops. A simple enough task? No! Unfortunately the load was far too heavy for a lift to be made. So most of the iron ore had to be transhipped to another wagon, standing alongside. Have you tried shovelling iron ore? It is difficult, to say the least, and took us hours and a lot of sweat before it was to the required weight for lifting. That day I rode home in the mess coach and enjoyed a three-course dinner, served up by our travelling chef (one of the fitter's mates!). I am sure he had missed his vocation! When Col John was superintendent and a call-out came to a derailment, say for instance, a wagon off the road in a station siding and not causing too much trouble, he would dash out to site in his old Wolseley car. In the boot would be a pair of re-railing ramps, jacks and wooden packing. By the time the breakdown gang arrived on the scene, he would very often have it almost re-railed. He would call on the local station staff and sometimes borrow a locomotive, if there was one handy, to help him. It was no good saying to him, 'I'm the station porter or shunter,' it just didn't matter. 'We are all working for the same company!', he would say. That is army training for you.

When it came to maintenance, one out-station I always enjoyed visiting was Harby and Stathern on the old GNR/LNWR Joint line. Not only was it set in the beautiful Vale of Belvoir, but also again it meant a lengthy footplate or guard's brake-van ride. This was the only means of getting there. By then the passenger service had finished except for the summer weekend traffic from Leicester Belgrave Road to the East Coast resorts. At the time, the line was being used by goods trains working to Colwick or Doncaster, from the Northampton area, plus iron ore trains from the Scalford and Waltham quarries. A water tank had been retained for supplying the water cranes on the platform and station, as the sidings were still handling goods and coal traffic for the local villages. There was also a turntable for turning the odd ex-LMS 0-6-0 which had worked in from the south. On a lovely day we would very quickly service the turntable and the water cranes, climbing to the top of the tank and making sure the ball valve was working correctly, then we would spend our lunchtime in the local platelayers' cabin, followed by a walk across the fields to the pub for half a pint, and gather mushrooms on the way back, and then wait for the afternoon return working home to Colwick - no travelling by road in those days. As far as I know the only road transport the 'Loco' possessed was a motorized three-wheel Lister truck, which spent most of its time trundling to and from Netherfield and Colwick station, collecting stores that had arrived by train. Even supplies came by rail.

I also have wonderful memories of renewing the wire ropes on the coaling plant – a Sunday job of course, as it was too busy to do it on a weekday. I think this was one of the dirtiest jobs I ever tackled. The ropes were covered in thick oil and coal dust. The new ones after replacement had to be painted with new thick black tar-like oil to protect them. You finished up black from head to foot, your overalls stood up for themselves, and it took a week of scrubbing before you were clean! You had to have no fear of heights either as the plant stood 100 ft, the top being reached by iron steps on the outside.

A view of Doncaster locomotive works in the mid-1930s showing the 'Crimpsall' erecting shop centre right, with its four main bays and smaller machine bays in between. *Author's Collection*

This view looking over the plant works at Doncaster was taken from a high-rise block of flats in 1970, the Crimpsall erecting shop can just be seen at the top left, and the long buildings in the foreground are the offices; Sir Nigel Gresley's was situated beneath the clock. *John Clarke*

Chapter Two

Doncaster Works (The Plant)

In the days of steam on the Eastern Region of British Railways, it was the duty of every running shed apprentice to spend part of his six years' training at one of the main locomotive works, usually for a period of six months. When my turn came, being a Colwick lad I was sent to Doncaster. I was not particularly looking forward to it at the time, especially as I had to lodge away from home, and would also lose the freedom of the running shed, in exchange for a factory type environment.

To most railwaymen and residents of the town, Doncaster works was always known as 'The Plant'. I would be based in the main erecting shop - 'The Crimpsall', where the locomotives came in for their major overhauls and modifications.

I was given instructions to report to the machine bay foreman at 7.30 am on a Monday morning, as they would be expecting me. But before then my lodgings had to be arranged, and this was done for me by an admin. office clerk at Colwick, after seeking advice from his opposite number in Doncaster. They carried a list of landladies who were willing to take in young apprentices from the running sheds. Arrangements were made for me to stay with a Mrs Winters at 52 Wentworth Road, situated on the edge of town. I had to travel up to Doncaster on the Sunday evening, in my own time, not the company's. As I lived at Radcliffe-on-Trent I travelled via Grantham, and I did this on most Sundays for the next six months, just occasionally going from Nottingham Victoria via Sheffield, to break the routine, but always returning home on a Friday via Grantham.

I remember arriving on that first Sunday at Doncaster station around 9.00 pm. I had not been to see the lodgings previously, so had to find my way there, no map or instructions having been given to me. After enquiries I caught a Becket Road trolleybus from the town centre and alighted 10 minutes later at Wentworth Road. I was soon made welcome by Mrs Winters, and she had waiting for me a cold meat supper, which she did every Sunday for the next six months. She had taken in several Colwick apprentices in previous years, and it was a bit like home from home.

On the Monday morning Mrs Winters called me out of bed at 6.30 am, and after a quick breakfast I was on the trolleybus by 7.00 am, with my overalls and Oxo tin of banana sandwiches under my arm. At the time I thought it was a bit early for a 7.30 am start, but soon found out why. If you did not arrive in the town centre by 7.15 am, it meant you were going to be late at your place of work. The Crimpsall was situated at the west end of the site. Walking over the station footbridge and past the gatehouse entrance, it was a further 10 minutes before you could clock on. I was soon carried along on the tide of hundreds of men, rushing to their work posts. After making a few enquiries I found the foreman's office, in the middle of No. 2 bay.

The clerk issued me with my new works number. Then I was shown how to clock on each day, including the lunch break between 12.30 and 1.30 pm. The

A 'V2' class 2-6-2 under overhaul in the erecting shop, the frame is standing on jacks and the horn blocks and stays for the axle-boxes can be clearly seen, the spring hangers and con-rods are lying on the floor along with rest of the junk. No wonder it was a dangerous place to work in!
Copyright Rail Archive Stephenson (Photomatic) N881

This class 'A3's' overhaul is now completed and it is waiting to be taken to the paint shop.
Syd Hancock

foreman introduced me to the chargehand in the axle box gang, working in No. 1 bay. He then put me into the capable hands of fitter Tom Snowball, who was to be my guardian for the next two weeks. Tom had served his apprenticeship in the works so knew it well. Every section in the erecting shop was split up into groups of men called 'gangs'. I had never worked in such a large workshop before, amongst so many men. To me it seemed like a human ant hill, men everywhere working at lathes, machines, and crawling over tenders, boilers and locomotives, plus those that operated the overhead cranes, which trundled up and down the lifting bays. Men of all grades from foreman, charge-hands, fitters, boilersmiths, turners, machinists, labourers, crane-drivers, store-keepers, slingers, boiler-laggers, joiners, white-metallers, even the odd electrician and not forgetting the wheelwrights in their shop at the west end of the Crimpsall, plus a few odd grades I may not have mentioned. No doubt the conditions had not changed for decades, although by then most of the machinery was being driven by electric motor, no longer overhead line shafting, and some of the larger hand tools by compressed air piped around the bays. I am sure that if the likes of Ivatt and Gresley had put in an appearance, they would have felt quite at home.

It was a noisy place - as well as the noise from machinery, most of it was due to the boilersmiths constantly riveting inside and outside boilers and fireboxes. By 7.40 am you had difficulty in hearing what the fitter was instructing you to do, so I had to get used to it. This continued until 10.00 am, then a hooter would sound and everything went quiet for 10 minutes, whilst we all had a tea break. The hooter would sound again and it all started up until 12.25 pm. Then everyone was allowed five minutes to wash their hands at the long sinks situated in the centre of each bay. You had to provide your own soap and towel, but most men cleaned their hands in paraffin and sand.

By 1.35 pm in the afternoon the whole procedure was in motion again until 5.25 pm. This time we worked through without a tea break. It was quite amusing when, in the middle of the afternoon, you would often see men creeping down to the water boiler, with a mug in their hand, usually held behind their backs, and dodging behind machines and benches in case they were caught by the foreman. This also applied towards the end of the shift, when they were making sure they would be first at the sink by 5.25 pm. These were the primitive conditions we worked under.

One big change for me from working in a motive power depot was the extra pay I received. Everyone in the works was earning a bonus, so the apprentice was paid a percentage, according to the gang he worked with at the time. Protective clothing was either a pair of overalls or a boiler suit; these had to be provided by yourself. But most of us belonged to an overall scheme, where for a small fee they were cleaned each week. No hard hats and yellow vests were worn in those days, just a cloth cap, usually covered in oil and grease, and footwear was normally a pair of hobnail boots, but some men even wore wooden clogs.

The axle box gang was responsible for fitting and bedding in the boxes to the axle journals. It was heavy work, the white metal bearings had to be scraped in to a perfect fit. This meant lifting them on and off the axle several times.

Admittedly we did have the use of a wall-fitted crane. During my time with the gang, I spent a small part of it in the brass finishing section, handling those famous Pacific nameplates. Little did I realise at the time what a price they would command in today's enthusiasts' market.

After two weeks I was moved into the motion gang in No. 2 bay. Here they fitted bushes into the side rods, as well as many other tasks associated with the locomotive's drive motion, especially scraping and bedding in of the big-end bearings. As an apprentice I was given the job of repairing and fitting the side-rod and con-rod brass oil caps. I would be sent with a two-wheel barrow to the stripping shop, situated to the rear of the Crimpsall. There I collected a bucket full of caps and brought them back to the bench and duly set about repairing them, which meant a lot of tedious filing of the hexagon flats, bringing them back to their original shape in order that a spanner would fit them correctly. You can imagine what they looked like after having been in traffic for a number of years, and knocked about a bit by a few drivers when oiling round. I found the stripping shop a fascinating place and often hung around for a while watching the fitters at work. A locomotive would arrive and within a short time it was stripped, frame and parts cleaned, and these were then sent to the relevant sections in the Crimpsall for overhaul. A few weeks later they passed through the erecting shop, leaving at the east end as a complete locomotive, ready for testing. Before I completed my time in the motion gang, I was involved in the fitting of die-blocks into the radius links and helped fitter Ernie Whalley with the scraping in of the big-end bearings, especially those fitted to the Pacifics. These were skilled jobs, requiring the careful use of the hand tools, such as files and scrapers, which had to be kept in tip-top condition. Ernie was a real expert and it was a joy to watch him at work. He had scraped in the bearings of *Mallard* in 1938 before it did its record run. The job became a bit tedious at times, but we were often cheered up and entertained by one of the turners. Stan was a comedian and told music hall jokes and sang to us; I am sure he had missed his vocation. In the machine bay the benches were arranged down one side and the lathes, etc., down the other. Mr Andrews the bay foreman, who always wore a trilby hat, was a hard task master: at 7.35 each morning, he would walk the length of the bay, making sure that everyone had started work. If you were late the clock was locked and you went home and returned at lunchtime, the next time it was unlocked. This meant you forfeited half a day's pay and bonus, unless of course, you were a favourite of the foreman, or you managed to talk him into unlocking it. Most men made sure they were never late. Before I left the motion gang I was permitted to work at the bench of former professional boxer Bruce Woodcock, who had served his apprenticeship in the works and worked as a fitter before becoming a world class boxer.

My third move was at the other end of the bay to work alongside one of the machinists. He operated a planing machine, profiling crosshead slipper blocks, after they had been re-metalled. It was the apprentice's job to re-drill and cut out the oil ways, which had to be done with great care. If the chisel slipped and dug into the white metal, the whole thing had to be sent back and re-metalled, unless you were skilled with a blowtorch, a stick of white metal and a scraper.

So you made sure it didn't happen. Near to the bench, next to a lathe, stood the bell from 'A4' class 4-6-2 No. 60010 *Dominion of Canada*. One of the men used to say to me, 'See that, it is mine, so keep your eyes off it!' He was only joking, or I think he was! Mind you, I often wondered what happened to it, because I have never seen it come up for sale. Maybe it's in the National Railway Museum.

At last the time arrived for me to move out into the lifting bays, working on the rebuilding of the locomotives - first into the cylinder gang, helping to fit the slide-bars and cylinder covers. The fitting of the slide-bars was quite an intricate job. A line was fixed to the centre of a bar fastened across the cylinder front; it then passed along the cylinder barrel and out through the piston gland to a fixed point. Once the correct alignment had been attained the slide-bars were aligned to it, making sure they ran parallel to the piston rod. They were then bolted to the rear of the cylinder casting and support bracket. For the lining up, the light used was from a candle. In fact candles were used for many tasks, especially those in dark places. Electric lead-lamps were only used for really specialized jobs. There was candle fat everywhere. It was the apprentice's duty each morning to go to the stores and collect the day's supply. On the Pacifics the cylinder covers had to be fitted face to face with the cylinder, again having to be scraped in until there was an all-round fit. This meant lifting the covers from the floor on to the cylinder studs by hand, quite a number of times - it was heavy work as each cover weighed well over a hundredweight. The lifting had to be done by the fitter and the apprentice, not a crane, so you had to be fit. When the time came for the cover to be bolted to the cylinder, the only seal between them was a coating of boiled oil, painted on the surface with a brush.

As the locomotive progressed down the shop various parts were fitted. Very often whilst you were working on the frame, especially when underneath, it would suddenly start to become dark, you looked up and realized that the boiler was being lowered into position. No one bothered to tell you to move out of the way. On one occasion I even saw a boilersmith jumping out of the firebox as the boiler was being lifted. No one seemed to take much notice of health and safety regulations, and accidents occurred regularly. Whilst I was in the Crimpsall there were numerous minor ones, and several major ones. A man had his fingers crushed between the boiler and a lifting chain, and in another bay a man was killed when a steel plate fell on top of him. They were hard times. Today's health and safety inspectors would have had a field day, but no doubt it would slow down progress. In those days speed was essential.

Before the frame could be re-wheeled, the axle-box horn blocks had to be assembled and ground in; this was done with a heavy grinding machine, held by hand - after a few minutes your arms felt like dropping off. I think it was the worst job I ever tackled in all the time I was there. Eventually the locomotive was re-wheeled and the springs fitted; these were also lifted and fitted by hand. Next it was the turn of the valves and pistons to be placed in the cylinders, the covers were then bolted up and the motion assembled. Then it was time for the valves to be set, a task carried out by a highly skilled tradesman known as a valve setter as it was a specialized job. The driving wheels were placed on a revolving rig, which turned the wheels by the aid of an electric motor, operated by the setter as and when required, as he adjusted the valves.

The Doncaster works footbridge crossing over the station. This brings back memories to me of rushing across in the early morning to make sure I would be on time at the Crimpsall erecting shop to clock on, and then in the evening trying to be first to the trolleybus. 'A4' class 4-6-2 No. 60025 *Falcon* is waiting to depart at 4.30 pm with the up 'White Rose' to King's Cross on the 14th August, 1962. The train I travelled on to Grantham every Friday on my way home for the weekend followed this train at 4.40pm.
John Clarke

Standing down the north side of the 'Crimpsall' in 1963 is 'A3' class 4-6-2 No. 60103 *Flying Scotsman* waiting for preservation. The tall building behind the locomotive is No. 1 bay and the lean-to is the brass finishing shop where the name plates were polished, note also the pile of main steam pipes on the right, no doubt waiting to go for scrap.
John Clarke

Time was drawing close for me to return to the running shed. My final six weeks were spent in the smoke-box gang, where I worked with fitter Cyril Symonds - once again he too was a joy to work alongside, and taught me a lot. Twenty years after leaving the Plant, I returned on business connected with my duties as an engineering inspector (more later) and met Cyril again in the Crimpsall; this time he was working on the overhaul of travelling rail cranes. He recognized me straightaway. Either I had not changed or I had made a lasting impression on him at the time I worked with him in the 1950s, considering the number of apprentices that must have passed through his hands over those 20 years. Whilst I was in the gang, I learnt to fit smokeboxes to the cylinder casting saddles; the box was already attached to the boiler. I also helped assemble the main steam pipes and superheater headers, plus the fitting of the chimneys and cowls. During this time I was lucky enough to be involved in an interesting project, the conversion of the class 'A3s' from single to double blastpipes. I think it was one of the most enjoyable periods of my time spent in the works. Normally working in a locomotive smokebox in the running shed was considered a punishment because it was such a dirty place, being covered in soot and ash. But in the main works it was one of the most keenly sort after jobs in the shop.

These are just a few of the many tasks I was involved with, it's not possible to name them all. At times we did have moments of light relief and the pressure came off. This is when we were allowed out of the Crimpsall, to attend to jobs outside. As soon as a locomotive left the erecting shop, it would be re-coupled to the tender and taken to the test house, for steam-test and weighing. If a fault were found, a fitter would be called to put it right, usually the one that had carried out the repair in the first place. If I was working with him at the time, I went as well to help rectify the fault. The locomotive would then be sent to the paint shop for painting and lining out, followed by a test run on the main line, usually to Barkston Junction, north of Grantham, where it would turn on the triangle and return to Doncaster 'Carr Loco' running shed. After further inspection, if a fault were found, it was the fitter from the Plant that had to put it right, not one of the running shed staff. Whilst I was working in the motion gang, the fitter and I were sent over to the shed to attend to a 'K3' class 2-6-0. To leave the works during working hours was like trying to escape from Colditz. First you had to obtain a permit from the section foreman. This you presented to the Hexthorpe gatekeeper, before he allowed you to leave the premises. Then it was a walk across town, carrying the tools, no motor transport in those days. The 'K3' in question had been reported groaning badly in the right-hand cylinder casting, and on stripping it down we discovered that someone had forgotten to drill out the oil-ways.

During lunch breaks I would wander round the yard, taking a look at what was being cut up on the scrap roads, and if it was a nice day I would sit and watch the old 'J52' class 0-6-0 saddle tanks shunting locomotives and wagons around the site. The Plant had quite extensive sidings and most supplies for the various shops and stores were moved in rail vans, not like today in road transport. I would often take a look inside the other shops, especially the paint shop, where I would stand and admire the gleaming Pacifics as they stood waiting to go on their test run.

The 'Crimpsall' No. 4 bay on 12th October, 2007 the only part of the erecting shop still in use carrying out light repairs on the class '91' electrics. It was in this bay that I worked with fitter Cyril Simons on the conversion of the class 'A3's' to double blast-pipe. *Author*

The 'Crimpsall' erecting shop on 12th October, 2007, just a few months before it was demolished. *Author*

Occasionally I would be called up to the top office to collect a letter or to see a clerk in connection with my apprenticeship. Clerks would be sitting at rows of desks; I doubt if the office had changed very much since the days of Gresley and Thompson. One of the things that I always found slightly amusing, was payday on a Friday. We always finished early and clocked off at 4.30 pm. Everyone formed a queue in each bay, in number order, and you would be handed your pay in a packet as you left. I was earning around £3 per week plus the extra bonus. But it was the way that it was brought down from the office to the Crimpsall that caused the amusement. A clerk and a labourer would wheel it along on a two-wheel flat barrow, the packets arranged in trays, with no means of protection. I suppose today it would have to be brought in by Securicor.

These are just a few memories and my impressions of working at Doncaster Plant, plus the many different locomotives I worked on at the time, which are too numerous to list by name or number. But amongst them were classes 'A2', 'A3', 'A4', 'K3', 'K1', 'B1' and 'B17'. Three I remember well were 'B17' No. 61623 *Lambton Castle*, no doubt in for its last major overhaul, 'A2' class Pacific No. 60530 *Sayajireo* and 'A3' class 4-6-2 No. 60095 *Flamingo*, being two of the last I marked off in my trusty 'ABC'. Although I didn't work on it, but in for repair whilst I was there was the unusual 'W1' class 4-6-4 No. 60700, in its earlier days known as the 'Hush-Hush', when it carried the experimental Yarrow water tube boiler, and numbered 10000. It would be interesting to know what my fellow apprentices thought of their time at Doncaster works. One thing for sure they would all agree that the work was heavy, hard and dirty.

I would not be telling the truth if I said I was sorry that I was leaving the Plant to return to my home depot, although it had been an interesting and often exciting period in my life. Lodging away from home for the first time had given me independence and confidence for the future. But being at Mrs Winters' was really like being at home at times, because she very often tried to mother me, maybe it was because I was so young at the time. As well as myself there was another apprentice sharing my room, Bob from Staveley GCR engine shed near Chesterfield, a sub-shed under the jurisdiction of the superintendent at Colwick. He too was on his six months' training course. Mrs Winters looked after us well when it came to food, but there was one snag, if you told her that you liked a certain type of meal, she gave it to us for the next two weeks, until one of us was brave enough to tell her that we would like a change.

A view of Leicester Belgrave Road station on 12th May, 1951 with the locomotive shed off the picture on the left. The water tank can just be seen, it was little changed when I was sent down, after I came back from Doncaster, to help rescue the stricken 'J39' class 0-6-0 that had run a hot big-end bearing.
Charles Bayes/Author's Collection

At Colwick standing on the ash pit is '4MT' class 2-6-0 No. 43060, it was another member of this class that I rode on down to Leicester Belgrave Road to rescue the 'J39' and then tow it back to Colwick for the wheels to be removed and the big-end journals to be turned.
Frank Berridge Collection

Chapter Three

Back to Colwick

On my return I was soon out in the district, being sent to Leicester Belgrave Road, to assist one of the fitters to strip down the big-end bearings and con-rods on a 'J39' class 0-6-0. One bearing had run hot causing damage to the big-end journal, and it was a case of having the locomotive towed back to Colwick for the wheel set to be removed. Once more it meant a lengthy footplate ride via Melton Mowbray North and Marefield Junction on the joint line. The locomotive chosen to take us down and to tow the 'J39' back was one of the recently allocated class '4' 2-6-0s, in the 43000 numbering series. The footplate was crowded; besides the driver and fireman, the fitter and myself there was a spare driver, sent as a rider for the 0-6-0, plus the box of tools. It took all morning to get there, and all afternoon to strip down the rods and bearings, no easy task given the conditions we were working in. The locomotive stood over a pit in the old disused shed. The first thing we had to do was clear the pit of rubbish, before we could get underneath, then came the laborious job of knocking out the tapered big-end bolts, using a long handled 7 lb. hammer, always difficult on a 'J39' as the bolts had shallow tapers. Between us we managed the job, and by teatime set forth on the return journey back to Colwick. I stayed on the footplate of the class '4' whilst Jim the fitter rode with the rider on the 'J39', just to keep an eye on things as we progressed home. It was late in the evening by the time the locomotive was shunted into the erecting shop for lifting. Mind you, everyone was happy with the extra overtime! Except Jim, who had arranged to take his wife out for an evening meal. I wonder what she said!

Soon after this, I was summoned to the foreman's office. My immediate reaction was: what had I done wrong? I was asked if I would like to work on my own as a tradesman with a fitter's mate to help assist. Although I still had 18 months of my apprenticeship to complete, I jumped at the chance to prove myself. 'We will not give you too many difficult jobs!' he said. This was a Friday, and I reported to him first thing on the Monday morning. To my surprise he gave me the job of overhauling the 2 to 1 valve gear on a 'K3' class. She stood at the bottom of 'Big Shed' on No. 6 road, in full view of everyone, as they walked past the locomotive. The gearing runs across the front of the engine beneath the plates below the smokebox door. Every time the door opens for cleaning out of the ash, quite a bit of it falls between the plates, onto the main central pin. After a time this becomes seized and the grease-ways blocked, causing the bearings to wear. It took me two days to get the pin out, nearly broke my heart. But I completed the job to the satisfaction of all concerned. Quite a few jobs tackled involved the cleaning out and repairing of sand valves, situated below the sand boxes. The sand often became wet, blocking the valves; no matter how much the driver worked the steam sand valve nothing came out of the end of the pipe, except a blast of steam. To get to the valve meant pit work - not very clean places at the best of times. Very often you would have to shovel

Above: A wheel from a 'J11' class 0-6-0 lying on its side in the Colwick erecting shop after it had broken its driving axle, whilst working a freight train on the Derby Friargate line.
Sid Checkley/Author's Collection

Right: The author and his mate having fun, in 1959, after carrying out a repair on the 'WD' class 2-8-0 which can be seen in the background. This was at the time when I was asked to do tradesman's duties while still an apprentice.
Author's Collection

away piles of ash and clinker, and unblock the drains, as there might be six inches of water in the bottom - even chase away a rat or two. And in the winter, break away several inches of ice that had accumulated under the locomotive, whilst it had travelled through the cold air. The pits also acted as wind tunnels, and to alleviate this, coal-burning braziers would be placed along the front of the shed to try and keep the weather out. So not only did we have to contend with the cold wind, but acrid smoke as well.

Running sheds were not tidy places, as well as rubbish and litter there would be fire irons lying around. Despite having labourers, it always remained untidy. Every so often, Col John would have one of his cleaning and white-line-painting campaigns, another throw-back to his army days! For a while everything looked neat and tidy. No driver dared park an engine across a white line. But within a few weeks things were back to normal.

One of my last jobs at Colwick was the renewal of a set of super-heater elements in the smoke-box of a class 4 - what a lovely place to work. Before we could start, the box had to be cleaned of ash, self-cleaning plates removed, then a good spray out with jets of hot water. Sacking was placed over the blastpipe and the box bottom, making it just about bearable to work in. First the elements would be released from the header, and that is not an easy job, especially if the bolts were corroded. Then we might find them held solid inside the super tube, blocked with the build up of soot and ash. The only way to remove them was by sling and pull-lift, fixed to an iron bar across the front of the box doorframe. Oh, what happy days! Although it was sometimes cold and dirty, working at the Loco had its lighter moments, like the day they pulled down the Inspector's Office. A locomotive was placed each side of the building (two 'WDs') and a chain fastened between them. On the word of command, the engines moved forward and the office disappeared in a cloud of dust, leaving a heap of rubble. It was up to the labourers to complete the rest with an empty wagon.

Many tricks were played on the apprentices in the early days. 'Go to the stores for a long weight,' or 'Fetch a tin of red and white striped paint', or 'A rubber hammer for knocking in glass nails'. Or the classic engineering one, 'Hand me a left- handed spanner'. Mind you, the apprentices got their own back especially in the winter. They would wait until a crowd gathered around the GCR stove in the machine shop, then climb on to the roof and pour paraffin down the chimney. When it hit the fire it exploded and smothered everyone in hot ashes. No apprentices were to be seen for hours after! At the end of the day, we all departed for home good friends. It was this that kept the job going.

A few characters I remember besides the ones mentioned were George Levick, the shed master, who stalked the Loco like a general. Most people kept out of his way. Arthur Harvey, the 'artist' boilersmith: if there was a funny incident that had taken place, you could guarantee Arthur would draw a cartoon. In my early days there was Herman Wood, one of the fitters who had served his time in the Lincolnshire, Derbyshire & East Coast Railway (LD&ECR) works at Tuxford. No apprentice dare call him by his Christian name, always 'Mr'. It was said that on one of his days off, he was taking the family to the seaside for the day, when the locomotive broke down. The enginemen knew that Herman was on the train, and called him up front.

Standing by the side of the sand house is Colwick-allocated 'O4/3' class 2-8-0 No. 63859. Note the loco fire irons leaning by the side of the sand house wall and the amount of ash lying on the ground. Although we had wet ash pits very often fires were thrown out where the locomotive stood, the same sometimes applied to the inspection pits in the shed, especially when we needed to work beneath a locomotive to carry out a repair!

J.F. Davies Copyright Rail Archive Stephenson (Photomatic) N7937

A view looking across the front of 'Big' and 'New' sheds in 1959 with a few locomotives fouling the walkway. This would never have happened when superintendent Col John Blundell was in charge. White lines were painted each side of the walkway and no driver was allowed to park an engine across them.

Frank Berridge Collection

Managing to scrape a few tools together, he got them out of trouble. Good for the passengers, but not for his suit. I understand the railway rewarded him with another. Now that is dedication to duty!

In those days men carried out all kinds of skills, not thought about today. If you could not get a spare, there was a chance that it could be made on the bench, to keep the wheels of motion turning. Without these dedicated men, the railway would have ground to a halt.

As well as all the hours spent at work, there were also social activities, including sport, and the luxury of travelling the country on a free pass or privilege ticket.

A poor quality image from a newspaper cutting of Colwick fitters working on a locomotive in Colwick shed. *Author's Collection*

A plan of Colwick marshalling yard and locomotive sheds in the parish of Netherfield.
Author's Collection

Chapter Four

Colwick and its Locomotives in the 1950s

I thought it might be of interest for the reader to know a little about the allocation of steam locomotives at the time, plus many other classes which visited the shed from other areas. This is a period I remember well and I am sure most readers will too. After all, steam was still in its heyday.

Although I previously gave details on the layout of the 'Loco', along with a brief history of its construction, I feel it will do no harm to mention it again, as this will set the scene for the following account.

Very little seems to have been written about Colwick in the railway press. I suppose most enthusiasts regarded it as rather a mundane place and tended to ignore it. No doubt it did not have the same appeal as the sheds at York, Grantham and King's Cross, especially as they had their thoroughbreds racing up and down the East Coast main line. Colwick locomotives were more the carthorses of the railway system, plodding through the countryside on the many mixed freight and mineral trains. But thrown in for good measure were the local passenger workings on the routes radiating from Nottingham Victoria. It made quite a change in the summer months, and no doubt came as a bit of light relief to the footplate staff, when the seasonal workings came into operation. These were required to cope with the extra traffic to the coastal resorts, especially at weekends.

The 1950s were the era of the British seaside holiday, and many trains ran to the East Coast, mainly from Nottingham, Derby and Leicester. These three cities often had special holiday fortnights when most of the local factories shut down and the work force would take daily excursions to many places of interest. Skegness and Mablethorpe were amongst the favourite destinations. Colwick locomotives played a significant role in the haulage of these trains and very often carried a headboard attached to the smoke box door, i.e. 'The City of Nottingham Holiday Express', etc.

I suspect the shed was regarded as being a bit of a backwater, tucked away in the fields to the east of Nottingham. Colwick is not a name that conjures up ideas of an exotic area, more a medical complaint. Admittedly it was not a depot you could easily gain access to, certainly not one for 'bunking' as the old number takers would say - although when pre-arranged, groups could be conducted round at certain times, mostly weekends!

The Great Northern Railway arrived on the scene in the Nottingham area at the beginning of the 1850s when they took over the running of the Ambergate company's line, which ran between Grantham and Colwick. From there it had running rights over the last three miles of the Midland Railway's (MR) Lincoln to Nottingham line. This gave them access to a shared station in the town, situated in the Nottingham meadows, close to the river Leen.

After a disagreement between the MR and the GNR, the GNR with the Ambergate company decided to construct their own station; this they did adjacent to the London Road, and at the same time a three-mile extension line

Looking east across Colwick marshalling yards from the engine shed in October 1954, in the centre can be seen one of the many ex-GNR 'J52' class 0-6-0ST allocated to Colwick for shunting the yards and local trip workings. *John Oxley/GNR Society*

The end of steam at Colwick in 1966. By then the allocation was mostly ex-LMS '8F' class 2-8-0s and '5MT' class 4-6-0s but the odd 'WD' class 2-8-0 did remain to the end. *Syd Hancock*

COLWICK AND ITS LOCOMOTIVES IN THE 1950s

The Colwick Estates Light Railway with the daily pilot locomotive 'J5' class 0-6-0 No. 65486. Several of this class were kept at Colwick long after the rest of the class had been scrapped, they were the right axle loading for the estates line. Nos. 65483 and 65498 were the last to go in 1957.

Charles Bayes/Author's Collection

Aerial view of Colwick locomotive sheds in 1936. On the right the original turntable the stores and twin roofs of 'Old Shed' constructed in 1876, in the centre the tall building is the two-road erecting shop and workshops, with the eight-road 'Big Shed' (1882) and on the left the four-road 'New Shed' and wagon repair shop (1897). The main entrance and offices are along the front on Victoria Road.

Author's Collection

Standing outside the 'Big Shed' at Colwick is 'J50' class 0-6-0T No. 68975. These engines were gradually replacing the older type 'J52' class 0-6-0STs as they were taken out of service and sent to Doncaster to be scrapped. *Copyright Rail Archive Stephenson/Photomatic/N8429*

A line of ex-GNR 'J52' class 0-6-0STs outside the 'New Shed' at Colwick in the 1950s. It must have been a Sunday, as they were normally brought to the shed at weekends for servicing before returning to the marshalling yard for their next week's work. *J.H. Gibbons/Author's Collection*

was laid from Colwick, running parallel with the MR. The station and line opened in 1857.

Coal mines were also opening up on the Nottinghamshire/Derbyshire border. And in order to obtain their share of the transporting of the traffic, the GNR constructed a branch from a junction at Colwick, off the Grantham line, via Mapperley tunnel and Daybrook, firstly to Pinxton in 1875, and then from the Pinxton line with a junction at Awsworth, to Derby Friargate in 1878.

With the opening of more mines, coal traffic increased so a decision was taken to construct a locomotive depot at Colwick, east of the Pinxton line; this was to help cope with the extra trains. The first shed of four roads opened in 1876, later to be known as 'Old Shed'. In the fields east of the depot a marshalling yard had also been laid down and by 1879 it was handling almost 914,000 tons of coal annually. More trains meant that more locomotives were required, so a second much larger shed was added in 1882. This had eight roads and at the side incorporated a two-road workshop with overhead crane; eventually this became known as 'Big Shed'. By 1892 the depot had an allocation of around 100 locomotives to handle this traffic, including those required for hauling the daily passenger services.

More new sidings were added to the marshalling yard in 1884 and the final extension was made to the locomotive depot in 1897, when a new four-road shed and a small two-road wagon repair shop were constructed to the west of 'Big Shed'. This obviously became known as 'New Shed'. The depot now comprised a total of 20 roads. The final extension to the marshalling yard came in 1900. It then had a capacity to handle 6,000 wagons. It became one of the largest marshalling yards and locomotive depots on the GNR system. At the end of World War I in 1918, as many as 900 to 1,000 personnel were employed in various grades, and at its busiest up to 250 locomotives were based at the shed.

After the takeover by the LNER in 1923 changes came to the depot, when a new coaling plant, wet ash pits and a 70 ft turntable were installed. At the advent of BR in 1948 Colwick was to remain the parent depot for the district with the allocated number 38A. The district included Annesley 38B, Leicester GC 38C, Staveley GC 38D and Woodford Halse 38E, plus two small sub-sheds at Derby Friargate and Leicester Belgrave Road. In 1958 it lost its status as the district head office and became a sub-shed under Lincoln, with the allocated number 40E – what a come-down! Its death knell was sounded in 1965 when to add insult to injury it was transferred to the London Midland Region. Steam finally finished in 1966, but the depot lingered on for the use of diesels until final closure came in 1970. Along with the marshalling yard, it was demolished the following year.

Nothing of the depot and yard remain today, except the old clubhouse near Netherfield Lane crossing, and the former canteen, now a social club, and a few rusty sidings on what was known as Spike Bank, plus a short length of the main line which ran through the centre of the yard from Colwick North Junction to Rectory Junction. This is now used as a siding for the unloading of oil tankers. The yard area is now an industrial estate and ironically the site of the locomotive sheds became a lorry and container park.

After the 'J52' class 0-6-0STs were withdrawn even more shunting engines were brought in to replace them. Standing on the sand road in 1959 is 'J69' class 0-6-0T No. 68570 and 'J94' class 0-6-0ST No. 68074. *Midland Railway Trust/Author's Collection*

On loan 'J11' class 0-6-0 No. 64375 from Leicester, a sub-shed of Colwick, at the north end of Nottingham Victoria waiting for the road. On the left is the hydraulic accumulator pump house and tower which powered the hydraulic buffers in the bay platforms and station lifts, all maintained by the P&M department. *Author*

Before we make a study of the locomotive allocation, it might be worth taking a look at the many different routes that the Colwick footplate staff signed for at the time. As the depot was central in the country it meant that routes radiated out to most points of the compass. To the west, as well as the local branches, they would work as far as Burton-on-Trent and in summer months to Stoke-on-Trent with a through train from Nottingham Victoria to Llandudno.

Back in the old days they even went to Stafford. The GNR had a shed there at the end of a branch which left the North Staffordshire Railway line west of Uttoxeter. Routes to the north included the former GCR main line to Sheffield and before electrification to Manchester, plus many ex-GNR and GCR lines to the north of Nottingham and in the Mansfield area.

Leaving Colwick yard to the east of Rectory Junction gave them access to a vast amount of route mileage; into the north-east via the 'Lowfields' branch joining the East Coast main line at Newark, they reached Doncaster, York and Hull. One working I remember well was the 'Burton Beer' train to York, which ran most evenings. Lincolnshire was covered with the freights to Boston, and of course in the summer months, the passenger services to Skegness, Mablethorpe and Cleethorpes. To gain access to East Anglia, trains would be worked to March (Whitemoor Yard) via the Great Eastern/Great Northern Joint line from Sleaford. Both March and Colwick depots had fast turn-round duties in each direction. Talking of joint lines we must not forget the old LNWR/GNR line, branching off at Saxondale Junction on the Grantham line and running via Melton Mowbray North to Welham sidings, north of Market Harborough. Most of this traffic was coal or iron ore from the quarries in the Vale of Belvoir. They also worked the former GNR branch to and from Leicester Belgrave Road station, especially in the summer, when the holiday trains ran to the Lincolnshire coast via the joint line to Bottesford. The once-GNR main line south of Grantham was well frequented by Colwick men, again mostly with mixed freight and coal trains to Peterborough and Ferme Park, just north of King's Cross. They also worked down the GCR main line to London Marylebone from Nottingham. These were some of the various routes covered. The different areas were divided up into 'links' and not all men signed for all lines, but I stand corrected if they did.

The following is a record of my observations during the 1950s, showing the allocation of locomotives at the time. By no means is it meant to be a full and comprehensive history of Colwick and its locomotives, just a series of jottings and notes from the pen of an enthusiast at the time.

As I have already mentioned, the yard was handling all types of traffic, but mostly coal and iron ore. The ore was conveyed to Stanton Iron Works near Ilkeston in Derbyshire. I suppose most enthusiasts can be forgiven for thinking that Colwick's allocation at the time was just the class 'WD' 2-8-0s, and ex-GCR 'O4' 2-8-0s, after all they were mostly seen trundling around the area to the local colliery branches, and on freight trains to March, Peterborough and Welham sidings. Admittedly there was quite a large number of both classes based at the depot. But most trainspotters would be surprised to find that at the beginning of 1951 there were 200 locomotives allocated in 19 different classes.

Most of the major freight traffic was being handled by the 'WD' and 'O4s', plus the 'J39' class 0-6-0s; the faster workings were in the hands of the 'K2' and

'B1' class 4-6-0 No 61264 is approaching Bingham on the Grantham to Nottingham line on Saturday 25th October, 2003 with the 'Lincolnshire Poacher' from King's Cross to Lincoln via Nottingham, Sheffield and Worksop. This is the closest I could get, in modern times, to photographing a Colwick engine working a seaside train in the 1950s. *Author*

Many visiting engines from other depots and regions came to Colwick mostly working freight trains into the marshalling yard; amongst the most frequent were the 'B16' class 4-6-0s from York, both the original NER-type and the rebuilt ones. 'B16/1' class No 61477 is seen standing outside the 'Big Shed' on 13th May, 1956.

J.F. Davies/Copyright Rail Archive Stephenson/Photomatic/N7877

'K3' class 2-6-0s. Incidentally one of the Colwick 'K2s' had a side window cab, No. 61729. But on the lighter and local freight traffic, one would very often find the ex-GNR 'J5' and 'J6' class 0-6-0s; in fact the whole class of 20 'J5' class were at some time during their lives based at Colwick. Although the 'J6s' were, according to the records (Ian Allan ABC), a standard design, this was not exactly true as No. 64183, compared with the rest of the class, was termed as being long-fronted, which meant that the distance between the firebox door and the tender was greater. In other words it had a slightly longer cab. Shunting duties were in the hands of the ex-GNR 'J50' class 0-6-0Ts and 'J52' class 0-6-0STs, with help from a couple of ex-GCR 'N5' class 0-6-2Ts.

On the passenger side the fast trains, especially those working on the old GCR main line, were worked by the 'B1' and 'B17' class 4-6-0s. Colwick had four 'B17s' on the books in 1951, Nos. 61652 *Darlington*, 61653 *Huddersfield Town*, 61657 *Doncaster Rovers* and 61662 *Manchester United*. The local branch line services were in the hands of the last two ex-GNR 4-4-0s to remain at Colwick, 'D3' class No. 62148 and 'D2' No. 62172, plus the 'A5' class 4-6-2Ts and four 'N2' class 0-6-2Ts plus a few ex-GNR 'J1' and 'J2' class 0-6-0s. Very often the 'J6s' and 'K2s' could also be found on these duties, especially on the Nottingham/Grantham line. Strangely enough at the time only one ex-GCR 'J11' class 0-6-0 was on the books, plus an ex-GNR 'C12' class 4-4-2T. I think that had been used on the remaining part of the Nottingham Suburban Railway, to work a few specials before the line finally closed in 1951. Even then the line was only open from the north end at Daybrook as far as Thorneywood station, as the south end near to Trent Lane Junction had been damaged in World War II by a bomb.

In the summer months the many East Coast seaside trains were mostly hauled by the 'B1s', 'K2s' and 'K3s', but when times were busy the 'J6' and 'J39s' would be called into service. By mid-1952 the allocation had risen slightly to 207, but the class numbers had been reduced to 16. The 'B17s' were now down to one: No. 61657. The four 'N2s' had been transferred away, and arrived to take their place were four ex-Great Eastern Railway (GER) 'N7' class 0-6-2T's. The two 'N5s' had also disappeared from the list and sadly the two ancient 4-4-0s had been sent to the scrapyard.

My early 1954 records show an allocation of 204 locomotives. Surprisingly 'B17' No. 61657 was still there, but most of the older ex-GNR 0-6-0s in classes 'J1' and 'J2', like the 4-4-0s, had gone to the scrapyard leaving only one 'J1' in service, No. 65002. But an extra few 'J11s' had been added to the list, bringing the total up to five; no doubt this was a move to replace some of the old GNR types. I also noted that my records show only eight of the 'J5s' remaining. And four 'N5s' had reappeared on the scene, but for some reason the 'K3' allocation had been reduced to three. On the shunting side the 'J50s' had also been transferred away and replaced by more' J52s'.

By January 1955, just after I'd started my apprenticeship, more changes had taken place. The lone 'B17' had finally left the area, but there had been an increase in the allocation of 'K3s' to eight, and the 'J11' numbers were now seven. On the reduction side the 'J5s' were down to three. Regarding the tank engines, the 'N7s' had gone back to East Anglia, but replacing them eight of the ex-GNR class 'N1' 0-6-2Ts had arrived on the scene. The different classes now numbered 14 with the allocation of 198 locomotives.

Colwick also supplied the station pilots at Nottingham Victoria. 'J6' class 0-6-0 No. 64235 is shunting empty stock on the east side in 1959 and in the background can be seen the south end turntable. *Author*

Standing outside the old LNWR loco shed at Colwick are two 'Super D' 0-8-0s. There is no date on the photograph but it could be the late 1920s just before the shed closed. The 'Super Ds' worked up from Northampton to Colwick via the joint line almost into the 1960s and on occasions as many as three could be seen standing on the shed. *Frank Berridge Collection*

COLWICK AND ITS LOCOMOTIVES IN THE 1950s

Two years later, in January 1957, there was again a slight decrease in locomotive allocation to 196, now 13 different classes. Gone were the 'N1' and 'N5s' and the last remaining 'J5s'. Two of them, Nos. 65483 and 65498, lingered on for almost two years after the rest had been scrapped; they had been kept in service to work the Colwick Estates Light Railway daily shunt - apparently they had the right axle loading for this lightly-laid line. Two new classes arrived in the shape of five 'L1' class 2-6-4Ts and three of the ex-GER 'J69' class 0-6-0Ts, and there was a re-appearance of five 'J50s', no doubt to replace the ailing 'J52s' which at the time were disappearing to Doncaster works at quite a fast rate.

My final record shows mid-1958, at the time when Colwick was transferred to the Lincoln district. The allocation by then was down to 166; the burner's torch had been hard at work, but there were still 13 different classes on the books. Again, two new ones had been added, in the shape of a '9F class 2-10-0 No. 92186 and a 'J94' class 0-6-0ST No. 68033. Towards the end of 1958 more 'J94s' arrived, along with the first of the '4MT' class 2-6-0s in the '43000' numbering series. After this I made very few notes; maybe it was because I was unhappy about the transfer to Lincoln.

As for the visiting locomotives working into the depot from other districts, the list makes very interesting reading. The ones I always looked forward to seeing were the ex-LNWR 'Super D' 0-8-0s - these worked in over the old GNR/LNWR Joint line from Northampton. Out of East Anglia came the 'J17' 0-6-0s from South Lynn, 'K1' 2-6-0s and 'O1' 2-8-0s from March and on their fast turn round freight service, they used the 'K3' class. I heard of a story told one day of the Stratford-based, lone 'K5' class 2-6-0, working in on one of these turns, and the driver sending the fireman underneath the locomotive to oil the middle big-end bearing. (I will leave the reader to work that one out for themselves!) Grantham would often produce a 'O2' class 2-8-0 on an iron ore train, as well as providing 'B12' class 4-6-0s on the Grantham to Nottingham stopping passenger service. If one of them failed at Victoria station, they would be brought to Colwick for repair. I remember seeing on shed, at different times, Nos. 61554 and 61580, both stabled in 'New Shed'. As I have already mentioned, this also applied to the ex-GCR 'Director' 'D11' class 4-4-0s off the Lincoln line, working the stopping trains between Lincoln St Mark's and Nottingham Midland.

York, on their workings to Colwick, mostly supplied 'B16' and 'B16/3' class 4-6-0s; at times as many as two or three would be seen standing outside the 'Big Shed'. Doncaster could be relied upon to send quite a variety of motive power, as they often used locomotives fresh from overhaul in the works, on running in turns. Sometimes in the early 1950s the newly constructed BR '4MT' class 2-6-0s would arrive, and even the odd 'B17' made an appearance and I remember seeing on one occasion No. 61656 *Leeds United* standing on No. 1 road 'Big Shed' after one such working. As I previously mentioned, my biggest surprise came in the early 1950s, when one day I noted 'K4 class 2-6-0 No. 61997 *MacCailin Mor* passing through my home station, Radcliffe-on-Trent, on its way into the marshalling yard with a mixed freight. When I told my railway enthusiast school friends, no one would believe me! But I realized later that when it was required for a general overhaul it was sent to Doncaster or Darlington, and not Cowlairs, unlike many of the other locomotives allocated to Scotland.

Colwick workings were widespread with many going to the local collieries around Nottinghamshire and Derbyshire. Colwick-based 'WD' class 2-8-0 No. 90037 is taking empty wagons to Annesley colliery on the old GNR Leen Valley line, in 1960, and is passing the site of the closed Linby station, the church can be seen on the left; the passenger service on this line finished in 1931.
Author

Waiting to leave Nottingham Victoria and head north is Colwick 'K3' class 2-6-0 No. 61982, which may have been a replacement for a failure especially as it's carrying an express head code.
Author

COLWICK AND ITS LOCOMOTIVES IN THE 1950s

On summer Saturdays there was an East Coast seaside passenger working from King's Norton in the West Midlands via Derby Friargate and the back line through Mapperley tunnel. Locomotives would be exchanged in the marshalling yard. Very often it was hauled by an ex-MR '4F' class 0-6-0 or a '5MT' class 4-6-0, and from Colwick to Skegness it would have up front either a 'K2' or a 'K3'. The Midland Region locomotive would then run light to the shed for servicing and turning and then wait for the return working.

In the days just prior to the 1950s, it was not unknown for an ex-Great Eastern Railway 'D16' class 4-4-0 to put in an appearance, after having worked a horsebox special from Newmarket to Nottingham Hall Sidings, near to the racecourse.

As Colwick was the parent depot, it meant that from time to time locomotives from around the district would be brought in for major repairs, i.e. valves and piston examinations, which also included a motion overhaul - especially on the 'A3' class 4-6-2s allocated to the old GCR main line and based at Leicester, and on occasions a few of the 'V2' class 2-6-2s from Woodford Halse. It is of interest to note that the Leicester allocation of 'A3s' over this period was nearly always eight, but numbers varied from time to time between the following, Nos. 60039/44/48/49/52/54/59/60102/103/104/106/107/108/ 111 - No. 60107 *Royal Lancer* being one of my favourite locomotives. No doubt swaps took place between the GCR and GNR main lines when needs arose. All had been transferred back to the East Coast main line during 1958. Annesley and Staveley would also send some of their allocation for repair. I have already mentioned the '9F' class 2-10-0s and the fault with their pony wheels. But ones that were always a delight to see in the erecting shop, were two 4-4-2Ts, an ex-GNR 'C12' class No. 67363, which was used on the 'Dido' staff working between Annesley and Bulwell Common station, and an ex-GCR 'C13' class No. 67419 from Staveley. They also came in for valve and piston examinations.

In 1955, after the accident involving the 'W1' class 4-6-4 No. 60700 at Peterborough, all Gresley Pacifics had to have their bogie centre pins examined for cracks. These were quickly sent to various depots with repair shop facilities and overhead cranes, and a number of 'A3s' found their way to Colwick erecting shop. I well remember working on No. 60074 *Harvester*.

Towards the end of the 1950s a number of King's Cross 'A3s' and 'A4s' came up from London via Grantham, for their valve and piston examinations. This was due to a shortage of maintenance staff in the London area. Amongst some of the most celebrated visitors to the depot were two preserved Midland Railway veterans, single-wheeler No. 115 and 2-4-0 No. 158A. These were being towed back to Derby, after having been on exhibition at Leicester Belgrave Road station. They stood in 'Old Shed' having their axle box oil pads changed before continuing their journey. After Colwick transferred to the Lincoln District, several of the Immingham 'Britannias' also came in for repair.

When Colwick was taken over by the Midland Region, the ex-LMS '8F' class 2-8-0s seemed to be the mainstay of the depot, until the end of steam in 1966. But by then I had moved away to work in London, so have very few details about their activities. Even some of the numerous 'WDs' lingered on to the end and finished their days at Colwick.

Colwick erecting shop had the capacity to carry out quite major repairs especially as it had a 35 ton overhead crane. Waiting to enter the shop in the 1950s is Leicester (GC)-allocated 'A3' class 4-6-2 No. 60054 *Prince of Wales* needing a front end repair. On the left can just be seen the edge of the locomotive inspector's office. *Author's Collection*

Three of the present day locomotives to have been preserved, have at some time or other been allocated to Colwick: 'N7' class 0-6-2T No. 69621 seen here arriving at Holt on the North Norfolk Railway on Saturday 7th March, 2009 and 'B1' class 4-6-0 No. 61264. *Author*

My enthusiast friends sometimes tell me that, in later years, on odd occasions even a GWR 'Hall' would be seen on the ash pits. I never saw one, so have no way of confirming this. But I do know that a Southern Region Pacific came on to the shed in the early 1960s, after having worked a special to Nottingham.

It's worth mentioning that whilst I was working in the depot, the star locomotive was always 'B1' No. 61111. Whenever one was required for a special working, it was almost certain that it would be called into service. I remember seeing it burnished up one day, as a standby for the Royal Train, when the Queen was paying a visit to the area. It is also interesting to note that at least three of the present-day preserved locomotives spent part of their time based at Colwick: 'N7' class No. 69621, in 1954/1955, which at the present time is based on the North Norfolk Railway; 'B1' class No. 61264, which finished its working days at Colwick, ending up as the depot stationary boiler, which I am sure saved it from the burner's torch; and a 'J94' class 0-6-0ST, but at the moment I cannot recall its number.

The men who worked with the locomotives very often referred to some of the classes by their nicknames, not using their class numbers: 'WDs' were always known as 'Austerities', 'O4s' as 'Tinies', although the original ones had been the ex-GCR 0-8-0s, 'J11s' were 'Pom-Poms', 'K2s' 'Ragtimers' and 'K3s' 'Jazzers'. Very often a 'B1' became a 'Bongo', and the old GNR 0-6-0s were nearly always referred to by their GNR classification, the 'J6s' and 'J5s' as 'A' and 'B' engines. Visiting locomotives from East Anglia became 'Swedies', especially the old 'J17s', and those from the North-East as 'Yorkies'. All locomotives from other depots were known as 'Foreigners'; in fact, we had a foreigners' pit.

Many railway enthusiasts thought that Colwick was a boring and mundane place, but my few records show a large and interesting variety of locomotive classes. From my point of view it was one of the finest locomotive sheds on the Eastern Region of British Railways, but then I would say that - after all I was employed there for six years.

'O2' class 0-4-4T No. 24 *Calbourne* is departing Ryde Pier-head station on the Isle of Wight with a train for Ventnor in the summer of 1956. *Author*

Sandown station with train departing to Ventnor hauled by 'O2' class No. 17 *Seaview*. It was at Sandown that I spent a week's holiday with a friend in 1956 touring what was left of the railway system and visiting the sheds and works at Ryde and Newport. *Author's Collection*

Chapter Five

Travelling on a Free Pass

Becoming a railway employee meant that I would now be entitled to free and privilege travel after one month's employment, and I was able to use as many privilege tickets as required, at a quarter of the normal fare. But to obtain a ticket you had to first fill in a form at the office, and then get the foreman to countersign it before you could travel. This was the easy part, because you had to decide beforehand where you wanted to go, and which route you were taking, and if spending a week away on holiday it often meant filling in a number of forms for various routes, just in case you wanted to take days out. Very often you would return home with half of them not used. After three months' service, I was granted one Regional pass. As Colwick was in the Eastern Region of BR, it meant I could travel to any destination in the eastern counties, between the Humber and the Thames, including London. After six months I received two and after nine months three, of which one was classed as a foreigner. In other words, I could travel anywhere in Great Britain, but not in Europe. To obtain a pass for Europe, I had to complete five years' service. Again a form had to be filled in, at least three months prior to travel. When filling in the forms for passes, you always made sure the destination was well beyond the one you were actually travelling to: for example if your holiday was to be taken in Inverness, the destination would be either Wick or Kyle of Lochalsh, just in case you wanted a day out during your stay. Free passes were valid for three months and you were allowed to make a break of journey, but had to travel by the most direct route. The same system applied to the European pass. It was much better in later years when the system altered and you had coupons instead of tickets and an ID card to buy privilege tickets (PTs). At the same time the passes changed to 'all lines', which was a big help as far as I was concerned, as it gave me more scope to pursue my hobbies and interests.

My new friend Gordon and I soon put these facilities into good use. In the summer of 1956 we decided to take a week's holiday in the Isle of Wight, in order to travel on the lines that were still open, and also visit the tourist sites, but especially to see the 'O2' class 0-4-4Ts that were still in service hauling the passenger trains, plus the four 'E1' class 0-6-0Ts used for the freight and shunting duties. Before departing we had taken the precaution of applying for permits to visit the locomotive sheds and works. Obtaining the permits had been made easy by the help of the area assistant superintendent, Mr Glennister, who had said to us, 'Any time you require a shed permit, lads, just let me know by letter and I will make sure you receive them'. He was as good as his word, and over the next few years we visited many locomotive sheds around the country, especially those in the Scottish, North Eastern and Eastern Regions.

Before travelling to the Isle of Wight we had to work out how many privilege tickets we would require to cover the lines on the Island. Our accommodation had been booked in a guest-house at Lake near Sandown, at a price of £2 10s. 0d. for the week, half board. It was a bit expensive at the time, because I was

A delight whilst on a tour of Scotland in 1957 was seeing the old Caledonian Railway '72' class 4-4-0 No. 54486 on Perth shed. *Author*

Hawick in Scotland in 1961 and standing by the side of the shed is 'D34' class 4-4-0 No. 62484 *Glen Lyon*. It was in 1955 that I first visited Hawick on a trip from Carlisle and was hauled from there to Hawick by 'D30' 'Scot' class 4-4-0 No. 62440 *Wandering Willie*. *Author*

only earning £1 19s. 6d. a week. We travelled down to Sandown from Radcliffe via Grantham, King's Cross and Waterloo to Portsmouth Harbour, crossing to the Island on the Solent ferry to Ryde Pier Head. Here, an 'O2' class tank locomotive and train was waiting to take us on to Sandown. The ferry service at the time was still operated by paddle steamers. Arriving at Sandown on the Saturday afternoon, we were met by a team of boys who, for a fee of 6d., would transport our luggage to the guest-house on four-wheeled wooden trolleys, which to us was a big help as Lake was over a mile down the road.

On the Sunday morning we presented ourselves at the station ticket office with our first form for a return ticket to Ventnor. Standing behind the booking clerk was the station master who, realizing we were railway employees, asked if we required a weekly runabout ticket. When we told him we had not applied for one, he called us into his office, made out a PT form and countersigned it. This made travelling easy and saved us money, which we put to good use during the week - so much for railway protocol.

During the week we managed to travel on all the lines still open and saw most of the 'O2' class locomotives, being hauled by several of them, plus the four class 'E1s', and visited the sheds and works at Ryde and Newport. Sadly the lines from Newport to Freshwater and Newport to Ventnor West, along with the Bembridge branch, had closed a few years earlier. To visit the west of the island, we had to travel by Southern Vectis bus. We even had several rides on the Ryde Pier Tramway.

In 1957 we both embarked on an extensive tour of eastern Scotland, covering and visiting as many of the ex-North British Railway (NBR) and ex-Great North of Scotland Railway (GNSR) lines and sheds as possible. I had already visited the sheds in the Carlisle area in 1954, when staying on holiday with another friend and his family at Windermere in the Lake District, having travelled there by train from Nottingham. The journey to Carlisle was my first over the Shap Bank. I even managed to take a ride behind an ex-NBR 4-4-0 to Hawick on the Waverley line.

Our idea of going to Scotland was to see as many as possible of the ex-NBR locomotives, especially the 'D30' and 'D34' class 4-4-0s. Of the GNSR only one of the class 'D40s' remained in service, No. 62277 *Gordon Highlander*, which we saw at Huntly on the weekly shunt, after having passed it en route to Keith. At Keith we caught the next available train back to Huntly, in order to have a good look at this stylish locomotive before it was taken out of service and preserved. We rode over the line from Keith to Elgin via Craigellachie, hauled by a 'B1' class 4-6-0. It was market day in Elgin and the train was packed with passengers. Sheep and small calves were being transported in the luggage van, along with all kinds of feathered fowl. We returned to Keith and Aberdeen on the coast line via Buckie and Tillynaught Junction, passing on the way several of the 'K2' class 2-6-0s, a class of locomotive we were used to working on at Colwick. At Aberdeen Kittybrewster (GNSR) shed we were lucky enough to see the old class 'Z4' and 'Z5' 0-4-2 dock tanks. Unfortunately we missed out travelling on the branches to Fraserburgh, Peterhead and Ballater, as we were running out of time and had a lot to pack in during the rest of the week. But I must admit that we were really chasing the locomotives and not doing so much line bashing at that particular time.

Many visits to the North-East with my friend often brought up a few surprises. When visiting York we called in to the old roofless Midland Railway shed near the station on a number of occasions, several of the ex-North Eastern Railway tank engines were stabled there, and on one visit we even saw an old Stockton & Darlington Railway wagon standing on one of the roads being used for waste. Here, two 'J72' class 0-6-0Ts, Nos. 68677 and 68726, rest between duties.
Author

The main shed at York, now the site of the National Railway Museum, usually had a variety of locomotives stabled around the turntable. In this 1958 view we see 'A1' class 4-6-2 No. 60152 *Holyrood* of Haymarket shed and a 'J27' class 0-6-0 No. 65844 from Malton depot.
Author

Other sheds visited were Aberdeen Ferryhill, Dundee Tay Bridge (NBR) and the Caledonian Railway (CR) shed at Dundee West, where our digs overlooked the railway. At Thornton Junction (NBR), to our surprise we saw the last 'V4' class 2-6-2 and two of the 'K4' class 2-6-0s, from Glasgow Eastfield. And in Stirling Shore Roads (NBR) one-road shed, we managed to 'cop' our last 'D30' class No. 62426 *Cuddie Headrigg*. Both LMS sheds at Stirling and Perth revealed a large variety of classes, including a few of the ex-Caledonian Railway 4-4-0s. Around the Edinburgh area we managed to pull in the main line shed at Haymarket, the home of the locomotives which worked most of the expresses to Aberdeen and the East Coast main line towards London. St Margaret's shed south of Waverley station was far more interesting as it still had a quite large allocation of the smaller ex-NBR classes, including one of my favourites, the little 'Y9' class 0-4-0 dock tanks, used in and around Leith docks. The suburban sheds visited included Bathgate, Dunfermline, Alloa, where the shed foreman allowed us to walk through the tunnel leading to the docks, to 'cop' one of the ex-NBR 0-6-0s at work, and Dalry Road, the old CR shed which supplied locomotives for trains working out of Princes Street station, now long disappeared. Other classes seen during the trip, besides the many ex-LNER Pacifics and 'V2s', were the Scottish 'D11' class 4-4-0s, 'D49' class 4-4-0s (the 'Hunts' and 'Shires'), the 0-6-0s in classes 'J35', 'J36', 'J37' and 'J38', and the stately 'C16' class 4-4-2Ts. On shunting and station pilot duties at Waverley station, we found the 'J88' class 0-6-0Ts and 'N15' class 0-6-2Ts, which also from time to time worked local passenger services. Most of the suburban trains were in the hands of the 'V1' and 'V3' class 2-6-2Ts.

It had been an excellent holiday, even if we had not managed to achieve everything we set out to accomplish, it certainly brought back to us lots of happy memories, especially of the places we visited. We returned home via the East Coast main line, with a lot of extra underlining in our trusty Ian Allan 'ABCs'.

Our main interest in chasing locomotives was mainly confined to finding those classes that made up the former LNER, hence our reason for sticking to the eastern side of the country, although we did at times make excursions into other parts. Between our holidays, when time and money allowed, we took day trips, mostly on a Saturday, to East Anglia or the North-East of England. If we were going to the North-East areas, Gordon would catch the early morning train out of Nottingham Victoria at 5.25 am and I would join him when it stopped at Radcliffe at 5.41 am. Changing at Grantham we didn't have to wait long for a connection to Doncaster and York, which departed at 6.25 am and arrived Doncaster 7.57. If travelling on to York the connection departed at 8.15 am and ran into York at 9.04, just in time for breakfast. This usually meant that we sat on a platform seat and ate a few of the sandwiches that our mothers had packed for us, and then washed them down with cold tea or water. No going to the buffet in those days, as we could not afford the prices. When visiting sheds in the Newcastle area, we always made a point of catching 'The North Briton' from York, which departed at 9.51 am and conveyed through coaches to Glasgow. With only one stop at Darlington it covered the distance in 90 minutes, which gave us plenty of time in Newcastle before returning home. As there were so few trains in the evening going south, it usually meant leaving Newcastle at 4.30 pm, in order to catch the Nottingham connection at Grantham; even then it was nearly 9.00 pm before I arrived home. If we were only visiting the Doncaster or Hull areas we occasionally had a change and travelled from Nottingham Victoria to Sheffield Victoria on the old GCR, and changed there for Doncaster, travelling via Rotherham and Mexborough. On these trips I had to be the early riser and catch the train from Radcliffe at 5.25 am, meeting Gordon in Nottingham, where he would be waiting with the carriage door open, just in case my train was late and I had to make a last minute dash for the 6.00 am stopping train to Sheffield, which took nearly two hours to complete the journey and didn't arrive until 7.43 am. This gave us a 17 minutes connection into the 8.00 am departure, arriving in Doncaster at 8.48 am.

When going south to East Anglia, most of our trips were either to Cambridge or London. If it was Cambridge, we changed trains at Huntingdon instead of Peterborough and usually caught the through train from Nottingham Victoria to King's Cross, which departed at 7.33 am. Again I joined it at Radcliffe at 7.49 am. Although it was classed as an express, it was allowed plenty of time to reach Huntingdon, making several stops en route, including Little Bytham and Essendine, plus an engine change at Grantham, where the usual 'A5' class 4-6-2T which had hauled the train from Nottingham was exchanged for an 'A3' class Pacific. Arrival time in Huntingdon was 9.36 am, which gave us just enough time to dash across the yard to the East station to catch the Kettering to Cambridge train, departing at 9.41 and arriving at 10.20 am. This was usually hauled by a BR class '2MT' 2-6-0 and quite often double-headed as far as Huntingdon, where the leading locomotive was removed, owing to the weight restriction over the wooden trestle bridges between there and St Ives. Returning home was not quite so easy as we had to change at Huntingdon, Peterborough and Grantham. Journeys to London were made on the same through train, which arrived in King's Cross at 10.50 am, having taken 3 hours and 17 minutes. Today the journey can be done in less than two hours, including a change at Grantham. It seemed strange at the time that there was a through train to London from Nottingham in the morning, but no return working in the evening without having to change at Grantham. I can never remember the privilege ticket rates for all these journeys, except for the one from Radcliffe to King's Cross, which was 8s. 6d. return. By 1960 it had risen to 12s. 6d. It doesn't sound like much, but in 1955 it was nearly a quarter of my weekly wage!

As mentioned earlier, the idea of travelling to these places was to chase the locomotives and see as many of the older ones as possible, before they were taken out of service. I had already spent quite a bit of time in the East Anglian area when as a young boy, in the late 1940s and early 1950s, I went to stay each year during school holidays with an aunt and uncle at Beacontree near Dagenham. I used to spend a lot of the time sitting by the side of the Liverpool Street to Norwich main line at Chadwell Heath, with my notebook and pen, jotting down the locomotive numbers. The only section electrified in those days was as far as Shenfield, so the trains to Southend and Clacton were still steam hauled.

In East Anglia it was the locomotives of the former Great Eastern Railway that we went looking for - the elegant 'B12' class 4-6-0s and 'D16' class 4-4-0s, and the maids of all work, the 'J15' class 0-6-0s. Of special interest to us at Cambridge were the 'E4' class 2-4-0s, the only ones left on BR of that wheel arrangement still hauling passenger trains. Another class of locomotive, with special interest to me and amongst my favourites, was the handsome ex-LNER 'B17' class 4-6-0, at the time still hauling many of the expresses out of Liverpool Street, along with the BR 'Britannia' Pacifics. A visit to Stratford shed and works in east London revealed a variety of different classes; as well as those already mentioned there were the heavier type of freight locomotives in the classes 'J17', 'J19', 'J20' and the ex-LNER 'J39' 0-6-0s. The tank engines seen were the 0-6-0 'Coffee-Pots', in classes 'J67', 'J68' and 'J69', and the classes 'F5' and 'F6' 2-4-2Ts, used for working the Epping to Ongar branch. The suburban services out of Liverpool Street were in the hands of the 'N7' class 0-6-2Ts, to me ungainly looking machines, and the ex-LNER 'L1' class 2-6-4Ts. The works shunting locomotive was a 'Y4' class 0-4-0T No. 68126. As well as wandering around East Anglia, on the way home we very often spent time on the end of the platform at King's Cross, with all the other trainspotters, watching the ex-GNR 'N2' class 0-6-2Ts bringing in and taking out the empty coaching stock of the main line expresses, as well as hauling the many suburban trains. It fascinated me watching them plunging into the tunnel, after having made a stop at York Road station, on their way to Moorgate; and then on the west side of the station, seeing them climb out of the 'Rat Hole' tunnel on the return working, usually to Hertford North (but this could only be witnessed on a weekday, as Moorgate was little used on a Saturday).

I always enjoyed our trips to the North-East, especially to York, to see what must be one of the finest railway stations in the country, if not the world, and to visit the beautiful Minster city. At the time, the old GNR station, within the city walls, was still being used as a goods depot. And at the south end of the station stood the ex-Midland Railway roundhouse locomotive shed, still in use as a stabling point for the station pilot and shunting locomotives, but by then it had lost its roof. On one trip Gordon and I had permission to pay a visit, and to our surprise, standing on one of the roads was an old Stockton & Darlington Railway wagon, being used to hold the rubbish swept up from the shed floor. Once again it was the older locomotives that we were chasing. On York shed, as well as the numerous Pacifics, 'V2s', 'B1s' and 'K1s', there were the un-rebuilt and rebuilt ex-North Eastern Railway (NER) 'B16' class 4-6-0s, always a joy to see, the ex-LNER 'D49' class 4-4-0s for working the local semi-fast and stopping trains. On the tank engine side the ex-NER 'J71' and 'J72' class 0-6-0Ts were used for shunting and station pilot duties. One of these had been repainted into its original NER livery of green with the coat of arms on the side tanks. Highly polished, it looked splendid standing in the centre of York station, waiting for its next turn of duty.

Selby was another interesting place to visit, and on a trip there we found quite a collection of old NER stock in the shape of the solid looking yard shunting locomotives, the 'T1' class 4-8-0Ts. Although large in appearance they were stylish and every inch a workhorse. The lighter shunting locomotives there were the 'J73' class 0-6-0s, but of special interest to me were a few of the last remaining 'D20' class 4-4-0s; they were very elegant and just as good looking as

My friend and I enjoyed visiting the branch lines in the North-East especially the ones leading to the coastal resorts where the trains were very often hauled by one of the 'A8' class 4-6-2Ts. Inside Scarborough shed in 1958 is No. 69881 resting between duties. *Author's Collection*

Always a joy to see were the numerous 'Q6' class 0-8-0s freight locomotives and seen here, ex-works at Darlington, is Tyne Dock's 'Q6' class No. 63437. *Author*

the 'D40s' and 'D34s' in Scotland. We came across two others when we did a tour of the sheds in Hull - first visiting the main shed at Dairycoates, then Springhead, the old Hull & Barnsley Railway shed, where we came across the remaining ex-NER 'A7' class 4-6-2Ts, similar in appearance to the 'T1s', but built for passenger work; if I remember rightly they were in store. Botanic Gardens was the shed which provided the locomotives for the passenger duties, and the shed foreman made us most welcome, conducting us round and even supplying a list of locomotives allocated to the shed at the time of our visit. I still have the list today and it makes interesting reading. Of those seen on shed or round the station were three 'A5' class 4-6-2Ts, five 'A8' class 4-6-2Ts, five 'B1' class 4-6-0s, six 'D49' class 4-4-0s, plus four from the sub-shed at Bridlington, two 'D20' class 4-4-0s and two class '3MT' BR Standard 2-6-0s Nos. 77000 and 77010. Other tank engines were two 'G5' 0-4-4Ts, and six 'V1' and 'V3' class 2-6-2Ts, plus a solitary 'J73' 0-6-0T, almost the entire allocation, and only 12 were not seen.

Owing to the long distances we would have had to travel to the North-East, we made several day trips over two years. One was even by bus when we joined in one Sunday with the RCTS tour to visit the sheds at Northallerton and Darlington, plus the locomotive works. Darlington, like York, was always an interesting place for the trainspotter, as there was so much to see. On another occasion Gordon and I went there specially to travel on the line to Middlesbrough and Saltburn, just to take a ride behind the 'A5' and 'A8' class 4-6-2Ts which dominated that service.

The main reason for going to Newcastle was to see the workhorses of the NER, the 0-6-0s and 0-8-0s, mostly based in the industrial areas around Newcastle and Sunderland. Coal trains were hauled by the 'J27' class 0-6-0s, mainly in the area north of the Tyne around North and South Blyth, but could be found anywhere in the region. To the south of the Tyne it was the 'Q6' class 0-8-0s that seemed to do all the work, with help from the smaller 'J25' class 0-6-0s. The large 'Q7' class 0-8-0s were mostly reserved for working the iron ore trains from Tyne Dock to Consett, and were based at Blaydon and Tyne Dock sheds, until their duties, at a later date, were rostered to the new BR '9F' class 2-10-0s. Almost the entire class of 'J26' class 0-6-0s were hauling freight trains in and around the Middlesbrough and Hartlepool areas, and a good many of them could be found on the shed at Newport, now renamed Thornaby. Again, another of my favourite classes was the small-boilered 'J21' class 0-6-0s with their tall graceful chimneys. I was pleased when they preserved one at the Beamish Museum. By the time Gordon and I visited the area only a few of the class were left in service, so it was a case of chasing round for them. There were two or three based at Blaydon, and these from time to time worked into Newcastle, plus a few based at Tweedmouth in the north, which we saw from the train on our way to and from Edinburgh. Darlington shed also had one and we managed to 'cop' that on our visit with the RCTS. Also based at Darlington and Blaydon were the 'K1' class 2-6-0s used for mixed traffic work. And let's not forget the other reliable freight workhorses in the North-East, the class 'WDs'. No matter where you went in the country, one somehow always seemed to pop up.

On the passenger side, the expresses were in the hands of the Pacifics and 'V2s', with the 'B1s' working the trains on the line between Newcastle and Carlisle. The 'J72' class 0-6-0s did most of the shunting and station pilot duties, and like York one of them had been repainted into the green livery of the NER. Local passenger and branch line trains, besides the Tyne electrics, were being hauled by the 'G5' class 0-4-4Ts, especially in the Sunderland area, and I remember riding behind one on the line from Durham to Sunderland via Penshaw, long since closed - although recently a short length of it has been reopened at the Sunderland end as part of the extended Metro system.

Of all the sheds visited the one I enjoyed the most was Borough Gardens, just outside of Newcastle by the side of the line to Sunderland. It was a Saturday and the shed was full of 0-6-0 and 'Q6' class 0-8-0 freight locomotives, and we had a wonderful time writing down the numbers. But it was in finding the place that we had the most fun. Although we always carried with us our Shed Directory Book, the locospotters' bible, it was still difficult to locate, as we first had to catch a bus from the city centre. The conductor put us off nearby, but there was no sight of the shed. Eventually we asked a lady the way, but gave up when we realized that we couldn't understand what she was talking about, owing to her speaking the local dialect. After wandering down several streets we found the entrance, and made ourselves known to the shed foreman, who also spoke the same dialect. We must have understood him, as we had no difficulty in getting in. Gateshead was another interesting shed to visit as it was a combination of both running shed and locomotive works, or that's how it seemed to us, and we found 'A4' Pacifics mixed in with freight and shunting engines.

As well as roaming the North-East and East Yorkshire, we ventured into the West Riding, especially to the Leeds and Wakefield area to visit the sheds at Neville Hill, which had a quite a large allocation of ex-NER and LNER locomotives, such as the "B16s', 'D49s' and the 'G5' and 'A8' tanks – and Copley Hill, the home of many ex-GNR locomotives, where it was a pleasing sight to see the 'N1' class 0-6-2Ts working some of the local passenger services. We even got in visits to the ex-LMS sheds at Holbeck, which supplied the power for trains working over the Settle & Carlisle line, and Stourton Junction, that provided locomotives for many of the freight trains running on the lines of the old MR. But the highlight of our visits to Leeds was to ride the electric trams, especially when we went out to visit Neville Hill shed.

Nearer to home I paid visits to Sheffield Darnall and Mexborough, mainly to see the remains of the old GCR classes, such as the 'J11' class 0-6-0s known as the 'Pom-Poms', and the 'O4' 2-8-0s, the 'Tinies'; and at Darnall, the 'D11' class 4-4-0s - the 'Directors'; but these later worked out of Lincoln. Of the local sheds, I visited them in my younger days whilst still attending school, usually by bicycle, because I couldn't afford the train fare. At Grantham I had no difficulty in getting around. I just went to see my uncle Sid, and when it was convenient he walked round with me. At the other places it was a case of sneaking in through the gate or a hole in the fence, and making sure you were not seen by the running foreman. In this way I visited Newark (GNR), both sheds at Retford (GNR and GCR), Tuxford and Langwith Junction, both former sheds on the

LD&ECR until taken over by the GCR. At Langwith it was the large shunting locomotives of classes 'Q1' 0-8-0 and 'S1' 0-8-4s that I especially went to see. I think there were two of each class based there, or that's what my records show. If I had plenty of time on the way home, a call would be made at either Mansfield or Kirkby-in-Ashfield. Somehow I never seemed to get as far as the sheds at Chesterfield (Staveley) or Annesley until I went to work for the railway, even though Annesley was close to Kirkby. I suppose it was because I saw most of their locomotives passing through Nottingham Victoria station.

Lincoln and the Grimsby area were well covered, again in my schooldays, especially when the family went to visit an old friend in Lincoln. If I went with them I would spend part of the day standing by the Durham Ox Crossing to the east of the station, a good vantage point for all trainspotters in Lincoln. The level crossing has now been removed and replaced by a road bridge, and the Durham Ox pub has been pulled down. Travelling to Lincoln, we always went by train, either via the MR line from Nottingham Midland to Lincoln St Mark's, which was the usual way, or via Grantham on the line through Leadenham. A few family holidays were spent with relations in Cleethorpes, again travelling there by train from Nottingham Victoria on a Saturday Special via the GCR route through Mansfield, Lincoln and then to Grimsby on the line through Market Rasen. If I were lucky enough, during the week I would be allowed a few hours' trainspotting in Grimsby and maybe see an odd GCR 0-6-0T shunting in the dock sidings. But the most enjoyable part of the holiday was the annual ride on the Grimsby to Immingham tramway, to view the ships in the docks. Also from Radcliffe I went on the annual church Sunday School outing, which was either to Skegness or Mablethorpe via Boston. There was always a reserved coach for us all on the train, which had started its journey at Nottingham, and picked up other school parties at stations en route. The train was mostly hauled by a 'B1' class 4-6-0, or a 'K2' class 2-6-0 locomotive. All this was before my days of using a free pass or a privilege ticket, but then I suppose I was travelling free, because my parents were paying for the tickets.

Sadly these scenes have long since disappeared and most of the lines in the North Eastern and Eastern Regions have closed. But I am pleased that we went when we did, and saw them in the latter part of their heyday.

Gordon and I never seemed to venture into other parts of the country, except on special trains; maybe it was because we only had one free pass per year which covered those areas. But we were mainly interested in the locomotives of the pre-Grouping companies that had made up the LNER in 1923. I can't remember ever going to Wales until after I was married, except in the early 1950s when I went on an outing to Llandudno with my local church choir. Although it was by road I did manage a ride on the Llandudno to Colwyn Bay Tramway, but missed out on seeing the narrow gauge lines until they were preserved.

However, in 1958 we decided to take a week's holiday at Wells in Somerset, but this time with a difference, as we pursued one of our other interests, church architecture, and there was no better place to go to than Somerset to see the churches in all their gothic glory - wonderful perpendicular towers, amongst some of the finest in the country. As I was a bell-ringer I had a dual purpose, not

Mablethorpe station on 26th November, 1960, not a train in sight on what appears to be a wet bleak morning, not as I remember it back in the 1950s when we arrived on the annual Sunday school outing, the platform would be a sea of people all making their way to the beach.
Derek Thompson/GNR Society

In my schooldays I would often go to Lincoln especially when the family went to visit an old friend there, and my favourite place for trainspotting was the Durham Ox crossing. Crossing over the road on it way from the GCR shed to Lincoln St Marks in the mid-1950s is 'D11' class 4-4-0 No. 62660 *Butler-Henderson*, now preserved, no doubt on its way to work one of the local trains to either Nottingham or Derby.
Robin Sharman Collection

only to see the church, but if I had the chance, to ring the bells. It didn't mean that we had lost interest in the trains, but just thought we would have a change. We travelled down on a free pass from Nottingham to Bristol Temple Meads via the old MR main line, and changed there into a semi-fast train going to Exeter, which stopped at Yatton for passengers to alight for the branch line trains to Clevedon and Wells. I can't remember what type of locomotives hauled the trains, except the one from Yatton, which was a 2-6-2 tank. Alighting at Wells Tucker St station it was only a short distance to the B&B. This time we had taken our bicycles with us to make it easy getting from church to church during the week, and besides it saved us money, not having to fork out for bus fares. We were always on a tight budget. It was a beautiful sunny week, and on the day we arrived it was so hot that we retired to the nearest hostelry and downed a pint of cider, which knocked Gordon out for the rest of the day. Returning home at the end of the week, we had the pleasure of a ride up the Lickey incline. We were riding in the first coach behind the engine, which was an ex-LMS 2-6-0 'Crab', although the train was being banked by three ex-GWR pannier tanks, the roaring sound emitted from the chimney of the 'Crab' was tremendous.

Of the special trains mentioned we rode on two of the many organized by the local RCTS branch entitled 'The East Midlander', the first to Crewe in 1955 and in the following year another to Swindon works. Both took roundabout routes and went on little used lines, including some for freight only. The 1955 trip on the 8th May, departing at 9.15 am, was hauled by an ex-GER 'B12' class 4-6-0, No. 61554, at the time based at Grantham. The route taken from Nottingham Midland station was along the main line west towards Trent, before turning onto the goods road at Attenborough Junction to run through Toton and up the Erewash Valley line to Dore and Totley South Junction, there turning left onto the Hope Valley line and through the famous Dore and Totley tunnel, the longest under land in Great Britain. At New Mills South Junction the direct route to Cheadle Heath was traversed before running onto the old Cheshire Lines Committee Railway to Northwich, where we turned south to Sandbach, on the main line to Manchester, and took the up line to Crewe. At Crewe the train took a diversionary route in order to gain access to the locomotive works. First it passed beneath the West Coast main line, north of the station, then ran along the goods road into Basford Hall sidings, and reversed onto the old North Staffordshire Railway line, once again passing beneath the main line. It was then facing in the right direction to enter the works off the Chester line, after first passing through the station. Two and a half hours were allowed for everyone to have a good look round the works. The journey back to Nottingham was along the North Staffs line to Derby via Stoke and Uttoxeter. At Derby the train departed to the north and then curved right onto the line passing through Chaddesden sidings, and joining up with the Nottingham line west of Spondon to continue its journey through Trent station, arriving at the Midland station at 7.07 pm. As far as anyone can recall, it was the first time a GER locomotive had ever entered Crewe works.

The following year, on 6th May, 1956, it was the turn of Swindon works to entertain 'The East Midlander', this time being hauled by an ex-MR '2P' class 4-4-0. Again the journey there and back was via a roundabout route. Departing

In 1955 my friend and I joined the RCTS 'The East Midlander' special to Crewe works hauled by Grantham-allocated 'B12' class 4-6-0 No. 61554. On Sunday 8th May it is standing in platform three at Nottingham Midland station ready to depart on its roundabout route, out via Dore and Totley tunnel and Altrincham and home via Uttoxeter and Derby.

J. Henton/Author's Collection

On display at Crewe works on the 8th May, 1955 was the ex-LNWR 0-6-0ST No. 1439. *Author*

No. 61554 is now seen standing in Crewe station platform No. 1 ready to depart back to Nottingham with the 'The East Midlander' railtour on 8th May, 1955. I think this may have been the first time that a 'B12' class had been seen at Crewe. *John F. Oxley/Author's Collection*

'B12' class 4-6-0 No. 61554 is standing at Uttoxeter with the returning 'East Midlander' railtour to Nottingham on 8th May, 1955. Whilst the locomotive was being watered we were allowed to alight from the train for a quick look round the engine shed, which if my memory serves me right contained a stored ex-L&Y 2-4-2T. *T.J. Eddington/Author's Collection*

On the 6th May, 1956 the 'The East Midlander' railtour to Swindon works is seen running into Swindon ex-GWR station, hauled by two '2P' class 4-4-0s Nos. 40454 and 40489. They were running tender first after reversing at Rushey Platt to gain access to the GWR main line, No. 40489 had been acting as pilot whilst travelling down the old Midland & South Western Junction Railway line via Cirencester, having been attached at Cheltenham.

T.J. Eddington/Author's Collection

On Sunday 6th May, 1956 at Swindon works the author is standing by the side of 'Castle 'class 4-6-0 No. 7010 *Avondale Castle* which had just received an overhaul. *Author's Collection*

the Midland station the train ran along the main line to Sheet Stores Junction and turned onto the goods line passing through Castle Donington to Stenson Junction on the Derby to Birmingham line. It then traversed the Birmingham line, via Burton-on-Trent and Tamworth as far as Saltley, where it bypassed Birmingham on the Camp Hill line to King's Norton. Joining the main line to Bristol, via the Lickey incline, we ran as far as Cheltenham Lansdown station, and turned left onto the GWR line towards Kingham and Banbury. After about 10 miles, at Andoversford, the train joined the old Midland & South Western Junction Railway main line to Swindon, via Cirencester. Both these lines have long since closed. This time we were only allowed one hour and forty minutes to look round the works. At 4.10 pm the train departed east along the former GWR main line to Didcot Foxhall Junction and turned north to Oxford. Leaving the GWR line there it ran onto the ex-LNWR line towards Bedford and Cambridge. In my days of working at Hitchin [more later], it was known as the 'Boat-race Line'. At Bletchley we turned north onto the West Coast main line and ran as far as Blisworth, and took the LNWR route to Wellingborough. The journey back to Nottingham from Wellingborough was via the Midland main line through Kettering, Oakham, Melton Mowbray and Old Dalby, arriving at 8.52 pm. The latter section between Melton and Edwalton, on the outer edge of the Nottingham suburbs, is now a test track.

As well as 'The East Midlander' trips, I attended the works open day at Derby and on one occasion amongst the locomotives seen was the ex-MR 0-10-0, 'Big Bertha' which had been specially constructed to operate on the Lickey incline, banking trains to the summit. She spent all her life based at Bromgrove, except for the times when she came to Derby works for a general overhaul.

Like all other trainspotters from the Nottingham area, when time allowed I travelled on a free pass or a PT to Trent station, a very popular place to catch not only the freight trains hauled by the LMS Garretts, but also the expresses working between London St Pancras and the North of England, via Nottingham, Derby and Sheffield. The other popular place I visited was the spotters' field at Tamworth, where you could kill two birds with one stone, as they say, by not only seeing the West Coast main line traffic passing through the low level platforms, but also the cross-country expresses, working between the West Country and the North, on the high level line. This was a good place to see the 'Royal Scots', 'Princess Royals', 'Coronations', 'Jubilees' and 'Patriots' mixed in with the 'Black Fives', '8Fs' and many other ex-LMS and BR Standard locomotives.

By 1958 girls appeared on the scene and I began to walk out with a young lady from Devon, who at the time was living with one of her friends in Nottingham. It was never going to work out as she lived too far away, and besides it really was only a friendship, as we often joined in with our pals and all went out together. I was also taking a greater interest in my bell-ringing activities, and chasing steam locomotives started to take a bit of a back seat. But I never gave up on them as Gordon and I from time to time still enjoyed a good train ride and no matter what happened I still used my annual quota of free passes. Also in 1958 I joined the Society of Rambling Ringers, a group of students who cycled round the countryside, staying at youth hostels overnight and ringing bells at different churches in the daytime. On my first trip the tour

No. 40454 is now on its way back to Nottingham from Swindon with the 'The East Midlander' railtour on 6th May, 1956 and is seen taking the west curve off the ex-GWR main line at Didcot in order to gain the line to Oxford. *J. Faithfull/Author's Collection*

Memories of spotting days at Tamworth as 'Royal Scot' class 4-6-0 No. 46122 *Royal Ulster Rifleman* hauling the 'The Mancunian' roars through the centre road at Tamworth Low Level, heading south. *Robin Sharman Collection*

started at Shrewsbury, and ended after two weeks in Cheltenham, having taken in the city of Bristol. A bell-ringing friend and I travelled to Shrewsbury by train from Nottingham to Birmingham New Street, cycled cross the city to Snow Hill Station and rode the old GWR line via Wolverhampton and Wellington, our bikes stowed in the guard's compartment. From Cheltenham we cycled cross-country to Woodford Halse, and before boarding the train to Nottingham, I took a quick look to see what locomotives were stabled on the shed.

The following year I did a tour of Oxfordshire, Wiltshire and Berkshire starting at Banbury and for me finishing at Faringdon, where I caught the branch train to Uffington, hauled by an ex-GWR 0-6-0PT; from there I went to Oxford via Didcot and picked up the cross-country Poole-Bradford express to Nottingham Victoria.

A few weeks later I met my future wife June at a bell-ringers meeting in Aspley near Nottingham; at the time she was living at Oakham in Rutland. She too was interested in the Society of Rambling Ringers, so in 1960 we both joined the tour to Hampshire, including the Isle of Wight, Sussex and Kent. Unfortunately we had to cut the tour short at Goudhurst in Kent and return home when June fell from her bicycle and broke her wrist after swerving to miss a group of people in front of her. After treatment in Tunbridge Wells Hospital, we caught the Hawkhurst branch train at Goudhurst, hauled by a 'H' class 0-4-4T, as far as Paddock Wood. Before the train arrived, we both had a tour of the signal box, after having been called in by a very friendly signalman. He must have realised I was a railwayman, maybe it was the way I admired the station buildings and furniture! At Paddock Wood we joined a train bound for London Charing Cross. Looking after two bicycles was not easy and somehow we had to cross London to St Pancras. Whilst June waited at Victoria I cycled over to St Pancras and left my cycle at the left luggage office, and returned to Victoria by underground. Then we both walked, wheeling June's cycle at the side. It was a long operation, but we managed it and were just in time to catch an express to Oakham, hauled by a Jubilee class 4-6-0.

From first meeting June to the summer of 1960 I spent my time on some Saturdays travelling between Nottingham Midland and either Melton Mowbray or Oakham, in order to be with her; other times it was on my bicycle. My one lasting memory of those journeys was the train stopping at Old Dalby, especially in the winter when it was dark. The station was dimly lit by gaslight and I shall never forget the porter walking the platform carrying his oil lamp shouting 'Dalby'. It could easily have been 1900 instead of 1960, very little had changed. The stopping trains were usually hauled by an ex-LMS '4MT' class 2-6-2T, or if it was a semi-fast it would be a 'Black 5' or a 'Jubilee'.

After returning from the 1960 bell-ringing holiday, June moved from Oakham to live in Felixstowe, on the sunny Suffolk coast, her father having moved there with his work. It now meant that I had a lot further to travel if I was still going to see her at weekends. I made one or two trips, before I too moved to live in London during August of the same year, travelling once again on the lines of the old GER. But this time instead of changing at Huntingdon, I went by way of Peterborough, March, Ely, Cambridge and the cross-country route via Bury St Edmunds to Ipswich, changing there into the branch train to Felixstowe. We

As well as a railwayman I was also a church bell-ringer so in 1958 I joined the Society of Rambling Ringers, a group of students who in the summer months cycled around the countryside ringing the bells of different churches. I later joined the Railwaymen's Guild of Church Bell-ringers and for two years was their Ringing Master. This photograph shows a group of Rambling Ringers outside the gates of Christ Church Swindon in 1958, the author is on the right next to the gate post. *Author's Collection*

On a tour of churches in Cornwall in 1961 with the Railwaymen's Guild my future wife and I returned home by train from Launceston. From there to Halwill Junction the train was hauled by an ex-LSWR 'T9' class 4-4-0, but sadly I never took a photograph of the locomotive, so to make amends here is one taken at Salisbury with No. 30729 standing outside the shed. *Author*

spent some enjoyable weekends, before we married in October 1961, travelling round by train, and at the same time doing a spot of bell-ringing. But I will talk more about those days later.

Falling off her bike didn't put June off and the next year 1961 we joined a successful bell-ringing tour to Somerset, Devon and Cornwall. During the tour, to cut out a long cycle ride and to save time, all the ringers boarded a train at Wiveliscombe to ride to Dulverton on the ex-GWR line between Taunton to Barnstaple. The three-coach train ran in, behind a GWR 2-6-0, and to accommodate our bikes we had to load them into empty compartments as there was very little room in the luggage van. The driver and fireman had a good laugh and joined in with the fun, shouting rude comments. Little did I realise at the time that one day I would meet the driver again, after I joined the 'Railwaymen's Guild of Church Bell-ringers'. Jack Thomas the driver was also a keen ringer at Taunton and remembered the occasion well. As well as driving branch line trains, Jack was in the top link, and often drove the 'Castles' and 'Kings' on expresses to Paddington. He and I became good ringing friends until I left the railway in 1980, and spent many an hour talking about our exploits working with the steam locomotives. June and I had to cut the tour short at Launceston to return home, as we had run out of time and work called. We chose to travel to London on the old London & South Western (LSWR) main line to Waterloo. To my delight on joining the train at Launceston, it was being hauled to Halwell Junction by an ex-LSWR 'T9' class 4-4-0. From Halwell I think it was an ex-Southern Railway 2-6-0 to Okehampton, but from there an unrebuilt 'West Country' Pacific was up front, and took us through to Waterloo.

As you see, although I was not chasing so many steam locomotives I was still putting my free passes and privilege tickets to good use and riding the trains of Great Britain. As soon as June and I married, it meant that both of us could then enjoy free and privilege travel. We didn't let the grass grow under our feet, and in the next few years visited Scotland, Wales and the West Country, especially riding the branch to Barnstaple and Ilfracombe, before it closed between Barnstaple Junction and Ilfracombe, cutting out the Mortehoe bank, which was a shame, because it was a joy to ride behind a steam locomotive as it climbed to the summit. But, as I said, those days are another story.

BRITISH TRANSPORT COMMISSION

BR 9211

BRITISH RAILWAYS

EASTERN REGION

15th. November, 19 60

Certificate of Apprenticeship

I hereby certify that

JOHN MEREDITH,

born on the 22nd. November, 1939 *has been employed as an Apprentice in the* Motive Power Department at Colwick

from 29.12.54 *to* 22.11.60

Trade to which Apprenticed FITTER.

for Traffic Manager,

District Motive Power Officer.

Chapter Six

Finsbury Park - The Learning Curve

At Colwick my apprenticeship was drawing to a close; I had only three more months to complete, so the management decided to send me to the recently opened diesel depot at Finsbury Park in North London, situated on the down side of the East Coast main line, south of the station. I moved there during August 1960 and straightaway was involved in the maintenance of the East Coast main line diesel locomotives, mostly the English Electric type '4s' (class '40s') and type '5s' (class '55' 'Deltics'). Unlike the steam locomotives, I have never quite taken the same interest in the diesels, so my memories of those first three months are scant, except for working on the prototype 'Blue Deltic' with the English Electric engineers. I think the only thing that the BR fitters were allowed to touch was the changing of the brake blocks.

I had found digs in Stoke Newington, with a lady whose father had been station master at Grimsby in north Lincolnshire, so she knew a little about the workings of the railway. It seemed strange living in the surroundings of a large city, especially after the wide-open areas of the countryside; having to catch a bus each morning to get to work, making its way through the London rush hour, was somewhat alien to me.

As my future wife, June, had moved from Oakham to Felixstowe in Suffolk with her parents during the summer of 1959, every weekend or whenever possible I would travel from London to Felixstowe to be with her. My journey was to cross London on the Underground to Liverpool Street station, where I would catch a Norwich-bound express to Ipswich, changing there into the branch train to Felixstowe. This was an interesting trip as the Norwich expresses were still being hauled by the 'Britannia' class 4-6-2s, with the odd type '4' diesel thrown in for good measure. Unfortunately the Felixstowe branch had changed over to diesel railcars by then, but the passenger service was still open to the Beach station on the dock branch. June and I did a lot of travelling around East Anglia, with me looking for the remaining steam locomotives and both of us finding new churches to visit, especially where we could ring the bells, very often returning back to Felixstowe Beach station and walking home from there along the sea front.

Whilst working at 'The Park', one of the most amusing things I noticed was the fitting staff arriving for work each day in suits, carrying a rolled umbrella and in some cases a briefcase. I thought those were reserved for the civil servants and office staff. At Colwick they would turn up for work dressed in jacket and flat cap, carrying a tin under their arm containing the sandwiches.

On 22nd November, 1960 my apprenticeship was complete and I was called back to Colwick to collect my certificate, pronouncing me to be a fully trained tradesman. I was also given my City & Guilds engineering certificates, having studied part-time at the local technical college over the past six years. I also received some disturbing news: there was no fitting job for me in the steam depot. Traffic in the area had been running down and the railways in the Nottingham district were

A view looking across the main line side of London Liverpool Street station from the central road bridge in 1959. This brings back a lot of memories for me, the days in the late 1940s and early 1950s when I travelled to Chadwell Heath to stay with relatives and in later years when I departed from there to Ipswich and Felixstowe to see my future wife. On the left is 'B2' class 4-6-0 No. 61644 *Earlham Hall*, in the centre 'B1' class 4-6-0 No. 61280 and on the right English Electric type '4' No. D234.   *Robin Sharman Collection*

English Electric type '4' No. D237 passing over Barnby Crossing near Newark with a southbound express to King's Cross in 1961, this was the locomotive I rescued with the seized cam shaft.   *Robin Sharman Collection*

losing trade, so no more staff could be taken on. I was given a choice, either to go down the road to the local labour exchange and look for an engineering job, which quite a few of my fellow apprentices had done, finding work at the pits with the National Coal Board, or stay where I was at Finsbury Park, or join the staff at Top Shed King's Cross, as they were crying out for fitting staff at that time. I chose to stay at Finsbury Park and returned to London a few days later.

I soon settled into the daily routine of being on the day shift and was employed on most types of jobs involved with the maintenance of diesel locomotives, from the one-day service to larger inspections and general repairs and breakdowns. Working on my own with a fitter's mate was not something new to me, as I had already spent a period of time on my own at Colwick when they were short of staff; but this time I had to take full responsibility for my actions if anything went wrong, which was no worry to me, as I've always felt quite confident in whatever I've done in my working life. I can't say it was exactly an exciting time whilst I worked the short time at the Park; we always seemed to be confined to the depot and rarely got out on breakdowns, except on odd occasions. I suppose I was somewhat lucky to be given the task of carrying out the first one of the three-monthly inspections on one of the new main line 'Deltics', No. D9003 *Meld*.

One day I got my chance to attend to a breakdown, when the foreman called me to his office and asked me to go to an English Electric '08' class diesel shunting locomotive which had broken down in Ashburton Grove siding. 'Good', I thought, 'at long last a trip to the country' - only to find that Ashburton Grove was situated on the opposite side of the main line to the depot, on the branch to Moorgate - what a disappointment.

A few days later I was called out again this time to the main line when type '4' No. D237 failed with loss of power. On investigation I found that one of the engine cam-shafts had seized - being 16 cylinder 'V' engines, they had two cam-shafts, with 8 cylinders on each bank. The shafts were chain-driven, and the damaged one had had all the teeth stripped from the sprocket wheel drive. There was nothing left to do but have the locomotive towed back to the depot for repair. I spent the next few weeks renewing the shaft and retiming the engine, which turned out to be quite a major job.

A big percentage of the work involved working on the Brush type '2s' (class '31') and BR type '2s' (class '24'), these by then being responsible for working most of the suburban services out of King's Cross and Moorgate. One class I came to know quite well were the BTH type '1s' (class '17s') in the D8200 numbering series, plus the English Electric type '1s' (class '20') and the type '2' D5900 'Baby Deltics'. These last two classes I got to know even better after I moved to Hitchin, some months later.

The steam locomotives from King's Cross were still responsible for maintaining a good majority of the main line passenger traffic, and one memory which will always stay in my mind was being allowed to stand outside the depot and watch the Royal Train pass on its way to York for the Duke of Kent's wedding in the Minster. The train was hauled by 'A4' class 4-6-2 No. 60026 *Miles Beevor*; she looked fantastic, highly-polished with a white painted roof and not a speck of dust in sight, a credit to the lads at Top Shed.

A view inside the new Finsbury Park diesel depot in November 1961 showing the upper level platform, across the ends of the roads, the offices and workshops were to the right out of the picture, and below the platforms were the raised track levels and the pits. On the left is type '5' 'Deltic' class No. D9009 *Alycidon* with its nose top doors open, '08' class 0-6-0 No. D3892, Brush type '2' No. D5650, a BR type '2' and another Brush type '2' No. D5641, I joined the team there in August 1960. *Midland Railway Trust/Author's Collection*

A Napier 'Deltic' 18 cylinder diesel engine from one of the type '5' locomotives, which is now on display in the National Railway Museum at York. They were not easy engines to work on especially when in the confines of a locomotive engine room. *Author*

After a few months I began to develop a keen interest in the train heating boilers, no doubt due to my steam training, and soon became quite knowledgeable on the various types in use, especially those manufactured by the firm of Spanner; these were a conventional type of boiler, oil fired with flue tubes and came in several different designs, i.e. Mark I, II or III. The Mark I had a vertical boiler, but the Mark II had a horizontal one and looked a bit like Stephenson's *Rocket*. These were fitted to the class '55' 'Deltics'. The firm of Stones produced another type of boiler, which were really steam generators, having a water coil fitted inside the firing chamber. Water was pumped through the coil and by the time it left at the other end it had developed into high-pressure steam. Again these came in several different designs. Due to my keen interest, I was very often called upon to carry out repairs or modifications to the boilers fitted on the different types of locomotives allocated to the depot.

During my time at the Park, I was sent on my first training course of many. This time it was to the Diesel Training School at Stratford locomotive works in east London, a three weeks' course on the maintenance of diesel locomotives and railcars.

On the third week, the training instructor came to me and said that there were quite a few vacancies for draughtsmen in the drawing office: would I be interested in applying for one of the positions? Why he selected me I'm not quite sure, I was good at drawing and we had been sketching out plans and diagrams during our course work, maybe he had noticed examples of my work and thought it good enough for the design office. I decided against applying as the pay for a junior draughtsman was below that of a tradesman, so I would be better off staying at the Park. Besides June and I were thinking about marriage at the time.

At the start of summer 1961 I was asked to go on relief work to Hitchin in North Hertfordshire. This was a sub-depot to the Park, 32 miles north of King's Cross and manned by a very small staff; they were chiefly involved in the daily servicing of the diesel locomotives and carrying out repairs and attending to breakdowns, on both steam and diesel. This sounded all very attractive to me so I agreed to give it a go.

Hitchin is a very pleasant market town, with some beautiful buildings and an ancient church. The original two-road locomotive depot was situated by the side of the station on the up side, but by 1961 had lost its allocation of steam, although it was still used for the stabling of steam locomotives visiting from other depots, having worked in on freight trains, mainly from the Peterborough area. It still had a usable turntable, the water softening plant, a coal hoist, rarely used, a water tank, situated on top of a cliff at the back of the shed, which supplied water to the shed and the various water cranes in the area, and the offices of the shed master, clerks, the running foremen, who were in charge of the footplate staff, and the signing-on point.

In 1960 a new two-road diesel depot had been constructed at the back of the down yard, next to the old Midland Railway shed, which by then had been long closed and converted to a road motor repair garage. The fitting staff were based in this new depot, under the control of a chargehand fitter; the allocation of men were four fitters, one on days and three on round-the-clock shifts, a semi-skilled fitter, an electrician, five mates and a labourer.

The allocation of diesel locomotives was quite small; although they really belonged to Finsbury Park, with a Park shed plate (34G), they were out-stationed at Hitchin for working the local freight trains, shunting the various station yards in the area, such as Hatfield, Welwyn Garden City, Letchworth and Huntingdon, working the London suburban passenger trains, especially those starting in the early morning from Letchworth, Baldock and Royston, and the Cambridge buffet expresses. Locomotives allocated were in four different classes, 10 English Electric type '1s' (class '20'), 10 type '2s' (class '23', the 'Baby Deltics') which made up the entire class in service, eight English Electric class '08' 0-6-0 shunting locomotives and six Drewry '04' class 0-6-0s. The '08s' were out-based at Hatfield and Welwyn Garden City and only came back to the depot at weekends for servicing. The '04s' were used at Hitchin to shunt the up and down yards, with two out-based, one each at Letchworth and Huntingdon. The Letchworth one returned to the depot for servicing, but a fitter had to go once a month to look after the one at Huntingdon.

This was the state of the depot when I arrived there one Monday morning in June 1961, acting as a holiday relief. I was told to report to the chargehand fitter at the new diesel depot and he would allocate me my duties. I soon found out that he had been a former Colwick fitter, as had the shed master and the foreman in charge of the road motor garage; it was like going home. I also found out that there was a vacancy for a full-time fitter; this was my chance to return to the country way of life. On returning that evening to the Park I immediately applied for a transfer, and a week later, to my surprise, it was granted and I became a member of the Hitchin staff, staying there for almost five years.

The lovely old market town of Hitchin in Hertfordshire. A view along the High Street, which in 1961 was a far cry from the congested streets of London, when I moved there to take up my post as a fitter at the then new diesel depot. *Author's Collection*

Chapter Seven

Happy Days at Hitchin

As the day shift fitter, I was mostly responsible for the servicing and carrying out of the various examinations and repairs on the diesel locomotives. I was also called on to deal with any repairs and breakdowns on the visiting steam locomotives, another reason why I was keen on a transfer. As it was a small depot one soon got to know the staff, especially the footplatemen who worked in the area, several of whom had transferred from Colwick and Langwith Junction, on the old LD&ECR and I became friendly with quite a few of them, which was to my advantage in the future.

On my arrival, the first and most important thing I had to do was to find somewhere to live, saving me the daily travelling from London. I was lucky and soon found rooms with a lady in Whitehurst Avenue, only a few minutes' walk from the depot. Now that I had these rooms and things were a bit more free and easy, and I could come and go as I pleased, I made another big decision in my life, when June and I decided to get married. There was no way we could afford to buy a house in those days, certainly not on railway pay, so we had to manage with what I had acquired. Our families could not make up their minds where the wedding should take place, in Felixstowe where June was living, or in my family church at Holme Pierrepont near Nottingham, so in the end we were married in St Mary's church, Hitchin, on Saturday 21st October, 1961; after all it was going to be our parish church and I had already joined the bell-ringing team by then. The reception was held in the Cock Hotel near the Market Place. We had a short honeymoon at Dorking in Surrey, the former home of my mother's family, where I had spent a lot of time in my younger days on holiday. We travelled down to Dorking by train, after having a real railway send-off at Hitchin station.

A week later I returned to work as a married man and continued with my responsibilities as the day fitter, with a certain amount of leg pulling from other members of the staff, who in the end gave up when they realised it was doing no good.

Although we were based in the new diesel depot, each morning we had to walk across the main line to the old steam shed to sign on at the time office, collecting a brass disc with our works number stamped on, which you carried round with you all day, returning it to the office at the end of the shift. A stop was soon put to this when they realised that it was too time consuming. My number was 280. We still retained the disc in order to collect our wages each week, handing it in to the pay clerk in the general office in exchange for the pay packet. (I retained mine as a souvenir when we finally did away with them and they were being thrown into the dustbin. No doubt today it is worth quite a bit of money as it was stamped with the company name, the London & North Eastern Railway, but there's no way that I would part with it, as it reminds me of those happy days spent working at Hitchin.)

The diesel depot had two roads, it was small but well fitted out, the two roads could accommodate one shunting and one main line locomotive on each road

St Mary's church, Hitchin where my wife and I were married on 21st October, 1961, we were also members of the bell-ringing team. *Author*

Hitchin diesel depot in 1966 and on the right the old MR steam shed which in the 1960s was being used as a BR road motor repair garage, on the left in the locomotive holding siding is the breakdown coach. Inside the depot on number one road is a Brush type '2' under inspection and standing on the fuel tank road a couple of spare '08' class shunting locomotives.
Frank Berridge Collection

and had doors which could be closed in the winter if required; this was very rare as locomotives were coming in and out most of the day, especially at night for servicing and refuelling, the refuelling pump and nozzle being between the roads in the centre of the depot. On the west side were the mess-room, chargehand's office, workshop and stores for both oil and spare parts. Outside stood two tanks for fuel storage and a siding for the tank wagons which brought new supplies as required. There were also two long sidings for the stabling of locomotives, after servicing or when not required. Being the main depot for the area it also had a breakdown train. Unlike the ones at Colwick or King's Cross, it did not have a crane in the formation, just a tool and packing van, plus a mess and riding coach for the men. This was kept at the steam shed in a siding near the water softening plant. Working in the breakdown gang was hard work - at the derailment of wagons or locomotives, you either had to jack them back onto the track or use ramps, very often with the use of a pulley block system known as the 'Kelbus Gear'; this was very heavy and needed a lot of setting up. If things proved to be difficult then the crane was sent for from King's Cross or Peterborough

After returning from our honeymoon, I was soon back into my stride down at the depot and it was not long before I had my first call out to a steam locomotive, in the shape of a '9F' class 2-10-0. It had worked up to the London area with a freight train and was returning to Peterborough, and had been brought to a stand on the down slow road just north of Cambridge Junction. A part of one of the right-hand cylinder rings had broken off and was jammed in the cylinder drain cock, causing it to remain open. The driver would not proceed forward until the cock had been repaired, as the clouds of steam it was causing at the front of the smoke box were impeding his vision; besides that the day was very foggy, with visibility down to a few yards. Walking up from the depot, it took the mate and me a good 30 minutes to find the locomotive, owing to the fog. I soon stripped down the offending drain cock and removed the damaged part of the ring and 30 minutes later the train was on its way. It was interesting that all the time I was working on the locomotive, we were only a few feet away from the down main line and trains were roaring past at express speed. We did not wear high visibility vests in those days and I often wonder if men would be allowed to work in those conditions today.

It had been a joy to do this job as it was well over a year since I last worked on steam. One of the amusing things that came out of it concerned the train guard – as we were walking past the Junction box, the guard, who was in the box reporting the fault to the control office, called down to us and said, 'When you have completed the repair tell the driver to go', which of course we did. Walking back to the depot we met the guard as he appeared out of the fog; he said, 'Have you done the repair and can the train carry on to Peterborough?' By this time it must have been half way to Biggleswade, so I said, 'If you put your skates on you might catch it up'. Panic set in and he rushed back to the box; what happened to him after that I do not know.

In between call-outs I would be carrying on with the normal everyday tasks on the diesels, the weekly and monthly exams on the type '1s' and the 'Baby Deltics', plus the routine repairs to the shunting locomotives. Another

The coaling plant at Hitchin's old steam shed, when I arrived there in 1961 it was out of use, but it must have been a bleak place to have worked on in the steam days, especially for our two fitters mates Francis (Nana) Hailey and Tom Worbey. *Malcolm Stevenson Collection*

The re-railing 'Kelbus Gear in action, this time it is the Colwick breakdown gang re-railing a derailed 'K3'class at Bulwell Common on the GCR main line north of Nottingham.
Robin Sharman Collection

A picture of Hitchin Cambridge Junction signal box which controlled the main line and the branch to Royston and Cambridge. It is where my mate and I saw the guard appear out of the fog after his train had departed for Peterborough. *Philip Millard/GNR Society*

interesting job that the day fitter carried out was the repair, servicing and inspection of the stationary plant around the district, connected with the steam locomotives, such as the water softening plants and tanks, the turntable, various water cranes at stations on the main line and the Cambridge branch and the water troughs at Stevenage. These were inspected by walking the track, between passing trains, looking out for any damage, such as loose bolts, water leaks and worn plates, etc. I would walk the down line first and then the up line, so that we were always facing the traffic, and my mate would be acting as the lookout. It's a miracle that neither of us was killed. If the passing train was hauled by a diesel locomotive, except for a type '4', we would stand by the track side; if it was a type '4' or steam locomotive, we would beat a quick retreat up the embankment - if we didn't, we would be in for an early bath. It is amazing what we found in the tanks, anything from fish to old prams; in the trough we even found part of an old bike.

By far the biggest part of the job was the call-outs and repairs; for call-outs the depot covered an area between Hatfield to the south and Huntingdon to the north on the main line and as far as Royston on the Cambridge branch. But the most interesting calls, as far as I was concerned, were to the steam locomotives. I was sitting in the mess-room one day, having a welcome cup of tea, when the door flew open and in dashed an out-of-breath fireman: 'Can you come quickly?' he said, 'We've ground to a halt on the down main line and lost the brake on the locomotive'. My mate and I grabbed the tool bag and hurried across the yard to the main line; standing there between the up-and-down yard was 'A3' class 4-6-2 No. 60063 *Isinglass* on a King's Cross to Leeds express. Sure enough when I tried the brake we could raise no vacuum, so first I had to find out if it was the train or the locomotive which was at fault, by isolating the

'A3' class 4-6-2 No. 60063 *Isinglass* standing on the scrap road at Doncaster works in May 1963. I often wonder if it had still got the temporary repair I carried out on the vacuum pan when I rescued it at Hitchin.   *Copyright Rail Archive Stephenson/Photomatic/N1713*

carriages. This done I tried the brake again and sure enough it was the locomotive. Whilst I walked round I got the driver to use the large brake ejector; this way I could tell if there was a broken pipe or damaged vacuum pan - on the 'A3s' there were three pans, or cylinders, two under the cab and one at the front between the driving wheels. By using the ejector, if a pipe was broken you could hear the air rushing in through the damaged part, and sure enough I could hear the rush of air near the front pan; a pipe had snapped in half between the chamber side (the top half of the piston) and the braking side (the bottom half below the piston) of the pan. What could I do? I crawled under the locomotive, passing between the driving wheels and lay flat on my back on the ballast; holding the two parts of the broken pipe together I could see that it was a clean break, thankfully the two broken parts were held firm, being attached to the pan and the train pipe. At this point a decision had to be made - do we remove the locomotive and replace it with a diesel, or do I carry out some kind of repair? Thinking quickly, I chose the latter option. I took a piece of cloth from my pocket and tore it into strips like a bandage, which I wrapped round the two broken parts of the pipe forming a kind of plumber's joint, which held them together; I then finished it off by wrapping electricians' sticky adhesive tape round the outside. I came up from beneath the locomotive and tried the brake, it blew up and held steady at the required 21 inches of vacuum; we re-coupled the brake pipe to the carriages and tried it again: it was fine. I told the driver to continue to Peterborough, if he was happy with the situation, and I would telephone through for a replacement locomotive there. He said he was willing to give it go. I heard no more about it, until one day I met the very same driver on the platform at King's Cross; he recognized me and thanked me for my help on that day and said that in the end the locomotive worked through to Leeds. Maybe it ran around like that until it was scrapped some months later!

By the early 1960s steam was beginning to be phased out in the King's Cross area and the locomotives allowed to be run down, although there was still a fair amount of freight hauled by steam and the Pacifics were still working at least 50 per cent of the expresses. But by 1962 this was becoming much less and breakdowns were occurring quite often. It was not long before I was out again to a failure on the main line, this time further north at Barford, just south of St Neots, where 'A3' class No. 60061 *Pretty Polly* had 'thrown her middle big end', in other words the centre cylinder con-rod main bearing had run hot and the white metal had melted. There was no chance of doing any kind of repair this time, it was a matter of stripping down on site and towing the locomotive and train to Peterborough. By the time I arrived with the tools, aboard a type '1' (class '20') diesel, the train had been standing quite some time. You can imagine how happy the passengers were, a great cheer went up, but little did they realize that before the train could be towed, I had got to strip down the con-rod and make the locomotive safe for travelling. It was lucky that it had failed on the down main and at the side ran the slow road, so following trains could pass by without too much delay to the daily service. I crawled between the driving wheels and got to work; after about one-and-a-half hours the job was completed, con-rod removed and strapped onto the footplate by the side of the boiler and the middle piston rod and crosshead fixed into the centre position, to stop it moving. Whilst this was taking place our type '1' had run forward to St Neots and reversed down onto the front of No. 60061, coupled up and was ready to proceed to Peterborough when I gave the all clear. It had taken almost two-and-a-half hours from the time of failure to me completing the job. I bet there were a few burnt dinners that day. The mate and I alighted at St Neots station and made our own way back to Hitchin, travelling on a freight train.

From time to time I had to do relief for the two shift fitters, who were both working 12-hour shifts at the time, due to shortage of staff. It was on one of the early morning shifts that I was called across to the station to attend to a 'V2' class 2-6-2 working the 5.55 am semi-fast train from King's Cross to Grantham. The train stood in the down platform and the driver complained that when he had been given the 'right away' and opened the regulator, there was a terrible roar of steam from the front end. I got him to try it again and sure enough the noise of the steam was deafening and I was nearly blown off the running plate. On further inspection I found that part of the front cylinder cover and the compression cock on the left-hand side cylinder had split away and lay on the ballast. There was nothing I could do but have the locomotive removed from the train and replaced with a diesel. A Brush type '2' (class '31') took the train forward to Grantham. The 'V2' was taken to the old steam shed and it was almost a week before I could fit a new cover, having to wait for one to be supplied from Doncaster works.

At Hitchin when there was no room at the diesel depot to stable the English Electric type '1' freight locomotives, we used the old two road steam shed which was convenient as the roads still had their pits if we were required to carry out any repairs. On shed are four engines, No. D8022 being the nearest one to the camera, they always ran in pairs.
Midland Railway Trust/Author's Collection

In between all my other work I was still on call for the breakdown train. This could happen at any time and it was not very pleasant when you were called in the night, especially if it was in the winter and you had just gone to bed. Most of the breakdowns I attended were to derailed wagons in the various station sidings or the up and down yards in Hitchin, very often caused by bad shunting or poor track. Occasionally it would be a wagon or a guard's brakevan that had been pushed over the top of the buffer stops. Locomotives did come off the track, mostly in the confines of the shed yard or the siding. One day a '9F' class 2-10-0 ran past the signal on the up slow road at Cambridge Junction and fell off the jack catch with all wheels. Re-railing was a slow process as we had to pull it back on with the aid of the 'Kelbus' gear, having to set up several times as the pulley blocks only worked on a ratio of 7 to 1: for every seven feet the re-railing locomotive travelled, the one being pulled back on moved one foot. But before this could be done, we had to dig the '9F' out of the ballast and jack it up onto wooden packing, at the same time having to contend with the passing expresses on the up main line.

Whilst I was in the gang we only had one major call-out when several freight trains became involved in an accident at Offord, south of Huntingdon, in which 'A1' class 4-6-2 No. 60123 *H.A. Ivatt* lost its bogie in the River Ouse, which flowed alongside the line. This was too big a job for the Hitchin gang and was cleared by the King's Cross and Peterborough gangs using their cranes, with the help of our manpower. I had gone to work on the Friday evening and did not return home until Sunday afternoon. June thought I had left her! One interesting fact to come out of this was the length of time it took to clear the debris - well over 100 wagons of various types were involved and at least 75 were non-runners, but by Monday morning the tracks were almost back to normal and trains were running past the site. If that had happened today, it would be at least 10 days before the line was clear, and they call that progress! All the time we were on site the area was guarded by the railway police, as one of the trains was carrying supplies for the major stores, mainly for Woolworths, electrical equipment such as radios and record players, etc., but lying around on the floor were thousands of pots of Shippam's fish paste - we were allowed to pick them up and take them home. For the next month everybody was bringing fish paste sandwiches to work, to eat during their mid-shift break.

A good many of the call-outs to the steam locomotives were for failed injectors or hot bearing brasses. Failed injectors could be attended to straight away, usually at the track side or in the goods yard, but hot bearings were a different thing altogether as the locomotive had to be taken to the shed. Most injector failures were on either the '9F' class 2-10-0s or 'WD' 2-8-0s, working into the yard from the Peterborough area, but hot brasses usually occurred on the Pacifics working main line expresses. I changed two sets whilst working at Hitchin, a tender brass on 'A4' class 4-6-2 No. 60021 *Wild Swan* and a carrier brass on 'A2' class 4-6-2 No. 60514 *Chamossaire*. In a depot with a wheel drop changing brasses was easy, but at Hitchin it was hard work; first I had to release the spring and then jack up the box before the brass could be removed, replacing it with a new one, after first bedding it onto the axle and then renewing the keep pad and oil. As we had no stores facilities for spare steam

'A4' class 4-6-2 No. 60021 *Wild Swan* in active service at Grantham in 1961 waiting to depart with an up express to King's Cross, this was before I carried out the repair on the tender brass.

Robin Sharman Collection

The gang that changed the tender axle bearing brass on 'A4' class 4-6-2 No. 60021 *Wild Swan* at Hitchin's old steam shed. The author is standing on the left, and my fitter's mate Tom Worbey is on the right, with a fireman in the centre.

Author's Collection

locomotive parts, the brasses, etc., had to be obtained from the main works. When I had completed the repair No. 60021 returned to traffic straightaway, but No. 60514 remained at the shed for several weeks. Finally the boiler inspector came and condemned the boiler and she was towed to the works to be scrapped; it seemed a waste of time changing the brass. Before she left, by permission of the shed master I removed a maker's plate from the cab side and he made arrangements for me to purchase it, with a firewood order, for 2s. 6d.; in those days everything you bought from the railway was paid for through a firewood order. I still have the plate today and I often wonder how much it is worth at today's prices!

I soon got to know the footplate staff and on my days off very often had a trip out on a locomotive; it made a change from always working with the tools. I became very friendly with an ex-Langwith Junction fireman, who had transferred to Hitchin some years earlier to gain promotion to the position of driver. Dennis Williamson took to me straightaway and he acted like a father to June and me. Maybe it was because I came from the same area and he knew Colwick quite well, having worked into there in his days at Langwith. At Hitchin he was renowned for being a good engineman, but a bit fast and hair-raising for the fireman - if he took over a late-running King's Cross train at Hitchin and provided he had a clear road, you could almost guarantee that most of the time would be made up before running into 'The Cross'. When driving a steam locomotive, the first thing he did was to find the largest lump of coal and place it in front of the seat for his feet to rest on, he would then open the regulator and it would be hardly closed before he reached his destination; it made hard work for the fireman, but everyone enjoyed working with him – at times he would even take his turn on the shovel, to give his mate a rest and a chance to take over the regulator.

Dennis and his fireman in earlier days had been awarded for their bravery whilst driving a 'B1' class 4-6-0 on a Cambridge buffet express. Between Royston and Cambridge the self-cleaning grill in the locomotive smokebox collapsed and fell across the top of the blast-pipe, causing a blow back of fire into the cab. Both men had the quick presence of mind to climb out of the cab and cling on by standing on the narrow footplate by the cab side. Dennis worked the brake handle through the window and brought the train to a stand, without any damage to the locomotive or train, thinking all the time about the safety of the passengers - the guard thought he had just stopped for a signal check.

I made several trips with Dennis to Peterborough and King's Cross, always on freight trains. I had plenty of opportunities to use the shovel and help out the fireman, even taking over the regulator if running light to the shed. Mind you, Dennis was keeping a close eye on me!

One footplate ride I really enjoyed occurred one afternoon. I was called over to the station to 'A4' class No. 60034 *Lord Farringdon* on an up express. The train had pulled up on the centre road. The driver told me that on leaving Peterborough the right-hand injector had stopped working and approaching Hitchin the left-hand side one had started giving trouble: could I help them out and find the cause of the fault? After 10 minutes I had sorted out the problem

A 'WD' class 2-8-0 departing Hitchin hauling a Peterborough to Ferme Park freight train of some considerable length, after the Peterborough crew had been relieved by a Hitchin set of men. In the background is the old steam shed by the side of the up platform. *Author's Collection*

Another 'A4' class I rescued at Hitchin when it was in trouble with its water injectors was No. 60034 *Lord Faringdon*. Here it is seen bursting out of Peascliffe tunnel north of Grantham with an up express for King's Cross in 1962. *Author* and soon had the injector working. I was just about to walk to the depot, when he called back: would I ride with them to King's Cross, in case the fault occurred again? I think he was a bit worried. I needed no second invitation and jumped up onto the footplate. By now the train was running late, the driver soon opened the regulator and set about making up for lost time. There was no further trouble and we completed the 32 miles in 25 minutes. It was the first and only time that I travelled on the footplate when the speedometer touched 90 mph; No. 60034 was riding as smooth as a carriage and it was a joy to watch two skilled enginemen at work.

One of the best opportunities to ride the footplate came about when I did my monthly trip to Huntingdon to service our resident class '04' shunting locomotive. We always travelled there on the 8.20 am train out of King's Cross, which departed Hitchin at 8.55 am. Top Shed usually provided an 'A3' or 'V2' on this turn and the drivers never refused you a ride - sometimes they were glad of your company, somebody different to talk to. On one particular trip the fireman happened to be an ex-Colwick lad, so in between firing we had a lot to talk about. A number of cleaners and fireman transferred to Top Shed from Colwick, in the days when there was a shortage of staff.

The servicing of the '04' at Huntingdon always took place on a Monday and on arrival we would find it stabled in the one-road engine shed, just east of the station on the closed branch to St Ives, of which a short section was still open for goods traffic as far as Chivers jam factory near Godmanchester. I would carry out the inspection and do any repairs, whilst the mate would do the refuelling, by hand, pumping the diesel fuel from 40 gallon barrels. By lunchtime we had usually completed our work and after eating our sandwiches, we would take a ride down to the Chivers factory to collect any full box wagons for dispatch to various destinations around the country. The line crossed the main road which ran between Huntingdon and Godmanchester. When we arrived at the road the driver stopped, whilst the guard walked forward and stood in the middle of the road, holding a long pole with red flags at each end, in order to stop the traffic, then the train crossed and waited on the other side for the guard to catch up. The whole process was repeated again on the return journey.

It's interesting to note that when I transferred to Hitchin in 1961 a passenger service was still running on the old Midland Railway branch to Bedford, once the main line before the line from Bedford to St Pancras was opened in 1868. Motive power was supplied by the Midland shed at Bedford in the shape of '2MT' class 2-6-2T's - diesel railbuses had been tried in 1959, but were found wanting as there were too many steep gradients. Train services on the line were normally worked by Bedford footplate staff, except on Sunday evenings when a train ran from Hitchin to Henlow, carrying the returning airmen back to their training camp. This was a Hitchin working and in the steam days was hauled by one of two locomotives, an ex-GER 'J15' class 0-6-0 No. 65479 or 'E4' class 2-4-0 No. 62785 (now in the National Railway Museum at York). By the time I arrived at the depot, a diesel railcar was being used to operate the service.

The passenger service finished at the end of 1961, but not before June and I had made several shopping trips to Bedford; we even rode back from Bedford on the very last service train. The line remained open for a further three years

106 STEAM, DIESELS AND ON-TRACK MACHINES

When I joined the staff at Hitchin the Bedford to Hitchin branch was still open with a regular passenger service and still steam worked although a rail-bus service had been tried. Arriving in the up platform is a local from Bedford hauled by a '2MT' class 2-6-2T No. 41245 on 9th July, 1955.
Frank Berridge Collection

Although not a clear picture, it does show BR '2MT' class 2-6-2T No. 84005 standing in the down platform at Hitchin with a train to Bedford on the last day of service 31st December, 1961. My wife and I rode on the very last train from Bedford.
Frank Berridge Collection

'3F' class 0-6-0 No. 43428 waiting in the up platform at Hitchin ready to cross over to the down side where it would stand outside the old MR shed whilst the footplate staff and the guard had their snack before working back to Bedford with the short train, not much doing that day!   S. Summerson/Copyright Rail Archive Stephenson/Photomatic/N4870

and was used by the daily pick-up goods, calling at all stations. This was worked by an ex-MR '3F' class 0-6-0 and would arrive in the up platform at Hitchin, where it shunted the wagons into the up yard and then ran light to the old GNR steam shed to take water and be turned, before returning back to Bedford with the afternoon empties. The footplatemen then took a break, but would never have a cup of tea or eat their sandwiches in the mess-room with the Hitchin men; they drove the locomotive over to the down side and stood outside the old two-road MR shed which, as mentioned before, was by then a road motor repair garage, but still rail-connected. Even in BR days ex-LMS men would not mix with their ex-LNER colleagues.

Towards the end of 1962 a new fitter joined the team, a young man who had been an engineer in the Navy, which meant that I would be filling the vacancy on round-the-clock shifts. I'm not sure if the other two liked this arrangement as it cut down their overtime, but nevertheless it was better pay for me, especially as I was recently married. We did three shifts, early mornings, afternoons and nights; there was one fitter and a mate on each shift, except on nights when we had two mates. This was a precaution, if we were called out to a breakdown; at least there was one left behind to fuel and water the diesels, so that they were ready to work their early morning diagrams. From 5.30 pm to 7.30 am you were on your own, any decisions to be taken were yours alone; in other words you were the boss. The kind of jobs we did in steam days was termed as running work. We serviced and did the daily examinations and any repairs as required on the in-coming locomotives, after they had finished the daily diagram. The busiest periods were between 11.00 pm and 2.00 am, when the suburban services out of King's Cross were terminating at Hitchin, Baldock and Royston. They would leave the stock in the various carriage sidings and then run light to the depot. But our main reason for being on duty was to attend to any failures or call-outs in the area, both on the main line and the branch. We were always busy in the early morning, especially in the winter, when the train-heating boilers stopped working; they would be working well when the locomotive left the depot, but by the time they coupled onto the train they very often refused to fire up. The driver would tell the signalman and he would telephone us at the depot and we would meet the train as it ran into Hitchin. So that there was no delay to the train, we climbed aboard and travelled, attending to the fault and carrying out any repair as required. As well as the tools we always carried a few spare parts. Very often it would only be a minor fault and within a few minutes the boiler would be working again; depending on where the train was stopping, we would alight and wait for the next train to Hitchin. But sometimes faults proved to be more difficult and the train was arriving in King's Cross before we had completed the repair. We would then return on the next available service, either riding on the locomotive, if we knew the driver, which was most of the time, or travel in the carriages. We always carried a riding pass for such occasions. The same applied if we were called to a main line train; the driver would pull up for us in the centre road of the station and we quickly climbed aboard, trying not too cause too much delay. If it was a train going north we usually ended up at Peterborough, as this was very often the first stop out of King's Cross. On the Cambridge branch it would either be Baldock, Royston or Cambridge, and on odd occasions Ely, especially if it was the afternoon Buffet Express which was worked by Hitchin men, usually with an English Electric type '2' 'Baby Deltic'. At the time it was the only train out of King's Cross which went beyond Cambridge. It was vital that we attended to these types of failures, otherwise the poor passengers would have been frozen by the time they reached their destination.

It was very noisy travelling in the engine-rooms of the locomotives, especially if it happened to be a 'Deltic'. On the small 'Baby Deltics' the boiler was situated at one end of the engine-room, but on the type '5' 'Deltics' it was between the two high-powered engines. The noise was deafening; although we carried a pair of earplugs, they were not adequate and I think this is what made me slightly deaf in later life.

As well as boiler failures we did attend to other problems, sometimes electrical, and although we were not trained as electricians, except for dealing with the boilers, we were expected to do our best.

I arrived on shift work just in time for the big freeze in 1963 - it started on New Year's Eve 1962. That evening I was working a 12-hour night shift as one of the other fitters was away on holiday. Towards midnight it started to snow and by the time my mate and I went home in the morning there were a good six to eight inches on the ground and it stayed for the next three months. During that time the steam locomotives came into their own, often deputizing for the failed diesels. I think it was their swan song, because 1963 was the year they were eliminated from the main line south of Hitchin, *Flying Scotsman* being one of the last ones to work an express out of King's Cross. I remember going across to the station to see it pass through.

The big freeze was at it worst during February, when the frost went down into the ground at least 18 inches. I remember trying to refuel a diesel locomotive one morning and nothing came out of the nozzle. At first we thought that the storage tanks were empty, but the chargehand informed us a new supply had only arrived the previous week: was there a blockage in the pipe? On closer investigation we found that the diesel fuel was frozen between the tank and the pump. That's the first and only time I have known diesel fuel to freeze. Nearly every morning for a week my mate and I spent most of the early hours at the station. The diesel locomotives working the suburban trains were freezing up as they ran along; owing to the very cold air ice would form in the pipes leading to the braking system. After a time we could thaw them out, but if the radiator froze then the locomotive was a failure, due to overheating; it was then replaced with another locomotive, if one was available - if not the train was cancelled, then the commuters were not happy. Unlike the class '04' and '08' shunting locomotives, which had anti-freeze in their cooling systems, the main line locomotives just had water mixed with a type of anti-corrosive oil, which gave it the appearance of milk, but did not stop them from freezing up in very cold weather. On certain days when the temperature fell well below freezing point, locomotives stabled in the sidings would have their engines continually running; this stopped the radiator from freezing and prevented the batteries going flat.

One particular morning when the temperature was at its lowest, the overnight expresses were arriving or passing through hauled by whatever steam locomotives the local shed could lay their hands on, including rusty old 'V2s' and 'B1s' that looked as though they had been in store for months. Most of them were stopping on the up main for us to de-frost the injectors, which are among the first things to freeze up as the locomotive travels along, especially where the cold water pipe from the tender enters the injector. To thaw them out we used burning rags soaked in paraffin, attached to the end of a steel rod; it looked like a flaming torch, and as it burnt down we replaced it with more rag and carried on the best we could. Icicles were hanging under the cabs and tenders, about 2 ft long. Not only were we having trouble with the locomotives, but the poor old platelayers were working flat out to try and keep the points from freezing, and signal engineers had also got their work cut out looking after signals, operating wires and point rods. In that cold period I think we spent most of our time in the early mornings across at the station sorting out failures and problems, often having to ride on the locomotives to cure a boiler fault and then return to Hitchin as quickly as possible to deal with the next one. Over those three months I hardly had a day off work, most of the time working 12-hour shifts. Not a good start for a newly-married couple, but June was very understanding. It was hard and very often cold work, but in a small way we did our bit to keep the wheels of the railway turning, and they did. In those days the work force struggled on and did their best, unlike the present times when they give in so easily and cancel the trains. I often wonder what would happen if we had the same kind of cold period today, the railway would be closed down for months, and they call it progress.

It was during the big freeze that I had my last call out to a steam locomotive. I was on nights and it was around 2.00 am when the running foreman called me over to the old shed. A 'B1' class 4-6-0 had worked in from Peterborough on a freight train, run light to the shed and had been turned and watered ready to return home. It was just approaching the outlet points, when it became derailed. Ice and snow had built up between the point blades and the rail, leaving a gap, the ice was so hard that the bogie and first set of driving wheels mounted the ice and they were on the ground before the driver even noticed it. When I arrived and saw what had happened, I suppose I should have called out the breakdown gang but, confident as I am, I was going to give it a go and see if I could re-rail the wheels. I was taking a chance, because bogies are notorious for spinning sideways if they run into an obstruction when being re-railed; then we would have been in trouble and I would have been up before the boss on a charge. We packed ice and snow behind the wheels and as much wooden packing as I could find. The theory was, that if it came off on the ice, it would go back that way. I asked the driver to reverse, very slowly, which is not easy when you've got wheels on the ground. Gradually they mounted the ice and wood packing and ran back on the rails. Everyone present breathed a sigh of relief; I was lucky, and had managed to pull it off. I bet there are not many steam locomotives around that have been re-railed using solid ice; it just goes to show what weight frozen water will withstand. I got into trouble next morning with the breakdown gang for not calling them out, because they lost out on some extra pay, but the shed master thanked me for saving him the money and not getting him out of bed on a very cold night, and he was pleased I had used my initiative. It was the last time I had anything to do with a steam locomotive, from now on it would be diesel power only.

It might be interesting to say something here about the men I worked with, as they were a good crowd and we all got on well together, which I suppose does happen when you are only a small staff.

The shed master, Bob Stevenson, like myself, originated from Colwick. Bill Lane the chargehand had also previously been a fitter at Colwick. I think they had both moved down to Hitchin during the war when there had been a shortage of staff in the London area. Bob was an easy-going shed master and very fair with his staff, but would be strict with anyone who stepped out of line. As well as the fitting staff, he was also responsible for the footplatemen and the general office. Bill was a quiet man who got on with the job, he looked after us all and handed out the work sheets to the men who worked on the day shift; part of his time was spent in the office, the other part working on the locomotives, mainly carrying out exams and repairs on the diesel shunting locomotives. When he was away on holiday or off work, the senior fitter took charge and the rest of us had to cover the shifts by working overtime; I occasionally did chargehand duties myself.

On days with Bill were four other members of the staff, a fitter, myself for 18 months, a semi-skilled fitter, an electrician and a general labourer. If any of those were away on holiday, etc., relief would be provided from Finsbury Park. The semi-skilled fitter was Jock, but I cannot remember his surname or where he originated from, except Scotland - his duties were re-blocking the locomotives with new brake blocks, as and when required, carrying out any minor repairs, helping the other fitters and looking after the refuelling tanks; he was also responsible for the water softening plant at the old steam shed, whilst it was still in use until 1963.

Ray Brown the electrician came to work at the depot just after it opened in 1960. He was an excellent tradesman and soon settled into railway work and ways. Very often he would go out with me on call-outs and breakdowns, we became good friends and nearly emigrated to New Zealand together when their railways were advertising for skilled craftsmen, but in the end thought better of it.

Jim the labourer was an old railwayman, I think he had been on the footplate, but I never did find out. When he was working with us, he was past retiring age and did the job to help out with his pension. He was always sweeping and tidying up, if you left something lying around it would soon be put away and he kept the mess-room spotless, the trouble was that if you were in there having a cup of tea or eating your snap, Jim would want to be sweeping under the table. One of the fitter's mates said to him one day: 'Jim, if I had not married my wife, I would have married you!' Like most of us, Jim cycled to work, but he rode so slowly that you could easily pass him whilst walking - how he kept his balance I don't know. One morning when cycling to the depot, he failed to stop at the halt sign at the end of the street where he lived. Unfortunately a policeman was standing at the corner on point duty and issued poor old Jim with a summons - he was most indignant.

Most of the fitters like myself had served their apprenticeships on the railway, except for the young man who had joined us after serving in the Navy as a junior engineer. He did not stay very long and left in the summer of 1963. Then a life-long friend of mine, Gordon Foster, who had served his time with me at Colwick and had moved down to Top Shed at King's Cross at the same time that I went to Finsbury Park, came to take the day fitter's job after Top Shed closed. Gordon too only stayed for a couple of years, transferring back home to the new diesel depot at Toton near Nottingham in 1965. Unlike me he remained on the railway for the rest of his working life and retired in 2003 after 49 years' service.

The other two shift fitters were Alwyn Sales and Tom Foster, who was related to Gordon by marriage, as Gordon married Tom's niece whilst working at Hitchin. Alwyn Sales, always known as Al, served his time in Doncaster locomotive works, and transferred to Hitchin on the completion of his apprenticeship, taking on the day fitter's job at the old steam shed, until he went on shift work when the new diesel depot opened. He was a born comedian and could sit telling jokes for hours, doing all the actions and putting in the expressions; he should really have been on the stage. I think he too missed his vocation. Being a Yorkshireman, he was a keen follower of the horses, spending a lot of his spare time studying form. At the betting shop he called himself 'Quentin Durward', much to the amusement of the girls behind the counter. He was also renowned for being a bit tight with his money and was always looking out for a bargain, especially if someone was giving anything away, and he collected all kinds of oddments. He and his wife became friendly with June and I, and we were both Godparents to their little girl. Other than Ray Brown, who lived at Hatfield and travelled to work every day on the train, Al was the only other member of staff who lived out of town, at Meppershall in Bedfordshire and he came to work in a clapped-out Ford 'Anglia' car. Many a time did we have to send someone out to rescue him when it broke down, usually because it had lost the water in the radiator. We tried hard to keep it running for him by getting parts from a scrap merchant's yard, situated close by the depot.

Tom Foster was a bit of a loner and kept himself to himself, not always mixing with the rest of the staff. Very often when he had a call-out he would go off and attend to it on his own, which was against the rules, especially if you were working on or near to the running lines. Whether he served his apprenticeship on the railway I'm not quite sure. He came originally from Ipswich and we understood that he could have served it at Ransome's. But there was always that air of mystery about him and he never let us know - I think he resented me going on to shift work and taking the extra pay away from him. Tom was a highly skilled tradesman and very clever at solving crossword puzzles, he would collect all the daily newspapers that had been left on the seats of the trains and would then sit over a cup of tea in the mess-room and solve them, the *Times* and *Telegraph* he could do in about 10 minutes.

On the strength of the staff were four fitters' mates, all on shifts, but for a time we did have five when for a few months an Irish mate came on loan to us from Finsbury Park; his name was Tim O'Flynn - now you cannot be more Irish than that! He came in for a lot of leg-pulling from other members of the staff, especially when he was telling tales about his early life in Ireland. The four mates on shifts were Peter Upchurch, Francis Hailey, Tom Worbey and Lenny, whose surname I can't call to mind. Unlike the fitters, they worked on a four-weekly system: days, afternoons and two weeks of nights, which meant the shift fitters never had a regular mate. You worked with each of them on a three weeks' interval basis.

Peter Upchurch started out on his railway career as a member of the footplate staff, but at an early age as a fireman failed his eyesight test and was transferred to the fitting department as a mate. His father was the manager of the local bacon factory, which was situated only a few hundred yards down the road from the diesel depot. From time to time we all got one or two cheaper cuts of meat. Peter lived on the east side of town, in a very smart house near to the famous Harkness rose gardens, and was the only other member of staff who ran a car, an up-to-date Vauxhall model, a little bit more reliable than Al's. Come to think of it, it was very often Peter that rescued Al when his old Ford broke down.

Tom Worbey, after leaving war service, joined the railway as a coal operator; in other words he coaled the steam locomotives when they came into the old shed for servicing. It was hard work, first you had to fill metal tubs by shovelling the coal from a wagon, and then the tub would be taken up on a hoist and tipped into the locomotive tender. Not only would it be dirty work, but when the weather was fine there must have been lots of coal dust flying around, worse than working down the mine. When not coaling locomotives, he was loading waste-ashes into wagons. He served the war years in the Navy on board frigates in Lord Mountbatten's fleet, joining in early 1940 at the age of 17. His ship was sunk twice, first in the Mediterranean and secondly in the North Sea whilst escorting the Russian convoys. The first time he said he could have stayed in the water most of the day, as it was so warm, but the second time he was lucky to be alive as the sea was freezing - he was only in for a few minutes, but still ended up in a military hospital for three months with frost-bite to his hands and feet. Like all the mates he was a great character and a super chap to work with, especially when things were not quite going to plan. He was a family man with two children, and there is a funny story about him when one day he decided to go on holiday to the coast. Instead of travelling on the train with a free pass, a friend of his had lent him an old car so he thought they would all travel in style. Now Tom lived on one of the council estates and opposite to his house was a patch of waste-land, so he parked the car there overnight, in order to get a quick getaway the following morning. He woke early, looked out of the window to find that during the night someone had jacked up the car, left it on bricks and taken the wheels - I expect they thought it had been dumped.

Francis Hailey, who was always known to everyone as 'Nana' (apparently this was the first word he spoke when a baby), was also a born comedian, like Al, a great leg-puller and player of practical jokes. He also after war service joined the railway as a coal operator and ended up as a fitter's mate when the steam shed closed. Unlike Tom, Nana served his war years in the army, also joining in early 1940, being posted to the Leicester Regiment at Glen Parva Barracks near Leicester. At first he thought he was going to Scotland, but was soon disappointed. After his basic training, he was sent to North Africa, joining the 1st Army, where he spent the next five years fighting his way across the north of the continent to Egypt. He was in the Salerno landing, finishing up in Austria at the end of the war. Out of the original company of men, he was one of only 75 to return home. He always said that he put it down to the fact that he was tall and could run faster then anyone else.

Both Nana and Tom were excellent at storytelling, and kept us all entertained at meal breaks by relating accounts of their exploits in the armed forces during the war. They really should have written a book, it would have made excellent reading.

Lenny, like the other two, had also served in the armed forces during the war, but said very little about it. Nana said that he was in the Pioneer Corps, digging trenches for the latrines, but Lenny always denied it; I think it was a bit of leg pulling on Nana's part. Lenny was an old railwayman and had started in London as a stable boy, looking after the horses which pulled the delivery drays around the streets of the capital. He, like the others, could tell a good story and often related the one about giving the horses their pills when they were sick. He said they placed the pill inside a tube, put the tube into the mouth of the horse, then blew it down its throat - one day the horse coughed and he swallowed the pill instead and he never stopped galloping around the yard for a week! He also transferred to Hitchin after the war, but I am not quite sure if he came to be a coal operator or a fitter's mate. As mates go, he was very helpful and always did his best, and was never lost for anything to do. In his spare time, between the servicing of the diesel locomotives, he would very often be found painting white lines on the depot floor, marking out the walkways and the edge of the pits so that they could be easily seen, especially in the dark. He would supply

From the front garden of our terrace cottage we had a wonderful view of the trains, the yard box, the cattle dock and bike rack! *Author*

Our end of terrace cottage in the station yard at Hitchin where we lived in 1965/66; our eldest son is in his pram by the front porch. *Author*

the paint himself and never claimed any money back from the company, a true railwayman.

On the domestic front things were going quite well and not long after June and I were married we made our first accommodation move. In early 1962 we moved from the rooms in Whitehurst Avenue to a rented furnished house at 15 Wilton Road. We lived there for almost a year until we were able to rent an unfurnished flat, just round the corner at Strathmore Court, in a recently-built block of six, three up and three down; we were lucky enough to have one of the upper ones. Thankfully we had managed to scrape together a few pounds and were able to purchase our first furniture, at the time June had a job and I was working quite a bit of overtime - that was the only way to do it in those days, unlike today when most young couples expect to have it all on the day they get married, even a house and a car.

On a cold winter's day just before Christmas 1964 our first son was born. David came as a bit of a surprise, as we were not expecting him until the end of January. Being five weeks early meant that he was quite small and should have been taken to the hospital, but as it was so cold we managed to look after him at home, with a lot of help from the midwife. The room had to be kept at a constant temperature of 70 degrees for almost two months, but he pulled through.

In March 1965 we were on the move again, this time to a railway cottage in Station Terrace - I had had my name down for one when we were first married. It was situated next to the main line and about 50 yards from the station entrance, which was very handy, especially when we'd been out for the day by train - we could be in the cottage before the train pulled out of the platform. But it did have its disadvantages, as the garden was at the front next to the path which led to the footplate-staff signing-on point. I could never get anything done, as most of the drivers on their way home wanted to stop for a chat. These were the problems you had working in a small depot, you tended to know everybody. Unfortunately we did not stop there very long, only a further year until March 1966, when I transferred to the plant and machinery (P&M) depot at Derby, but more of that later.

During our time in Hitchin we never socialized too much, as there never seemed to be any spare time, I was always at work. However, we found time to pursue our interest in church bell-ringing and managed to get in a few train trips around the country from time to time, especially during our annual holidays. My first trip overseas was in 1963, when a group from the depot visited Amsterdam for a four-day break. The odd days off or weekends usually resulted in us going to visit parents. In 1962 June's mum and dad moved to Leiston, on the Aldeburgh branch, and lived on the opposite side of the line to the Garrett works, but by then the branch was being worked by diesel railcars. Then later that year they moved down south and made their home at Hythe in Hampshire, living on the south side of Southampton Water. I always enjoyed the ride down, especially the section between Waterloo and Southampton, as most of the express trains to Bournemouth or Weymouth were being hauled by the Bulleid Pacifics. The walk across Southampton brought us to the town quay where a ferry took us to Hythe, alighting at the end of the pier, and meant either

At Southampton we would cross the city to the town pier and catch the Hythe ferry alighting at the end of Hythe Pier where we would ride on the pier railway to the shore terminus. The pier railway electric train is waiting to return to the ferry station, which can be seen to the left of the train. *Author*

Whilst we lived at Hitchin my wife's parents were living at Hythe on Southampton Water and whenever we had the chance we would travel down to Southampton to visit them. A journey I always enjoyed as the train from Waterloo was mostly hauled by a Bulleid Pacific, and on arrival at Southampton I would stand and watch it depart for Bournemouth. 'Battle of Britain' class 4-6-2 No. 34060 *25 Squadron* is waiting for the road in the summer of 1965. *Author*

a walk or a ride on the pier tramway, with its ancient electric locomotives and carriages. Thankfully it is still running today, in almost the same condition, it is the oldest continuously operating public pier train in the world. Occasionally we changed at Southampton and caught the Fawley branch train as far as Hythe.

The bungalow in which June's parents lived at the time looked out over Southampton Water and the docks, and when the great liners backed out from the Ocean Terminal, on their way to the States, you had a panoramic view of the whole procedure. I well remember seeing the two 'Queens' depart, at different times of course, and watched them as they slowly made their way down river towards the Isle of Wight. It was a wonderful sight - something that can be repeated today with the big cruise liners.

Going to see my parents meant travelling north on the main line to Grantham, changing there into a Nottingham train and alighting at Radcliffe-on-Trent. In the early 1960s most of the trains we rode on would have been hauled by steam, either a 'A3' or 'V2' class on the main line and on the branch by various types, whatever there was available at Colwick or Grantham sheds at the time. On the odd occasion we even had a Derby lightweight railcar. It was on one of these visits that I experienced one of the finest sights of a steam locomotive hard at work, something I shall remember for the rest of my life. We were returning home one dark winter Sunday evening and stood on the up platform at Grantham waiting for our train, which in those days stopped at Hitchin, cutting out the change at Peterborough. Looking south I heard a distant whistle and made it out to be an 'A3' class on a northbound express, running at speed, with the regulator open, it roared through the station; as it approached the fireman had the trap in the fire hole door open and was obviously putting a bit round

This is the up platform at Grantham in the early 1960s. It was whilst waiting on this platform one dark winter Sunday evening I had my finest sight of a steam locomotive hard at work as it roared through the down platform heading north. It was a glorious sight as the glow from the 'A3's' firebox lit up the exhaust and the night sky. I will always remember it to the end of my days. *Author's Collection*

As members of the bell-ringing team at Hitchin my wife and I enjoyed ringing at other local churches especially the one just outside of Hitchin at St Ippollyts, a real country church in a pretty village. *Author*

After bell practice on a Thursday at St Ippollyts the ringers would retire to the pub across the road; the pub is sadly no more, the building has been turned into a family house. *Author*

the back corners. The beam of light from the fire shone into the night sky and was reflected in the exhaust, it was a beautiful sight and to me summed up the power of steam, a vision that today is lost for ever.

On the bell-ringing front we both continued with our ringing at the parish church, but when time allowed visited other towers in the district; one of our favourite churches, in the little village of St Ippollyts, was about a mile outside the town. We would join the local ringers on practice nights and Sunday evening, if I were not at work. Practice nights were always enjoyable, especially when they finished and we all gathered in the village pub across the road from the lychgate. The pub was still Victorian and had no bar or pumps; Fred the landlord sat us all round a scrubbed table in one of the rooms, giving us a glass each, then he would disappear down the cellar with a large enamel jug and draw the beer out of a barrel, returning and filling our glasses as and when required, until we'd all had enough. Then we would pay him for whatever we'd had at the end of the evening before going home. Sadly today the village no longer has a pub, as it has been turned into a high-class dwelling.

After ringing on Sunday evening, we would stay for evensong specially to listen to the vicar's sermons. He was a wonderful preacher and to this day I have never heard finer sermons than the ones we experienced at St Ippollyts. In the winter and summer we walked both ways and after David was born, we pushed him there and back in his pram, leaving him at the base of the tower whilst we did our ringing, even when we rang at the parish church, which was usually on a Sunday morning. Today we would be regarded as irresponsible parents, and maybe even locked up in jail!

Now it's back to work, as they say, and I will talk about my time on shift work with the diesels, their problems, breakdowns and failures, and how we dealt with them. But before I do I would like to mention a most unusual derailment, which occurred at Hitchin, early one weekday morning; it involved a Birmingham RC&W Co. type '3' (class '33') locomotive and a cement train. During my time working at the depot, the new Forth Road Bridge was being built in Scotland and almost daily a bulk cement train ran between Cliffe in Kent to Uddingston, north of Edinburgh, via the East Coast main line. On this particular morning, as the train was approaching Hitchin, about a quarter of a mile south of the station, near to what we called Benslow Lane bridge, an axle on one of the tanker wagons broke, allowing the wheels to derail and collapse into the four-foot gap between the track. The driver, not knowing what had happened, kept going and the train stayed upright until the wheels of the broken axle hit the crossover points north of the station, near to the yard box, then all hell was let loose. The train broke in two and the trailing wagons ran onto the top of each other, spreading themselves over the tracks. Thankfully there were no other trains around at the time and the guard was not injured, otherwise it would have been a major disaster. I was on the morning shift and was called to the scene, but there was nothing I or the depot gang could do about it, so the breakdown trains and cranes were called out from King's Cross and Peterborough. Leaving the track at Benslow Bridge until it became derailed, the wheels of the damaged wagon had broken every track clip and damaged every sleeper. Afterwards the whole quarter of a mile had to be re-laid.

The author standing on the footplate of 'Baby Deltic' No. D5904, inside the diesel depot, before carrying out a daily inspection, and if I remember right D5904 was one of the better members of the class! *Author's Collection*

HAPPY DAYS AT HITCHIN 121

The servicing of the diesel locomotives that came into the depot from their respective trains each day rarely caused many problems - most types were easy to work on, except for the type '2' 'Baby Deltics', and they were a different kettle of fish. Whilst the mate fuelled, watered and topped up the engine oil tank if needed, I would get on and do the examination and carry out any repairs as required. When the 'Baby Deltics' arrived on shed, the first unusual thing you noticed about them was the strange sound they made, particularly when the driver shut the engine down and the oil pressure dropped. Then the engine gearing started to rattle; it was just like shaking an old tin can full of loose nuts and bolts. Regarding the servicing, they were reasonable in their use of fuel and water, but when it came to checking the engine oil level on average they would require topping up with at least 16 gallons per day. Most of this loss was unburnt oil, which had passed through the cylinders into the exhaust system, and coated itself on the inside walls of the exhaust silencer which ran along the underside of the roof in the engine compartment. After a period of time it would build up to a certain thickness and then catch fire, with spectacular results. Flames would shoot into the air out of the exhaust outlet to a height of around 10 ft. This was fine if the locomotive was running through the open country as it soon burnt itself out, but if it was standing in a station then that was a different story. I well remember one day a locomotive setting fire to Finsbury Park station canopy. On occasions we had complaints from a few farmers stating that their cornfields had been set alight. But there was no way of proving that it was the fault of the railway, especially as there were very few steam locomotives around at that time and certainly not on the Cambridge branch. But no doubt it was the 'Deltics' which were the culprits.

The mate and I had been called out one dark winter's morning to a boiler fault on a 'Baby Deltic', travelling to Royston to start its day's diagram. After remedying the fault, we were riding back to Hitchin, when suddenly the whole countryside lit up, and sure enough there was a column of flames roaring out of the exhaust. For about five minutes we had a spectacular fireworks display.

Carrying out any repairs on these strange locomotives was no easy task either, especially if it was anything to do with the engine. Being a nine cylinder opposed piston engine with two pistons in each cylinder, plus the fact that it was in the shape of a 'Delta', was unusual for a start. They had three main crankshafts, two at the top and one at the bottom driving onto a common gear wheel, which turned the generator. The fuel injectors were situated on the side of each cylinder and if any of them was at fault we had great difficulty in extracting them, especially the ones on the side, then it was a case of lying on your back in order to carry out the extraction. Like some types of steam locomotive, the man who designed them never thought about the poor chap who had to repair them. Having high-speed engines they were always in trouble and eventually the liners would crack and let water into the cylinder, pressure would build up and the engine then exploded, usually blowing a hole in the side of the crankcase. I was once called out to No. D5905 at Marshmoor near Hatfield; the message was that the engine had shut down and they had lost power. On investigation I found a hole in the engine almost big enough to crawl through and one of the pistons with its con-rod had shot through the inner

After the daily service and inspection or any repairs that were required, the locomotives would then be placed on the depot stabling siding waiting their next turn of duty. Here we see two 'Baby Deltics' and a Brush type '2'; the van was used as our overflow stores for large spares such as drums of oil and brake blocks, etc. *Author*

Even when I transferred back to Derby in the 1970s I was involved with 'Baby Deltic' No. D5901 seen here departing Nottingham hauling a Derby Research Centre test train. *Author*

casing of the engine room. After this incident they were regarded as being too dangerous to work passenger trains and were confined to freight work only until their engines finally gave out and blew up. Then they were dragged off to Stratford works in east London for storage, and were eventually taken to the English Electric works to have modified engines fitted, this time with new bronze-coated cylinder liners. Only one locomotive ran trouble-free, No. D5907, and if I remember rightly, used very little oil; maybe it was better constructed than the rest of the class in the first place.

It's a pity that one of these unusual locomotives was never preserved. One could easily have been, as D5901 ran for many years after the rest had been scrapped and was being used for test purposes at Derby Research Centre. I even got called to it at Derby diesel depot, some time in the 1970s, when I was working there as the on-track supervisor in the plant and machinery department. A fault had occurred in the braking system: I traced it to the driver's control valve, but there was nothing I could do about it, as the depot stores had no spares to carry out the repair. It's interesting to note that as far as I know the large 'Deltics' had no problems with their engines blowing up and ran mostly trouble-free. But then they had much larger engines fitted, two 18 cylinder ones to each locomotive. The 'Baby Deltics' were designed for working the stopping trains, which meant more acceleration and deceleration as they stopped at each station. Maybe the rapid expansion and contraction on their smaller engine put too much strain on the liners, and this is what caused them to crack.

The only one thing common to both classes of locomotive was the awful black smoke that shot out of the exhaust, each time the engines started and burst into life. I often saw it happen in King's Cross station, after the locomotives had been standing at the buffer stops. Having brought a train in, they would be shut down, to save on fuel and cut down on the noise. The engines would then be fired up and the station would be smothered in a thick black fog.

Breakdowns and call-outs to the diesel locomotives were just as frequent as those to the steam, especially in the winter months when the heating boilers were in use. We had more calls to the Brush type '2s' (class '31'), as their Spanner Mark I boilers always seemed to be in trouble and failed quite frequently, usually just as the train was departing on its journey up to London. This gave us time to meet them at Hitchin station, especially if they had started from Royston or Baldock. It has been known for us to make as many as three trips up to London and back during an early morning shift.

One boiler fault I attended was on a cold winter's morning in 1962, whilst I was still the day-shift fitter. Ray Brown the electrician and I had been asked by the chargehand to meet the 8.20 am King's Cross to Leeds express at the station. It had been reported that the boiler had failed en route and the passengers were beginning to feel cold. When the train arrived it was being hauled by a locomotive that we'd never seen before, the pioneer Brush/Sulzer type '4' (class '47') No. D1500, which was equipped with a Spanner Mark III boiler. It was not unusual at the time for Finsbury Park depot to use the 8.20 am train for test purposes, especially when new types of locomotive were being introduced into service.

Arriving at the driver's cab we found it full of engineers from the Brush works at Loughborough, wearing white overalls. My first comment to them was, 'If you can't repair the boiler fault, what do you expect us to do about it?' to which they replied, 'Boilers are nothing to do with us, we are only here to monitor the performance of the locomotive'. We climbed aboard and made our way through to the engine compartment, as the train departed north. On reaching the boiler, we were confronted with something unfamiliar to us, but we were prepared to give it a go. Bear in mind that a common fault with most Spanner boilers was with their firing electrodes, which often became dirty and shorted out, thus causing the boiler not to fire up and then fail to operate. We looked round and saw that the electrodes entered the firing chamber through a plate mounted on the end of the boiler. Undoing the holding screws we removed the plate and found to our surprise that a piece of thin metal had fallen across the ends of the electrodes and had indeed shorted them out. We were in luck. After cleaning and resetting them, we replaced the plate and switched on, the boiler fired up straightaway with a loud explosion. Apparently what had happened was that on the way to Hitchin the secondman (fireman in the steam days) had kept pressing the reset switch to try and get the boiler to work. Each time he did this the fuel pump pumped a certain amount of diesel fuel into the firing chamber before it cut out, thus the unburnt fuel built up in the bottom of the chamber and when we switched on and the boiler fired up, it tried to burn the diesel oil all in one go, causing the explosion. Black smoke poured out of the exhaust and darkened the countryside, but the boiler settled down and worked well and steam pressure soon started to build on the gauge, sending some heat through to the coaches.

Before long the train pulled up on its scheduled stop at Huntingdon. There the guard walked forward to the driver and said that several passengers had complained of being choked by awful smelly black smoke: was there something wrong with the locomotive and would he have to telephone for a replacement at Peterborough? After explaining the situation to him and how everything was now satisfactory, Ray and I beat a hasty retreat to the up platform and caught the next train back to Hitchin.

On another occasion I had a most interesting call-out. Whilst working on the morning shift, again it was to a faulty train-heating boiler, but it was the journey back home that created the interest. I received a message to say, 'Could you please meet the north-bound express to Edinburgh, as the heating boiler has failed to operate since leaving King's Cross'. The messages were usually conveyed to us via the signalman, after being given to him by the driver, who usually slowed the train down near the box and shouted, 'Get the fitters to meet the train at Hitchin'. It arrived in the centre road and I quickly jumped aboard. The locomotive turned out to be my old friend D9003 *Meld* and the driver happened to be the brother of one of the Hitchin drivers, who a year later became our next door neighbour when we moved to Station Terrace, so we had a lot in common.

The boiler fault was soon rectified within a few miles, but my mate Nana and I had to remain aboard until the next stop at Peterborough. That was fine by me as I always enjoyed riding in the cab of one those powerful and exciting locomotives. Besides, we had a lot to talk about with our new friend the driver, who invited me to take a ride with him at a later date. (I took up his offer and rode on one of the 'Deltics' from King's Cross to Grantham - he wanted me to stay with him through to Newcastle, but time did not allow.) On arrival at Peterborough we realized that there was no train to get us back to Hitchin for at least three hours, so decided to take the next available one to King's Cross and return from there, it would be much quicker. The train duly arrived, being hauled by a Brush type '4' (class '47'), and the driver was only too pleased to have us in the cab with him. Again it was someone to talk to and as it turned out later a big help as well. We soon got away and by Yaxley the locomotive was doing 80 mph, when suddenly the Automatic Warning System (AWS) horn began to sound for no apparent reason, which was rather strange as we were nowhere near a signal. The driver tried to cancel it but had no joy; I quickly turned round and pulled the isolation handle down on the relay box, otherwise the brakes would have been automatically applied. This now meant we had to proceed at caution; the driver said he thought there must be an electrical fault and would get the electrician to look at it on arrival in London. Just after passing through Huntingdon the brake started to be applied then released; this happened several times and the driver came to the conclusion that the guard was trying to get a message to us, so we pulled up, north of Offord. The guard alighted from the first coach and walked forward to the locomotive and climbed aboard. He said that he had received complaints from passengers, especially those in the front coaches, that they had heard a lot of bumping noises coming from beneath the floor of the coach. The guard went back to protect the train, placing detonators on the tracks, whilst I climbed down to investigate the cause of the problem. The first thing was to examine the locomotive. Walking round to the front, I found to my surprise that the AWS magnet had disappeared - all that was left was the retaining plate, a broken bolt and a few dangling wires, which was the remains of the electrical connection. This is what had caused the horn to sound when we were passing through Yaxley. Further examination of the coaches revealed that under the first three, the dynamos had been damaged and their drive belts were missing and this was the cause of the bumping noise beneath the floor. We decided to proceed to Hitchin, at reduced speed, and allow a further examination to be carried out by the resident carriage & wagon (C&W) examiner. So after all that Nana and I managed to alight, without having to travel through to King's Cross.

Our fleet of English Electric type '1s' (class '20') gave us very little trouble and I can only remember being called to one, when the driver reported that the engine was losing cooling water from the radiator. I had a good look round for the obvious causes, such as burst pipes or hoses, etc., but found nothing. I then asked the driver to turn the engine over by the aid of the start button and to my surprise found one of the cylinder heads moving up and down. All four retaining studs had sheared off, level with the cylinder casting. The locomotive was towed back to the depot and I spent the rest of the shift and part of next day renewing the studs. We first had to drill out the old broken ones, which was no easy task, bearing in mind the conditions we were working under at the time. The depot had no lifting facilities such as an overhead crane, everything had to be manhandled, and a cylinder head could weigh anything up to a cwt and even more. All this work had to be done between running repairs on other locomotives and call-outs. The English Electric type '1s' like their counterparts, the type '4s', had 'V' engines fitted with two banks of cylinders, four each side on a type '1' and eight each side on a type '4'.

You know the old saying, everything seems to happen in twos and it was not long before I was out again, attending to the same type of problem. A Brush type '2' (class '31') ran into the up platform on a King's Cross-bound passenger train. The Mirrlees 'V' engine was making the most appalling noise and radiator cooling water was cascading down the side of the engine from one of the cylinder heads. Sure enough all the studs had sheared off, and the head had been forced away from the top of the casting. A spare locomotive was attached to the front, an English Electric type '1', and the failed locomotive and train were towed to London. This time Finsbury Park could carry out the repair to the damaged cylinder head, especially as it was one of their allocated locomotives.

Not long after I had left Hitchin, the Brush type '2s' (class '31') were all rebuilt with new, English Electric, eight-cylinder 'V' engines - one member of the class had already been converted for a trial period whilst I was working at Finsbury Park.

It was during a call-out that I had one of my strangest experiences whilst riding in the cab of a diesel locomotive, and it made me realize the importance of the AWS system. I'd been called to a northbound night sleeping car express, hauled by a Brush type '4'. Again the train heating boiler was in trouble and had failed to operate after departure from King's Cross. It was a dark winter's night, no moonlight and thick with fog, you could only see a few feet in front of you. Eventually the train crawled into the station and the mate and I climbed aboard. The fault was only a minor repair and we soon had the boiler working, so now had the pleasure of a footplate ride to Peterborough. Sitting in the secondman's seat would normally have given me a clear view of the road ahead, but this particular night it was like running into a black wall, the only thing to be seen or heard was the green aspect of the colour light signal as it flashed past the window, and the AWS clear warning bell ringing in the cab. Without this facility the train would have run at slow speed, the driver trying to look for the signals from block post to block post, as they often did in the days of steam. It was even known for the fireman to climb the signal post to see if the signal had been pulled off. On this occasion we were travelling at the normal speed of between 80 to 90 mph. I passed a comment to the driver, 'What happens if there's a stationary train on the track in front of us?' His reply was, 'At this speed it doesn't matter, as we wouldn't know much about it'. I suppose he was right and it didn't seem to bother him anyway, so point taken.

One of the most unusual call-outs we had was to a 'Baby Deltic'. The driver reported that the Stones steam generator had suddenly shut down, pressure was dropping and they were losing heat in the train. The second man had pressed the reset button several times, but to no avail. The generator just refused to even attempt to fire up, as would have been normal practice, so they came to the conclusion that something was seriously wrong. What had happened was that the brick lining inside the firing chamber had collapsed and fallen across the generating coil, which then caused the coil to start and overheat, turning the steam into superheat. The overheat limit switch at the base of the coil should have cut in and shut down the generator as a safety precaution, but it failed to operate. The superheated steam reached such a high temperature that it had melted the steel generator coil into a solid lump and the steam heating pipe connections between the coaches looked like coil springs, and all their outer rubber casing had melted away. It just goes to show what high temperatures super-heated steam can attain, when it's capable of melting metal. If you had your hand in the way it would burn the flesh down to the bone.

It appears from my writing that we only had time for work and call-outs, but there was the amusing side to the job, when in our spare time we would have a bit of fun, or play a few tricks on one another. There were even times when we were called out that whatever we did caused a certain amount of amusement. I remember being called over to the station to the late night King's Cross to Aberdeen sleeping car express. On nights we were expected to carry out any emergency repairs on the coaches as well as the locomotives, as no C&W fitters were on duty - they only worked a morning and afternoon shift, based in their workshop and office in a wooden hut at the south end of the down platform. On this particular night a heating pipe between two of the coaches had burst and needed replacing. A couple of bolts also needed tightening on a clip which secured the metal heating pipe beneath the coach. This was situated just above the bogie, not a difficult job but a dirty one, as you had to crawl about on the ballast in order to carry out the repair. I crawled under the coach and removed the damaged pipe, my mate handed me the new one and after fitting it I was about to tighten the loose bolts, when a passenger on the train decided they required the use of the lavatory, which was immediately above where I was working. They flushed and I got the lot down my neck and back. My mates back at the depot wouldn't let me anywhere near the messroom for a cup of tea, until I'd had a good wash and changed my boiler suit.

On another occasion I was on the early morning shift, starting at 6.00 am. Between then and 7.30 am things at the depot were generally slack, as most of the locomotives had left to take up their respective diagrams and all we had to do was be on standby, in case of a call-out to the station. It also gave me a chance to do a bit of paperwork, like filling in and signing the previous day's examination forms. My hair was beginning to grow rather long and I'd already received complaints from June, so I decided to pop round the corner to the barbers, who always opened at 6.00 am in order to catch the early passing trade, men making their way to work, especially railway staff. It would only take a few minutes, as I thought, but halfway through my mate appeared in the doorway, 'Come on', he said, 'You are required on the next up train to King's Cross, the boiler has failed'. Luckily enough he had had the sense to bring my tool bag with him. I jumped out of the chair and said to the barber, who I knew quite well, 'I'll see you when I get back'. Thankfully I had my cap with me to hide the already started haircut, otherwise folk would have thought that I was setting a new trend in hairstyles. We rushed over to the station and just managed to get there as the train ran into the up platform. It was a limited stop working, so by the time I'd rectified the fault, we were approaching King's Cross. Dashing across to the suburban platforms, we managed to catch the next train back and arrived in Hitchin within one-and-a-half hours of departing. I went straight back into the barbers and had my haircut finished off; it was the first time he'd cut someone's hair in two goes. I suppose he would have been entitled to charge me a double fee!

At the depot we often had a bit of fun during our spare time or meal breaks. It was back in my early days, around the time of my marriage, when one day a driver walked into the messroom and said, 'I have an old bicycle at home - would anyone be interested in taking it off my hands?' Straightaway Al Sales jumped in with both feet, before anybody else could utter a word, 'It will come in handy if my car breaks down, then I can bike to work'. Next day the bicycle arrived as promised, but to everyone's surprise it turned out to be an old sit-up-and-beg type, not really what Al wanted, but bad luck, he had to accept it from the driver and do something with it, even if it ended up on the scrap heap next door. Unfortunately the following day, a Saturday, Al was going away for two weeks' holiday and asked if we would look after it whilst he was away, 'I will leave it in the workshop, it will be safe there until I return.' That was the worst thing he could have said, especially with certain members of the staff present. A meeting was held among a few of us and we decided that we would tart it up a bit and make it look a little more presentable. We went along to see the man who owned the neighbouring scrapyard and asked if we could have a few spare parts. 'Help yourself,' he said, after we'd let him in on our little secret. The first thing we picked up was the bonnet cover from a crashed Volkswagen Beetle: 'That will make a good canopy for the rider,' said Nana. Then we collected together a klaxon horn, to act as a warning bell, and a large oil funnel, which was turned into the rear exhaust pipe. Over the next two weeks, in our spare time we gradually put it together. The long side of the bonnet cover was welded to the back of the seat, which then curved over the top of the rider and was supported by a bracket fixed to the handle bars, forming the protective canopy. The klaxon horn was bolted to the bike and the funnel welded to the rear carrier, protruding out by about three feet. It looked fantastic, like an alien machine from outer space. One of the lads brought in some old tins of paint he'd had stored in the garden shed and we painted the machine all colours of the rainbow.

Now came the time to road test it, using the yard at the side of the depot of course, not on the main road. Everyone had a go, even Bill the chargehand. It was a good job that the shed master's office was on the other side of the main line in the old steam shed. If he had caught us I don't know what he would have said, but knowing him I think he would have joined in the fun, especially as a joke was being made at Al's expense! After a while we got used to riding this strange looking machine; it was fine whilst there was no wind, but as soon as the wind started to blow, you had a job to control it, wobbling about until you fell off. In the end one man managed to master the controls and decided to give it a road test. Ray Brown, the electrician, mounted the bike and rode out through the gate and made his way towards the town centre, whilst we all watched. Pedestrians stopped in their tracks and looked on in amazement. Everything was going well until a man driving a car could not believe his eyes and drove up on to the pavement, narrowly avoiding a lamp post. Ray dismounted and quickly wheeled it back into the yard, before being caught by the police and taken into custody.

Al returned from holiday and straightaway made enquiries as to why his bike was not in the workshop. 'We've locked it in the boiler house for safe keeping', said Nana. He had a shock when he saw it, but had a good laugh and even attempted to ride it himself. He agreed afterwards that it would have been too difficult to ride to work in any case, especially the distance he had to come from Meppershall. The scrap merchant didn't miss out, because not only did he gain his bits of scrap back, but also gained a bicycle! Before it was given to the scrap merchant Nana and his pals threatened to bring it to my wedding at St Mary's church. June and I were dreading leaving the church for the photographs, in case they were waiting outside. But thankfully they'd not kept their word.

Jock, like Al, was renowned for being a bit tight, or should I say careful when it came to spending money. I was on nights and it so happened that my two fitter's mates that week were Nana and Tom Worbey. Together they were two of the biggest tricksters on the depot. We arrived for work one evening and attached to Nana's locker door was a note from Jock, 'Could you please repair my boots, they need a new sole and heel, I've left them and a piece of old water crane leather on the bench in the workshop'. On seeing them, Nana realized that they were beyond repair and wanted confining to the dustbin. 'Leave it to Tom and me, we will do something with them'. I was busy carrying out an examination and doing a few repairs on a locomotive, whilst they both set about attempting to re-sole and heel Jock's boots. They found a piece of wood, about

Drawing of the bike. *June Meredith*

three to four inches thick, placed the boots on top and drew round the outside, forming the shape of a sole and heel. These pieces they cut out and nailed on to each boot and finally finished them off, by painting them in red and white stripes. They looked a picture and would have graced any circus clown's feet. Next morning Jock arrived at work expecting to wear his re-soled and heeled boots and was surprised to see what had happened to them. He should have known not to trust Nana and Tom. At first he was not too pleased, but in the end saw the funny side of it and joined in the fun. 'I will keep them in my locker, they may come in useful sometime in the future'.

Two weeks later, on a Friday, Nana and I were on morning shift together. It was customary for someone to go down the road to the fish and chip shop and collect the order for the lunch break. Nana said to Jock, 'You go down and whilst you are at it, why don't you wear your new boots?' Jock took up the challenge and put on the boots; being a short man it made him look four inches taller, he was seeing things he'd never seen before, like looking over hedges into the front gardens, as he made his way along the street. He only wanted a funny hat and a big nose and he would have been just right to enter the circus. People in the queue at the chip shop fell about laughing and refused to stand near him and if the lady serving had not known him, I think she would have sent for an ambulance to take him away. Never mind, it made a few people happy and cheered them up for the day.

As I mentioned before, Lenny was a good mate and a hard worker, but sometimes a little slow on the uptake, which meant he was a prime target for those wanting to play tricks. Again I was on the night shift, this time my two mates were Nana and Lenny. For his mid-shift snack, Lenny would bring to work two eggs to boil on the stove in the mess-room, and a packet of bread and butter sandwiches. He was always bragging about the eggs, 'These are the best you can buy in town, always up to date and fresh'. I don't know why he bothered to buy them, as he kept chickens, maybe they were not laying at that particular time. Nana, who also kept chickens, after a couple of nights got fed up with Lenny constantly bragging about these wonderful eggs he'd bought in town. 'I will shut him up, I've had a chicken sitting on some eggs for the last two weeks and a few have gone addled, I will bring a couple to work tomorrow and try and swap them over when he's not looking'.

The following night, whilst I took Lenny outside and got him to help with a repair on a locomotive, Nana did the swap, which was quite easy to do as we always left our snap boxes on the messroom table, ready for the mid-shift break.

About 2.00 am things had quietened down, so we decided to take our meal break. Lenny put the pan on the stove and when the water was boiling, popped in the eggs. After about a minute the shells cracked and the rotten eggs burst out into the water, the smell was awful. With us in the messroom were a group of footplate men from London, also taking their meal break; we all had to leave the room until the air cleared. Nana said, 'If I was you I would take them back to the shop and complain'. 'Good idea', said Lenny and drained off the water and put what was left of the eggs into a glass bottle. 'I will tell my wife never to buy eggs from the Co-op again'. The following night he turned up for work with a box of half-a-dozen eggs, which the Co-op gave him as compensation.

That night all three of us enjoyed a hard-boiled egg supper, as a thank-you for pointing it out to him.

Lenny's wife worked as a conductress and was very often on the early morning shift. If he was on the night shift at the depot with us, he had to pop home, with my permission, at 5.00 am to give her a wake-up call, which didn't take many minutes as he only lived a few hundred yards up the road. Unfortunately when this occurred he didn't get very much sleep in the day time, as he had to look after the children, so if we had a slack period in the night, usually between 2.00 and 5.00 am, I would let him get his head down in the boiler house. In there we stored the sacks of waste cloth and they made a comfortable bed.

One night around 3.00 am a locomotive arrived on shed, driven by my friend Dennis Williamson, who always came and had a chat with me and a cup of tea. Now Dennis was also one who loved playing a joke and asked me where Lenny was; 'In the boiler house trying to get a bit of shut eye', I said. 'Has he got to go and wake his wife up at 5 o'clock?' – 'Yes', I said. 'Okay', said Dennis, 'We will have a bit of fun with him,' and he told everyone present to alter their watches to 5.00 am, even the clock on the wall and Lenny's pocket watch. He then went and knocked on the boiler house door, 'Come on, Lenny, it's time to go and give your wife the early morning call'. After a few minutes, Lenny appeared in the messroom rubbing his eyes, 'That's a short night', and jumped on his bike and rode off home. Ten minutes later he was back. 'What lousy devil changed the time on my watch? My wife played hell with me for getting her up so early! She said to me, 'Can you not read a watch you fool? I will deal with you when I get home later in the day'.

Lenny turned up for work the following day, no worse for the previous night's experience. And there was not a mark on him, where his wife might have hit him. 'How did you get away with it?', we asked. 'I went and bought her a present to soften her up'. That night he made sure he kept his watch in his trouser pocket.

White lines were part of Lenny's life and when an opportunity arose, he would be out with his paint and brush, marking out the walkways or the edges of the depot inspection pits. Now when the locomotives arrived on shed, they were very often being driven in reverse. Main line diesel locomotives normally had two cabs, one at each end and the rule was that when being driven the driver should always be in the cab at the front, in the direction of travel, and if a reversal had to be made, then the driver should change ends. In the case of Hitchin, this did not always apply. When a locomotive came off a train and was running light to the depot the direction of travel was northwards via the down side yard, on to the Midland branch and then down through the depot sidings into the shed. At the point on the branch where the reversal took place, most of the drivers could not be bothered to change ends, so drove into the shed from the opposite end cab. They had to be very careful and inch their way in slowly, because very often one of the shunting locomotives was stabled at the bottom of the shed under repair and so there was then just enough room to accommodate one of the main line diesels over the pit. Lenny in his wisdom decided that he would be helpful, and paint a white right-angled line on the

The old Midland Railway shed at Hitchin in 1966 which was by then being used as a road motor repair garage, although still rail-connected. On the right can be seen the scrap heap where we obtained the parts to adapt the old bicycle. *Frank Berridge Collection*

Across the road from the MR shed was the Nightingale public house, which very often doubled up as the loco mess-room! When I arrived in Hitchin in 1961 it was known as the Leicester Railway Inn. *Author*

floor, and when the cab of the locomotive was level with the line, the driver knew he had to stop. That was fine, but when he came to paint the line, there was no shunting locomotive at the bottom of the road and the main line locomotive he used as a pattern had run further inside the depot than normal.

It was working well and most drivers said it was a good idea. We arrived for work one night and there happened to be a class '08' shunting locomotive stabled at the bottom of No. 1 road. We were all having a cup of tea in the messroom and heard a locomotive running into the depot; suddenly there was one almighty bang as it ran into the '08', pushing it over the wheel stops at the end of the rails, and almost through the wall at the back of the depot. The driver was fuming and said, 'What idiot painted the white line on the floor?' If Lenny had been on duty, I think he would have strangled him. Thankfully there was no damage done, except a couple of wheel marks in the concrete floor and Nana's bike, which he'd left leaning against the wall, was unfortunately squashed between the wall and the '08s' buffers. He was not pleased, because he had to walk home next morning and find himself another bike to ride to work on. For the next few weeks Lenny was not the flavour of the month with certain members of the staff, but in the end all was forgotten and they became pals again.

With the aid of the locomotive, we pulled the '08' back onto the track and then set about scrubbing out the white line. The paint and brushes were confiscated and never used again. Nothing was mentioned about the incident, until a member of the day staff noticed the grooves in the floor and then I had to make a report to Bill the chargehand. It was all smoothed over and Lenny got away with it as a little error of judgement.

On Christmas Eve it was the custom for us all to have a few drinks after work, in the pub across the road from the depot. When I first arrived in 1961 the pub was called the Leicester Railway Inn, named after the old Leicester to Hitchin Railway, which eventually became part of the Midland Railway. With the pub being situated across the road from the Midland engine shed, I suppose it was appropriate to name it after the railway. In 1964 when the line to Bedford closed, the name was changed to the Nightingale Inn. It's interesting to note that just before the branch finally closed, it was used for making part of the film *Those Magnificent Men in their Flying Machines*. The ex-Highland Railway 'Jones Goods' 4-6-0 No. 103 was used to haul the train.

One particular Christmas we were all together in the pub, when Nana and Tom Worbey were determined a get a few of the staff drunk. Jock got to the point where he could not stand and had to be taken home in Peter's car with the help of Al. They dropped him outside his back door, then knocked on the door and ran away in fear of his wife, who we understood was a bit of a battleaxe. Lenny on the other hand had to cycle home and went wobbling down the road trying to avoid the traffic. During the day he had been round the sidings gathering up bundles of straw. Bananas were unloaded in the down yard and as they were packed in straw, a lot of it was lying around on the floor. The yard foreman allowed Lenny, from time to time, to take a small amount home for use in his chicken run. The bundle of straw was strapped on to the carrier at the back of his bike and just as he pushed off, Nana put a match to the straw. And the last we saw of Lenny was when he disappeared under the railway bridge with three feet of flame trailing from the rear of his bike. He must have got home all right as he came to work on Boxing Day and said he'd had a good Christmas, but never mentioned what happened to the straw.

Nana and I used the Leicester Railway pub as our local, as well as most of the footplate staff, and whenever we were on day shift together, we would spend a couple of evenings enjoying a few pints and a chat. It was during one of these evenings that I experienced one of the worst thunderstorms in my life. When I set out from home to walk to the pub, the weather was very hot, just the kind of evening when you wanted a pint to cool you down. Around 8.00 pm the storm clouds began to gather and we could hear rumbles of thunder in the distance. By 9.00 pm it was overhead and it never stopped lightning; by the time Nana and I walked home we didn't need street lights or a torch to see our way, the lightning did it for us, but what was surprising was that there was very little rain. When I got home June had gone to bed frightened. The storm lasted well into the night and we learnt next morning that it had been one of the worst in living memory. Apparently three storms had run into each other over North Hertfordshire and then had difficulty in breaking up and dispersing.

Most of our work on the locomotives involved those working the regular diagrammed services; we didn't have many specials working out of Hitchin. If members of the Royal Family were travelling overnight between London and Scotland, we would be asked to go over to the station, complete with tool bag, and stand by whilst the train ran through, just in case there was a failure with the locomotive or the train-heating boiler. There would also have to be a spare locomotive standing ready, usually on the cattle dock siding behind the yard signal box. This would not be the complete Royal Train, but a coach attached to the rear of the 'Night Scotsman'. Depending on which member was travelling, we would receive a special code word from the control office.

The only time I was involved with the Royal Train was in 1964, when David Bowes Lyon, the Queen Mother's brother, died. His coffin was brought to Hitchin from Scotland in a special coach attached to the rear of the train. The rest of the family including HM The Queen, travelled in their normal compartments. The family home was at St Paul's Waldenbury, and Hitchin was the nearest station to the estate church where the funeral was to take place.

The first thing we did was clean and polish one of the class '04' shunting locomotives. This was used to remove the coach containing the coffin from the rear of the train after it had arrived in the up platform. The '04' then brought the coach across the main line and placed it in the cattle dock on the down side, where the coffin was transferred into a waiting hearse. In the meantime the Royal Train was shunted into the down platform close to the station's main entrance to allow the Queen and her family easy access to the waiting cars. For these movements all facing points had to be clamped and locked. The platelayers were kept busy that day. No trains were allowed into or out of the station until the Queen had left, so there was a certain amount of disruption to the normal train service. My mate Nana and I had to be present at the station all through the proceedings, wearing our clean boiler suits and having the tool bag at the ready, just in case something went wrong or broke down. Fortunately nothing did go wrong, and we both had a grandstand view of the whole event.

After the train had been serviced in the down sidings it returned to London. And the Royal Family, after attending the funeral, returned to Scotland by air.

One local train I was involved with was a special to Peterborough laid on for the employees of the K&L factory in Letchworth. The bosses had paid for them all, especially the children, to go and see the pantomime 'Mother Goose' at the Peterborough theatre. Like the class '04' used for the Royal Train we also had to specially prepare a locomotive for the occasion. A type '2' (class '31') was used this time. It would also be carrying a special headboard entitled 'K. & L. Children's Outing'. On the day, 15th January, 1965, Peter Upchurch and I had the honour of placing the headboard on the front lamp bracket. The local press were there to record the event and we had our photographs taken surrounded by children, as we carried out the operation. This was one of the lighter sides of the job, making a group of children happy. As the train pulled out they were all at the windows waving and cheering whilst we both stood on the platform feeling proud with what we had achieved.

Not exactly a special, but each weekday we had an unusual working out of King's Cross in the late afternoon - a departure for both Peterborough and Cambridge. It would run as one train as far as Hitchin, where it was split, the front half going forward to Peterborough and the rear to Cambridge. To work the Cambridge half a locomotive driven by Cambridge men would arrive at Hitchin in mid-afternoon on a freight train. After shunting the train into the down yard the locomotive would come into the depot for servicing, when the footplatemen would have at least a couple of hours' break to have their food

A poor quality image from a newspaper cutting of the headboard about to fitted onto the front of the locomotive hauling the 'K&L Children's Outing' on 15th January, 1965. The author is standing on the buffer beam and on the right fitter's mate Peter Upchurch holds the train headboard. *Author's Collection*

There was a steam-worked train in the afternoon out of King's Cross to Peterborough which split at Hitchin, the rear half going to Cambridge hauled by a Brush type '2'. Steam finished working this diagram on Thursday 18th April, 1963 and the honour fell to 'A4' class 4-6-2 No. 60022 *Mallard* and here it is ready to depart from Hitchin for Peterborough at 5.21 pm. *Author*

The next time I saw steam at Hitchin was in more recent years when I photographed 'A4' class 4-6-2 No. 60009 *Union of South Africa* passing through on a special from King's Cross to York.
Author

HAPPY DAYS AT HITCHIN 137

and a rest. They would then return to the station and have the locomotive standing in the siding behind the yard box ready to back down on to the Cambridge portion as soon as the Peterborough section had departed.

When I was working the regular day shift I got to know the Cambridge men quite well, especially one driver, Percy Fitzgerald. Percy was a gentleman and an engineman of the old school. In his earlier days he had fired and driven many of the East Anglia expresses, including firing the locomotives which hauled the Royal Train on the occasions when Royalty were visiting or staying at Sandringham House. He and I became very good friends and, like Dennis Williamson, he was also a bit of a father figure to me, always taking an interest in what June and I were doing and often offering good advice. Sadly in July 1965 on his way home from work Percy dropped dead in the passageway at the side of his house. It was a big shock to us all, especially as he was so close to retirement. I wrote a letter of sympathy to his widow and in return she wrote to me thanking me for my kindness to Percy, a letter I still retain to this day and treasure in my memories of a true railwayman, a gentleman and a very good and kind friend.

On the last day the train was hauled by steam out of King's Cross, the locomotive was none other than the famous Gresley 'A4' class 4-6-2 No. 60022 *Mallard*. We all rushed across to the station with our cameras to take a photograph as she departed on her way to Peterborough. Little did I realize then that one day I would be back again to photograph another 'A4' class departing Hitchin, but this time it was in the 1990s, when I went to see No. 60009 *Union of South Africa* depart on a special to York.

In the early 1960s quite a number of the fitters were being sent on special training courses, at various places around the country. As already mentioned, whilst at Finsbury Park I was sent to Stratford works for my basic diesel training, but from Hitchin I only attended one, a two-week course on the maintenance of Clayton train heating boilers, which were appearing on the new type '3s' (class '37s'). The course was being held at the training school in Doncaster locomotive works, which brought back many memories to me. On this course I met and made another life-long friend, Randell Webster from Keith in Scotland. Like myself Randell had served his apprenticeship on steam locomotives, but was having to change with the times. Unfortunately a few years after meeting him he was made redundant when the shed at Keith closed. He transferred to Inverness for a short time but left railway service and joined the Scottish Maltsters as a maintenance engineer, travelling to all the whisky distilleries in the north of Scotland.

June and I, and later our two boys, spent quite a few happy holidays with Randell in Keith, travelling there by train and on one occasion on the overnight 'Night Scotsman' from King's Cross - the only time I've used a sleeping berth on a train in this country. The first time we made a visit, we were lucky enough to witness the last steam working in the north of Scotland when Randell took us to see the branch being worked between Tillynaught Junction and Banff by the BR '2MT' class 2-6-0s. I just missed out on having a footplate trip when we arrived at Banff, only to see the train pulling out on its return journey to the junction. But with a fast car we soon caught it up and had some splendid views as it made its way along the branch.

The branch is now long closed, and is sadly missing from the face of the railway map, more's the pity. I expect the present day residents wish it were still running today, if only to take some pressure off the clogged roads in the area.

In the summer of 1965 a rash suddenly appeared on my left hand; I didn't take much notice of it at first, until it started spreading up my arm, then I went to see the doctor, who immediately sent me to the Lister hospital to see a specialist. It turned out to be a form of dermatitis, caused through handling diesel fuel. Straightaway he wrote a letter to the railway, telling them that I could no longer continue working on the locomotives until the rash had cleared up. This came as a bit of a shock: what was I going to do now?

When reporting to the shed master the following day, he was at a loss as to what kind of work he could find me. In the end he telephoned round the district and found me a job visiting the various out station goods sheds and inspecting their loose lifting tackle, a job I was to know very well in later years. This job lasted for about a month and I enjoyed doing it, especially as it was in the summertime and the weather was warm. Just as it was coming to a close, a vacancy occurred in the running department for a time and roster clerk, based on shifts in the running foreman's office. I was to team up with Jim, a former driver from Langwith Junction, so straightaway we had something in common.

The job involved signing the footplate men on and off duty, keeping a record of their hours worked, looking after their route cards and booking men on to special duties, dealing with the control office and generally acting as assistant to Jim when required. There were 50 sets of men to look after, and at times the job could get a little complicated, especially if the men had worked over 12 hours on a shift, which meant they could not return in time for the same shift the following day, so another set of men had to be rostered in their place. As we carried a certain amount of spare sets on round-the-clock shifts, vacancies were not difficult to fill. It usually happened on a Monday morning when men had been working long shifts over the weekend on civil engineers' ballast trains, and a track-relaying job had run late.

Again I enjoyed this work, especially as Jim liked talking and spent a lot of his time in the messroom exchanging views with the spare link footplate staff, which meant I was left alone to get on with the job. This suited me fine as I was gaining experience all the time, especially as Jim trusted me and we both got on very well together in the nine months I worked with him. As he lived on his own, June and I often invited him round for lunch or tea and we exchanged stories about Langwith and Colwick and the railways in the Nottingham area.

During this time I'd been visiting the hospital once a month and at the end of nine months the doctor declared me fit to return to my duties as a locomotive fitter, as the rash had disappeared. I took the doctor's letter to the chief clerk at the locomotive depot office, who then made arrangements for me to see the medical officer at Marylebone station in London. This was the normal thing to do if you had been on the sick list for more than six months.

The medical officer gave me a thorough examination and agreed with the doctor that the rash had cleared, but stated that he could not allow me to return to my former duties and that I would have to try and find another job that would not involve handling diesel fuel. The company were frightened that I might claim compensation if the rash happened to break out again, and they were not prepared to take this risk. This came as a complete shock to me. What could I do? The medical officer said he would help me all he could in finding another vacancy and suggested I stayed on my present duties until one arose. Straightaway I received a letter telling me that there was a position as a fitter in the road motors department in London, until I pointed out to them that this too would involve handling diesel fuel. So that idea was scrapped. In the end I wrote and asked if they could find me a suitable post in the Nottingham area, as it was a way of getting back to my old stamping grounds. Within a week I received a letter stating that there was a vacancy for a fitter in the plant and machinery department at Toton near Nottingham, based in the diesel depot: would I be interested? The job involved the general maintenance of the equipment used around the depot, such as the locomotive jacks, the central heating system, lifts and hoists, the old steam shed water softening plant, which was still being used in connection with the dispersal of waste oil, and the wagon retarders in the up and down sidings in the marshalling yard. And to my delight the maintenance of three cranes, two of them steam-operated, the ex-Colwick breakdown crane and a three-ton grab crane which had also worked at Colwick, on the wet ash pits. It was being used at Toton for transhipping goods from crippled wagons.

June and I talked the matter over and decided that we would go, even if it meant once again moving home, especially as we'd just got used to living in Station Terrace. A week later I was sent to Derby for an interview and told to report to Alf Echells, the chief foreman at the plant and machinery office. I thought to myself, 'Why Derby?' when I was going to be working at Toton, but it turned out that the Derby office was the headquarters.

I had the strangest interview I'd ever had in my life; the only question Alf asked was, 'Are you frightened of climbing ladders?' to which I replied, 'No'. 'Then you've got the job,' he said. He then told me that the vacancy at Toton would not be available for a few months, but in the meantime would I be prepared to take on a fitter's job at Derby, until such time as it became vacant? I agreed and returned home to await confirmation, which arrived mid-way through February, with instructions to report for duty to the mechanical foreman on Monday 6th March, 1966.

After nearly 12 years, five of them at Hitchin, I was leaving the locomotive department for good and entering uncharted waters; would I like it? - and would I fit in with the rest of the staff? But that's another story!

It was a sad day when June, David and I left Hitchin, as we had made so many good friends over the past five years, especially with my work colleagues and the local bell-ringers. I think most of them were also sorry to see us leave the district, but by then we had already lost one or two friends ourselves, especially Dennis Williamson and his family, who in 1964 emigrated to Australia to work with a friend of theirs, in his electrical business. Dennis always said that when the steam locomotives finished working on the railways, his railway career was over and he was true to his word.

Chapter Eight

Early Days at Derby

The first thing I had to do before leaving Hitchin, was once again find somewhere to live, which was a pity as we had settled down at Station Terrace. Within a short time I found a flat in George Road, West Bridgford near Nottingham, which was very handy for travelling to my work at Derby as there was a frequent train service from Nottingham station. In the meantime, June and David went to stay with my parents at Radcliffe-on-Trent. This gave her and my mother a chance to prepare the flat for us to move into. I stayed on in Hitchin to work out my time and help with the removal. Under the circumstances the railway company had agreed to move the furniture for nothing, provided everything went by rail.

On the morning of the move, Pickfords came and packed the furniture, etc., into a container, which had been delivered by a railway lorry the previous day and left on the road outside the house. Everything went well and by lunchtime the container was ready to be collected and taken to the goods yard at Letchworth, for loading onto a flat wagon. Just as the crane was lowering it down, the driver let the container slip and it hit the wagon with an almighty bang. I had visions of the contents being broken into a thousand pieces. June and I had no sleep for the next two nights, worrying about what had happened to our happy home - besides which the railway also had a bad reputation for losing trucks en route!

However, there were no worries as the container turned up on time in Nottingham London Road goods yard (the former Ambergate Railway and GNR station) and was delivered straightaway to the flat in West Bridgford. And when Pickfords arrived to unload it, to our great relief the only thing damaged was a leg on the kitchen table and that was only cracked - so much for Pickford's expert packing!

At 09.00 on Monday 6th March 1966, I reported to the plant and machinery depot in Litchurch Lane, Derby and started a new working life, and at the same time wondered what I'd let myself in for. I was going to find a different style of engineering from that of working on locomotives, although I had some experience of dealing with static plant, with servicing of turntables and water cranes, etc. On the Midland Region, unlike the Eastern, the P&M department was responsible for the maintenance of all types of plant, which included anything from sewing machines to the civil engineer's on-track plant such as ballast tamping machines, ballast cleaners and track relaying machines. I would have a lot of experience with these a few years later. I also had to get used to a new kind of pay structure, as I was to be paid a weekly bonus as well as a flat wage. Most servicing work was routine and given a time in which it was to be completed, giving the tradesman a 100 per cent bonus. Any breakdowns or unexpected repairs, and work carried out on track machines, was given an average bonus between 100 and 125 per cent, until some form of a time structure could be worked out, which never came about whilst I spent my time working with the P&M. The other policy in the P&M was for new starters to work with an experienced fitter for the first two weeks as a training period, during which time no bonus was received.

Alf Etchells, the chief foreman who had interviewed me, introduced me to the mechanical foreman, Derek Skidmore, who straightaway showed me round the workshop, found me a vacant tool cupboard and explained the workings and set-up of the area he covered, which included most of Derbyshire. He then took me to the School of Transport in London Road and introduced me to fitter Derek Mosley, who was working on a routine service task, maintaining the two central heating boilers. I was back on steam.

On the Tuesday I reported for work at the normal time of 07.30 and was placed with fitter Keith Barber, who at times acted as relief foreman when Derek was absent. This time I was to work with him on one of the chief civil engineer's (CCE) Plasser & Theurer class '04' tamping machines No. TT40, stabled in a siding at Trowell Junction station. A seal had burst on one of the four hydraulic squeeze cylinders, which pack the ballast beneath the sleepers. This was a common fault on these machines, as they were working under very high pressure and subject to excessive vibrations. Luckily enough it was one of the small seals and was easy to replace without stripping down too much of the cylinder. The repair was completed in a reasonable time and we finished the day by doing a few extra jobs that the crew required sorting out before the night shift reported for duty.

Wednesday turned out to be quite different and in a way more interesting. Again I was to be with Keith, this time working on another tamping machine, No. TT52, which was stabled in the sidings at the closed Castle Donington station, situated on what we called the back line, which ran between Sheet Stores Junction, near Long Eaton, and Stenson Junction, on the main line between Derby and Burton-on-Trent. The machine had been working during the previous night and again had been reported as having failed with a burst seal on one of the squeeze cylinders. But this time it was the large seal and we also found that the cylinder was cracked, which meant that we had a major repair on our hands as part of the tamping unit had to be stripped down in order to replace the damaged cylinder, a long job which could be completed in the day if only everything went well.

Whilst the van driver returned to the P&M stores at Derby to collect a new cylinder, Keith and I, with the help of the fitter's mate, set about removing the cracked cylinder. As the complete unit was so heavy, it had to be removed by the use of slings and a pull-lift, which had been attached to the roof frame of the machine, and then lowered to the ground to be worked on. Unfortunately when stripping the tamping tine arms from the cylinder, one of the bushes had seized on to the stub bearing, situated on the side of the cylinder. Keith struggled in trying to remove it, but nothing would move it and by the time the van driver had returned it was almost 16.00. I made a few suggestions, knowing how we had removed seized bushes when working in the locomotive department, but Keith had his own ideas. Staying any longer meant we would be on overtime, which Keith didn't want to do as he was booked out that evening at a party. This now put the foreman in a bit of a spot as he'd promised the CCE department that the machine would be ready to carryout its normal shift that night.

After consultation with Derek the foreman about various ways of doing the job, I agreed to work overtime and to return to the machine and see if I could complete the repair and have it ready for the night shift. The van driver, Joe Vowles, and the fitter's mate, Dave Simpson, were happy about working with me. With my own ideas I completed the job and we clocked off at 20.00 that evening, having made almost four hours' overtime, which suited the other two, as they were both family men like myself.

Reporting for duty next morning, Derek asked me how I'd got on, and when he realized that the work had been completed and the machine had worked its shift, he was over the moon. From then onwards I was working on my own with my own fitter's mate, John Cooke. Not only did I start on bonus straightaway, but got it for the previous evening's overtime - so much for the P&M's rule of working for two weeks on a training period without bonus. As far as I know I was the only one to break this rule; thereafter all newcomers had to work the two weeks.

Although we kept to the Derby area when working on the static plant, the civil engineer's on-track plant was a different matter. The tamping and lining machines were allocated to the Nottingham Division, but the larger machines, such as ballast cleaners, tracklayers and cranes, etc., were maintained on a regional basis, and their routine inspections and repairs were carried out by whichever P&M area they were working in at the time. The Nottingham Division had three P&M areas; as well as Derby there was Nottingham and Leicester, with Derby having two small out stations at Burton-on-Trent and Toton. In the case of Toton they just looked after the plant in the diesel depot and the marshalling yard.

The chief civil engineer had stated that it was necessary for only one of the divisional P&M depots to maintain the tamping and lining machines, as it would be easier to keep control of the spares and the records. As Derby employed more tradesmen than the others, this work was allocated to the depot, which meant we had to travel long distances in order to attend to any breakdowns and repairs. But for examinations and major repairs they were brought back to Derby, where we had covered facilities on a siding at the rear of the depot complete with inspection pit. The problem with travelling long distances meant that almost half the shift was wasted, especially if going south where the divisional boundary was just a few miles north of Bedford. In the east we travelled as far as Newark on the Lincoln line, Aslockton on the Grantham line and Ketton in Rutland. To the west and north distances were not quite so far, as we kept to our own P&M area, Sudbury on the line to Crewe, Millers Dale on the line to Manchester, a few miles south of Chesterfield on the Midland Main Line and Tamworth and Lichfield on the lines to Birmingham, plus the many branches in between all these points, including those in the Mansfield area, the line between Burton-on-Trent and Leicester via Coalville ('The Alps') and the remaining part of the old Great Central main line between Nottingham and Rugby.

On my fourth day, and now working on my own, I was soon to be acquainted again with the motive power department, when I was sent on a routine servicing job to Derby '4' shed, which was still open for the stabling of steam locomotives. Many of the freight trains in the area were being worked by the '8F' class 2-8-0s and '9F' 2-10-0s. There was even the odd passenger service still being worked by the class '5MT' 4-6-0s ('Black Fives'), especially between Nottingham and Manchester via Matlock. My task that day was to service the turntable, ash plant, coaling plant and water cranes, plus carrying out any repairs as required. This of course gave us extra bonus above the normal 100 per cent, the standard for the day - in some cases as much as 125 per cent, the gold star as everyone called it, but that depended on the foreman, as to whether he thought it was justified.

The other piece of apparatus belonging to the shed, which the P&M maintained, was the 45-ton steam breakdown crane. I remember being sent one day to renew a broken pin connecting the jib to the main frame of the winding drum. Unfortunately it was situated in a very awkward position next to the base of the drum and below the jib lifting ropes, which of course were coated in a thick black protecting oil; I had about six inches of space to work in, but after a long struggle, managed to carry out the repair. Emerging from beneath the ropes, I was covered from head to foot in black grease - if John the mate had been a bit thinner, I would have sent him in and shouted my instructions to him from outside; at least I would have kept myself clean. But in those days you had to take the rough with the smooth and get on and do the job to the best of your ability. It was no good going back to the foreman and saying, 'I can't carry out the repair, it's too difficult', you would have been laughed out of the workshop by the rest of the staff.

The very nature of the type of static plant we worked on meant that a lot of the time it was not available during the weekdays due to being in use, so many repairs had to be carried out at weekends, mostly on a Sunday. Fitters were allocated to these duties on a rota basis, to make sure everyone had a fair share of the overtime. Sometimes we were so busy that the entire fitting staff were often on duty at the weekend, in fact it was difficult to get a Sunday off. As well as the static plant, we had to cover for standby duties on the CCE track machines, when they were working in the area. This very often meant working long hours at night. Many a time I have started work on a Saturday evening at 20.00 and been on duty until Sunday afternoon, especially if it was with a ballast cleaner or the tracklayers and things were not going to plan, maybe the machine had broken down or they had hit a snag with the track. No matter how long it took, the job had to be completed.

A pair of wagons descending Sheep Pasture incline on the curve halfway down, note the inclined pulley wheels keeping the rope in between the tracks.

E.R. Morton/Author's Collection

The top of Sheep Pasture incline 26th April, 1963, with the engine house behind the train, and over the wall on the left is the field where the old tender buffers were rolled down like cheeses. The trains at that time were being worked by the old LMS 0-4-0ST as seen here with No. 47007 departing to the bottom of Middleton incline hauling two wagons and two water carriers. The engine shed by then had disappeared, and by the time I arrived there in March 1966 the trains were being diesel-hauled.

Author's Collection

Chapter Nine

Working on the old C&HPR

I had only been with the P&M two weeks, when I was asked by Alf Etchells, the chief foreman, if I was available to work on the Sunday as he had a special job for me. It was in the engine house at Sheep Pasture Top on the old Cromford & High Peak Railway (C&HPR). By then the line was operating in two sections. The northern section ran between the top of Middleton Incline and Buxton via Parsley Hay, and the southern section between the bottom of Middleton Incline and High Peak Junction on the Derby to Manchester main line. This section still used Sheep Pasture Incline and the sidings at Cromford Wharf. Middleton Incline had closed in 1963 as an economy measure and the steam beam engine and winding gear had been retained for preservation. It was the only original engine left on the line, constructed in 1825 by the Butterley Company. Although we didn't have to carry out any maintenance, we had to keep an eye on it from time to time to make sure it was okay and people were not breaking in and stealing parts as souvenirs. Even then the vandals broke in and smashed the doors and windows, which was a bit of a surprise seeing that it was situated in such a remote spot, that the house next door was occupied at the time, and the locomotive shed sidings were still in use. The wooden engine shed had disappeared some years earlier in a gale.

Just before I joined the P&M in Derby the Sheep Pasture winding engine had been converted from steam operation to electric and was now being driven by a large motor. As the gears began to settle down, the teeth on the pinion gear of the motor started rooting into the bottom of the gear on the large wheel, which operated the wagon haulage rope. After a time it became very noisy and set up a vibration in the whole machine. If not attended to straightaway, the teeth start to crack and break off. What Alf wanted me to do was jack up the motor and fit new shims beneath the retaining bolts, thus raising it and stopping the pinion teeth from rooting, which would then allow the haulage drive wheels to run smoothly without noise and vibration. Although I was new to the P&M, no one came with me to explain how to tackle the job; I had to work it out for myself. It sounds easy until you realise that the motor weighed almost one ton and was situated at the bottom of a pit about 20 ft deep. Not having been to Sheep Pasture before, I wondered what I was letting myself in for and how long it would take to complete the job.

As there were no trains running between Nottingham and Derby in the early morning on a Sunday, I had cycled - I was fit in those days. By 8 o'clock the van was loaded with the tools, jacks, wooden packing and pieces of plate of various thicknesses. It was going to take us around half an hour to travel to site, but what Joe the van driver failed to tell me was that the nearest point to the engine house was the climbers' car park at Black Rocks north of Wirksworth, about half a mile from site. From there everything had to be carried by hand along the track. If it had been a weekday the pilot locomotive could have met us and done it for us, thus easing the burden. The Black Rocks are used for training new

The bottom of Sheep Pasture incline at Cromford Wharf. Beneath the A6 road bridge can just be seen the catch pit as the tracks curve round it. On the left are two water carriers used for supplying water to the various cottages and engine houses along the line. Note on the old ex-LNWR tender there is a wooden buffer. *E.R. Morton/Author's Collection*

The Cromford & High Peak Railway in October 2003, the view looking down the Sheep Pasture incline trail towards Cromford Wharf; the track has gone and on the right the old catch pit can still be seen. Inside in the mud is a half-buried wagon that ran away in the 1950s and just beyond the pit is the A6 road bridge. *Author*

climbers and when we pulled into the car park and started unloading the tools and jacks, everyone looked surprised. Had we found a new way of rock climbing! The fitter's mate and I had to make two journeys, as there was too much to carry in one trip. I noticed that none of the climbers offered to help! By the time it was 10 o'clock and we were ready to start the job - we were both just about knackered.

Access to the motor was down an iron ladder beside the gear wheels which operated the wagon haulage rope. They were both 12 feet in diameter, one standing above the other. The only light I had was a lead lamp and a torch, so it was like working down a coalmine. Tools and jacks, etc., had to be lowered down on the end of a rope. With the help of my mate, I managed to fit the wooden packing under the ends of the motor and jack it up, having first released the retaining bolts; this then gave enough clearance to measure the distance required for the shims. These were then cut out by hand, using a hammer and chisel. After fitting the shims, the motor was lowered and bolted down. Now came the testing time: had I done enough to cure the fault? The foreman had made arrangements to have an operator present, Dan, who I got to know very well when he joined us in the P&M after the line closed in 1967. Dan operated the motor and the gears ran as smoothly as a sewing machine. It was a success and gave no further trouble the rest of its working life, which only lasted for the next 18 months.

By the early afternoon we were finished, the only thing to do was clean up, enjoy a cup of tea and eat our sandwiches. Although it was only March it was a beautiful day and we could sit outside on the shunters' seat and admire the wonderful view across the valley towards Cromford village and Matlock Bath. Sometimes the job had its drawbacks, but at others it had its compensations; this was one of them. Tourists were paying pounds to have the privilege of seeing such views, but we were being paid to enjoy them.

All we had to do now was return to Black Rocks car park where Joe would be waiting to take us back to Derby. Again we had to make two journeys in order to carry the tools, etc. It had been a successful day and I was highly delighted with what I had achieved on my first Sunday working for the P&M department. I had no difficulty in sleeping that night, especially after having cycled home as well.

Every few months we would be send to Sheep Pasture Incline to check that everything was operating correctly, but mainly to examine the endless steel haulage rope, which meant walking the length of the incline. As well as the rope we had to pay special attention to the pulleys, making sure they were turning and that the rope was not sliding over them - the rope would soon wear a groove in a seized pulley wheel. The large pulleys beneath the ground at the top and bottom of the incline gave very little trouble. It was the small ones that were fixed to the sleepers and open to the elements that caused concern. They had harsh winters in that part of Derbyshire and very often a lot of rain in the summer months. The pulleys were used to keep the rope central to the lines and were attached to the sleepers at the point where they curved halfway down the incline, and again where they passed by the side of the wagon catch pit. Whilst I examined the equipment, my mate would be oiling and greasing the pulleys and at the same time making sure that we were not in the way of any ascending and descending wagons. No one wore yellow vests in those days and we had very little warning of approaching wagons, except for the moving rope. One thing that stays in my memory was the size of the ants crawling around on the sleepers; they were at least three times the size of the domestic variety, almost an inch long. After the line closed the track bed was converted into a walking and cycling trail. A few years ago I took a party of friends to Cromford to walk the incline to see what was left of the old railway, and to my surprise the ants were still crawling around on the ash track; they must have been the descendants of those from way back in 1966!

It was a full day's job, depending where the van driver dropped us off; if it was at Cromford wharf, then we would walk up the incline, checking one side of the track in the morning, have our sandwiches at the engine house, and then complete the other track on the way down in the afternoon. If he dropped us off at Black Rocks we would do the whole thing in reverse, having our sandwiches at the workshops at Cromford wharf. By then the stone trains on the section between Middleton Quarries and Sheep Pasture Top were being worked by a diesel locomotive, but the old water crane at Black Rocks had been retained, although little used. It consisted of a water tank on top of a steel frame and was fed by a spring from the hillside via a wooden chute, and it was this we had to check to make sure it was not blocked with debris or had been tampered with.

I didn't realize on that Sunday in March 1966, that just over 18 months later I would be back at Sheep Pasture removing the very same motor that I'd fitted the shims beneath, and would be one of the last tradesmen from BR to work on the old C&HPR. The railway soldiered on until September 1967, then it finally closed and the scrap merchants moved in, first removing the track before descending on the rest of the equipment, such as the winding engine at Sheep Pasture and a few ex-LNWR locomotive tenders that had been converted to carry water to supply the various outposts along the line. Two of these tenders stood on a disconnected section of track, once used for stabling locomotives. It had been decided that the scrap merchants would remove the contents of the engine house in January 1968, but our chief foreman Alf was determined that we should try and salvage as much of the mechanical and electrical equipment as possible, especially the large electric motor. At the beginning of December Alf called electrician Ken Slack and myself into his office and said, 'Would you two be willing to go to Sheep Pasture and remove as much as you can from the engine house and bring it back to Derby before Wards of Sheffield get their hands on it? – I will give you three weeks to do it in and pay 125 per cent bonus'. We both agreed, especially as Ken lived at Middleton and had been given permission to go to site each day without travelling to Derby to clock on for duty. Each morning I would travel up from Derby in the van escorted by two fitter's mates and an apprentice, who were to help us with the lifting. This time we were able to drive right up to the engine house, as the track from Black Rocks had been lifted; it was a bit bumpy though, driving over the holes where the sleepers had been. During the first week it snowed to a depth of about six inches, which made it doubly difficult to negotiate the track bed, and it stayed with us for the rest of the time we were there.

Each day we removed as much equipment as possible, until in the end the only things left for the scrap merchant were the two large winding wheels and the steel frames. We even managed to lift the large driver motor from the bottom of the pit by the use of a 1 ton pull-lift and long slings, suspended from a steel beam in the roof. It was too big to be taken back to Derby in the van, so the P&M lorry had to be sent for - this caused a lot of fun, especially getting it to run over the track bed and through the snow, but we managed it with the help of old sacks and bits of wood. It was easier going back as it had the weight of the motor to hold it down. Our difficulty was loading the motor on to the lorry; this we did by building a wooden ramp through the entrance doorway, then lowering the motor on to it and sliding it across the wood by the use of jacks and manpower until it was on the back of the lorry. In this day and age of health and safety at work, we would never have been allowed to carry it out like that, but that's the way we did things in those days and it worked.

We made our headquarters in the old platelayers' cabin, situated at the top of the incline. Each day at lunchtime we ate our sandwiches in front of a roaring coal fire - at least we had somewhere to get warm, as working in the engine house was like being in a fridge.

To me it was sad seeing the end of the old C&HPR, but it did have its lighter moments. One day when I was clocking on Alf called me into his office and asked if I would remove the wooden buffers from the water carriers and bring them back to Derby. Apparently they were the original ones, from the time when they were built as locomotive tenders in the 19th century. 'They require them at the Railway Museum at York, as part of their collection', he said. It happened to be a Friday, and in the afternoon I managed to remove four from one of the tenders and placed them in store over the weekend, inside the engine house, until I could remove the others on the Monday. Over the weekend vandals broke in and stole the buffers, but instead of taking them away, they rolled them down the field opposite, like a set of round cheeses. I guessed it was a group of local children having a bit of fun. Unfortunately the slope in the field was very steep and when we arrived on the Monday morning the four buffers lay at the bottom looking like four large snowballs. We happened to have plenty of spare rope with us, at least enough to reach the bottom of the field, so we set about retrieving them. But who was going to slide down the field and tie on the rope? One of the mates volunteered and scrambled his way down as best he could. By the time we'd retrieved them and pulled Dave the mate back up the hill, half the day had gone. I removed the others from the second tender and that evening we took them all back to Derby. We certainly weren't going have the same thing happen again overnight. When we arrived next morning the kids had broken in again, but this time we were two steps in front of them and had spoilt their fun, the buffers had gone. It may have been adults after all, because I don't know how they found their way up to the engine house in the dark, it would have been a difficult walk to such a lonely place.

We finally completed salvaging the various useful parts between Christmas and New Year 1967 and I never went back to the old C&HPR until some years later, when I walked the trail with a group of friends, between Cromford wharf and Middleton Top. Parts of the old railway still exist today: most of the

Right: Sheep Pasture incline engine house in 1998, now just an empty shell but at least it has been preserved for all to see as this part of the old C&HPR is now a public trail.
Author

Below: Remains of the old Cromford & High Peak Railway can still be seen to this day. This is looking across the Cromford Canal at the wharf showing the workshops and locomotive shed, the tall building on the right, which still contains on the pit road the original belly bottom rails from 1830. The tall post on the left is the remains of a LNWR signal post.
Author

buildings at Cromford wharf, including the transfer goods shed between the railway and the canal, and the workshops, which have been turned into a museum with many artefacts from the line itself. There are even the original rails each side of the locomotive inspection pit, that were laid down when the railway opened in 1830. At the bottom of Sheep Pasture Incline are the old water tanks and the water crane hose, which was used to fill the water carriers and the locomotive tanks. The large pulley beneath the ground at the base of the incline, which the steel haulage rope ran round, is still there and in good condition, as is the indicator on the bank side, used for indicating to the engineman at the top when to start or stop the winding engine after the wagons had been attached to the rope. Starting from the bottom, the two tracks of the incline passed under the A6 main road, but today the space beneath the bridge has been narrowed as a wall has been built on each side to act as a re-enforcement, due to the large amount of heavy traffic using the road above. Just beyond the bridge is the catch pit and still in the bottom is a wagon that ran away in the 1950s, now half-buried in the slurry, which had drained down the incline over the years since closure. At the halfway point, where the tracks curved, stood a timber-constructed platelayers' cabin. This is now used as a shelter for the ramblers. Sheep Pasture engine house still stands, but is now an empty shell with the engine pit filled in and concreted over. The trail continues on to Parsley Hay, passing on the way Black Rocks, the Killers branch junction at Steeple House near Wirksworth, where the branch ran up to the Middleton Quarries. Part of the trackbed is now used as a preserved narrow gauge railway, operated by old diesel-powered locomotives, once used in the coal mines. Between Steeple House and Middleton Incline you pass the new National Stone Museum and at the top of the incline is the restored engine house, complete with the 1825 beam engine, now in full working order. On certain weekends in the year the engine house is open to the public and the engine operated by means of compressed air, at a pressure of around five pounds per square inch. The old steam boilers were taken out of use in 1963 when the incline closed and have never been restored, but are still on site. Where the locomotive shed once stood a visitors centre has been built. Here you can hire bicycles, purchase refreshments and books, and see a video telling the history of the railway and showing scenes of it in operation during the early 1960s. From Middleton the trail passes through Hopton tunnel and then up Hopton Incline, which for most of its life was adhesion-worked. At the top stands a row of former railwaymen's cottages, which in the old days were supplied with water from the water carriers, brought up from Cromford Wharf each day. From Hopton to Parsley Hay, there is very little to see, except the sites of the old stations and the odd signal post or lineside milepost, but above the portal of the short tunnel at Newhaven is the badge of the C&HPR showing a wagon and bearing the date 1825, five years before the line opened. Was someone being over-optimistic?

Other jobs we carried out were the fitting of either water or fuel pipes at various locations around the district so occasionally we had to act as plumbers as well. The author and his mate John Cooke constructing a new diesel locomotive fuelling system at Avenue sidings south of Chesterfield. *Author's Collection*

Chapter Ten

Back to Derby

The family soon settled down to life in the flat at West Bridgford, which was the second floor of a semi-detached Victorian villa, so there was plenty of space, which we needed at the time, especially as David had just learned to walk and June was expecting our second son Paul, who came into this world at midday on 9th July, 1966 and had the privilege of being born in the same street as the famous comedian Leslie Crowther. I had been doing a night standby duty with one of the tamping machines and the job had run late, so it was 10.30 by the time I clocked off, and as I walked through the front door I heard Paul take his first breath and cry. I knew then that everything was all right. My mother and the midwife had been with June most of the night, so what could go wrong!

Being a bell-ringer I soon made myself known at the local parish church of St Giles and joined the team. But my attendance at ringing for the Sunday services was a bit limited owing to my working so much at weekends, but then there was always the midweek practice. One particular Sunday I was off duty, so I'd been ringing for the morning service and had decided to stay on and join in with the congregation. Partway through, the sidesman tapped me on the shoulder and I turned round and there standing by his side was Joe, the P&M van driver. 'Can you come quickly, a tamping machine has broken down at Nottingham station and there's no one to attend to it. I've got your tools and overalls in the van'. I didn't even have a chance to go home and change into my work clothes. In those days we had no telephone, so it was difficult to contact you when off duty. Derek had sent Joe to call me out, not knowing whether I would be at home or out for the day. On arrival at the flat, June sent him round to the church and he'd managed to attract the sidesman's attention. Even the P&M could penetrate the barriers of the church! The breakdown turned out to be a minor fault with one of the operating control valves, which from time to time would stick in the closed position. I soon sorted it out and Joe dropped me back home, just in time for my lunch.

The flat was handy for the Nottingham Forest football ground, only a short walk away. I'd been a keen supporter of the team in my younger days and now living so close to the ground I started to take a renewed interest in their games on Saturday afternoons and became a season ticket holder. At the P&M there was great rivalry between myself and other members of the staff who were all Derby County supporters. I jokingly told them that when Forest lost, I went home and drew the curtains for the rest of the day, as a form of mourning and respect for the team. Quite a few of them believed me and at the same time thought I was mad!

In my early days I loved the summer months when we were sent out to inspect and service the water cranes and tanks in the area. If we were sent to Trent Junction it was usually a full day's job as there were cranes at each junction and three large tanks supplying water to various points around the district, especially the station and railway cottages. We carried spares with us, such as water crane bags, and if necessary would have to change them if required. Other popular places were Millers Dale station and Ambergate Junction, both situated in the beautiful Derbyshire countryside. Travel to these sites was usually by train, having to carry the tools and spare bags with us, and making sure we didn't sit too close to any of the passengers and dirty their clothes. These duties soon finished when steam traction was eliminated from the area. Then I had the sad task of removing the bags from all the water cranes at Derby '4' shed.

One of the most interesting and the oldest places to work at in Derby was the civil engineer's workshops at Derby Friargate station. They were built and equipped by the Great Northern Railway in the 1870s and as far as I know had never been altered or changed since that time. It was our job to service and repair the various items of machinery, such as saws, drilling machines and lathes. Most of the machinery was driven by the line shafting and operated by leather belts. From time to time the belts would break, then we had the job of fitting a new one. First we measured out a length of leather belting and then fitted it round the driving pulleys, joining both ends together with metal clips which looked like a set of pointed teeth and were hammered into the ends of the belt forming loops; these were then fastened off with a metal pin, which slid through both clips and held them firm. I'd not seen line shafting and belt-driven machinery since I was an apprentice at Colwick.

Unlike most engineering workshops where the line shafting ran overhead, at Friargate it ran in a channel beneath the workshop and sawmill floor, which made it difficult to access for servicing purposes. The bushes in the support bearings of the long metal shaft were made out of hard wood, and over the years they had worn away so much that you could get your fingers in between the shaft and the surface of the bush. With generous use of thick grease the play could be taken up and the shaft would run quietly for a day or two. Whilst I checked the machinery, my mate John would crawl along the shafting channel, oiling and greasing the wooden bearings, his only means of light being a paraffin flame lamp called a Smoky Joe. With all the sawdust and wood chippings on the floor of the channel and cobwebs on the walls, it was surprising the place never went up in smoke. The present day Health & Safety Inspector would have had a fit.

In the corner of the sawmill stood a vertical steam boiler, used in the winter for heating the workshop and a place where men working outside could come in and have a warm. But its main purpose was to burn the sawdust, wood chippings and old bits of waste timber, which was its only source of fuel. Its working pressure was 15 lb. per square inch, and the boiler water level was maintained by the use of an injector. Once a month, on a Saturday morning, the boiler had to be washed out by the P&M staff. It was an easy job, which paid six hours' overtime and 100 per cent bonus, so every fitter was volunteering to do it, especially those who lived in Derby. They could have six hours of easy pay and still have time to go to the football match in the afternoon. But the foreman was very careful to allocate it to us on a rota basis, which meant that everyone had a turn and a fair share of the overtime.

The lifts on Derby station, the chief mechanical and electrical engineer's offices in Nelson Street, and in the old North Staffordshire Railway goods shed on London Road, were also serviced and repaired by the P&M staff. Some were operated electrically, but the majority were water hydraulic, with the water pressure maintained by a pump and large accumulator situated in the locomotive works, which was their responsibility. The three on the station platforms were the ones which gave the most trouble and we were constantly being sent to repack or tighten up the leaking glands on the lifting ram cylinders. Before we dared venture into the pit beneath the lift, we had to make sure it was empty of water. Although there was a submerged electric-powered sump pump to keep the pit free of water it seldom operated, owing to the failure of the float switch. The pit then flooded, sometimes above the lift floor level and if you weren't careful you could have ended up drowning in 6 ft of water. If the gland required new packing the flooded pit had to be emptied, by manually operating the sump pump. Then I would get my mate to operate the lift, taking it to the upper level, whilst I went down into the pit and placed two wooden props inside the lift guides which were situated on the side of the walls; the lift would then be lowered on to the props and these took the weight. Provided the lift gates were left open it was safe to work and I was free to release the gland and repack it with a thick kind of asbestos rope, soaked in graphite. Sometimes the old packing was difficult to remove, so if you closed the gates and operated the lift control valve the upward pressure would blow it out for you - if you were not careful you ended up getting soaked. It was no good jumping out of the pit to dry off, you had to carry on in your wet clothes until the job was completed, because the lifts were only to be out of service for the shortest time possible. The lift was put back into service in the reverse order, gates closed and the lift taken to the upper level, the props removed and I would jump out of the pit as quickly as possible, and the lift went back into normal service. Very often a gang of post office workers with their trolleys were waiting to use it, shouting down through the gates, 'How long will you be, we've got so-and-so train to meet.' If a lift was out of service for any length of time, mail and parcels, etc., had to be loaded by the postmen and porters into a box wagon which was then shunted from platform to platform as required, where it was unloaded; or it had to be carried over the footbridge by hand - this meant a lot of hard work on the part of the station staff, so you could see their anxiety in getting the lift back into service as quickly as possible.

We had several unusual items of plant to service and maintain, and three of them were located in buildings on the station. In a small room at the south end was a vacuum pump used to operate the communication system between the various offices. Pipes ran along the walls in each office and if a letter or a message was to be sent from one office to another, the piece of paper on which the message was typed or written was sealed inside a round cylinder. A flap valve was opened in the vacuum pipe and the cylinder was placed inside; within minutes it would travel along the pipe to the required office, where a clerk would retrieve the cylinder and remove the message. In theory it saved a lot of time, cutting out the need for the clerks to be walking from one office to another, but it was so old and worn out that it rarely worked correctly. Pipes often leaked at the joints and the message cylinder got stuck inside them between rooms, and we were always repairing the pump to stop it from falling to bits. The only other times I came across this type of system were in a large department store in Nottingham, in the 1940s, and in the old Co-op at the North of England Museum at Beamish in County Durham.

In a room in the area manager's office at the north end of the station was a large shredding machine, used for shredding up railway tickets. All the used and redundant tickets from almost the entire BR system were sent to Derby for disposal and sacks full would arrive daily. In those days they were mostly of the Edmondson card type. It was a full-time occupation for one lady - even then she had a job to cope with the amount of sacks arriving and they would pile up in a corner of the room. Often it meant she had to work at the weekend to clear the backlog. The machine frequently broke down, usually caused by pressure of work. If it did, then we were sent for straightaway to repair the fault, which often turned out to be jammed cutting blades, due to the volume of tickets passing through. This meant stripping it down, which took time. No matter what time of the day it was, Josie the operator would take her meal break, so that she could catch up with her work when we'd completed the repair. Although we serviced it once a week it made no difference. Members of the office staff would call in during their lunch break and sift through the tickets to see if they could find the odd rare ones to add to their collections. I even picked out a few for myself for my own collection.

Next to the area manager's office was the footplatemen's hostel, accommodating the men who were on lodging turns and taking their required rest between shifts. As well as being provided with a bed they were given free meals, and it was the P&M's responsibility to look after and repair the potato-peeling machine. As far as I know it very rarely went wrong and if it did it was usually an electrical fault. I can only remember attending to it twice, once to renew the bearing on the rotating drum and once to service it. The drum on the inside had a rough surface and didn't peel the potatoes, but rumbled them round until the skin was rubbed off. Some one then had to cut the eyes out by hand, so I'm not sure if it actually saved a lot of labour. We also maintained the one in the kitchen at the School of Transport on London Road.

In all the time I worked at the P&M, I only refused to do a job once. It was not my policy, as I would be prepared to tackle anything within reason. I arrived at work one morning requiring a new duty and Derek the foreman asked me if I would go to the old MR goods depot at St Mary's, near to the Nottingham Road station in Derby. One of the wagon traversers had been stripped down in the summer and was now ready to be rebuilt, as the new parts had arrived in the stores. The traverser was a tram-like machine, which ran on rails across the front of the goods depot, and took its power from an overhead cable. Attached to the front was a platform on which were two railway tracks. Wagons would arrive in the yard to be sorted out and each one would then be shunted on to the traverser and placed into whichever road they were required, by the use of a fixed capstan. The maintenance of the capstans was also the responsibility of the P&M. When unloaded or loaded the reverse operation would take place.

I arrived at the depot to find the shell of the traverser parked at the end of the track. Whoever had stripped it down had left the parts scattered around on the ground. Nothing had been stored in boxes for safekeeping and locked inside the cab, as was the normal rule. Small parts and nuts and bolts were missing, no doubt taken by the kids who very often trespassed in the yard during the evenings. It looked as if a bomb had hit it, and to rebuild the machine would have taken months trying to put it together like a giant jigsaw. I returned to the office and suggested to Derek that he might give the job to the fitter who had stripped it down in the first place, and let him sort it out. He had tried it on with me, knowing that I never normally refused to tackle any kind of job, no matter how difficult. But this time he had come unstuck. He laughed and said, 'Thanks for going to have a look at it, as everyone else has refused to go anywhere near the machine!' It never did get rebuilt and eventually ended up on the scrap heap, which I suppose was the cheaper option.

I don't know why, but it always seemed to fall to me to perform the last rites: was it because I was a churchman? In the summer of 1967 I was sent to disconnect the water supply to the old Rowsley locomotive shed and the water crane at the station. Rowsley is deep in the Derbyshire Dales north of Matlock on the now closed main line to Manchester. The storage tank which supplied the water was situated on the top of the bank by the side of the main A6 road, which ran parallel with the railway. But before I could disconnect the float valve and blank off the water supply, I had to find the main shut-off cock, which was somewhere at the bottom of a 30 ft hole in someone's private garden. After we'd been taken there in the lorry, Joe drove the mate and me up a long drive on the hillside to the front door of a large house, situated in its own grounds of several acres. When I knocked on the door, the owner was surprised to see us standing there and wondered what we wanted, until I explained to him that we'd come to turn off the water supply to the tank. Could he please tell us where the access was to the shut-off cock, which according to the plans was situated beneath the garden. At first he looked a little puzzled until he remembered that there was an inspection grate cover in the shrubbery at the bottom of the garden. He said that all the time he'd lived there, which was quite a few years, he'd never seen it open. After prising open the cover, I shone the torch down the 3 ft-square brick-lined hole and could just about make out the shut-off cock at the bottom. There were all kinds of creepy crawlies and cobwebs lining the walls. As usual it fell to my lot to climb down the rusty metal ladder. My mate, after having had a look down the hole, didn't even attempt to climb down. With the appropriate tools I descended into the depths and with a struggle managed to turn the cock and close off the water supply. A short passage led off from the bottom of the hole. I shone my torch along it and could see water; before my eyes was a large underground reservoir. How long and deep it was I don't know, but the water level was almost up to the passage. I beat a retreat before some kind of Loch Ness monster appeared!

Blanking off a pipe and removing a float valve may sound easy, but before it could be done, the tank had to be drained of water, then the supply pipe disconnected from the side and sealed off, the float valve unbolted and lifted out and taken back to Derby. The following week the scrap merchant came and cut it up. Then it was the turn of the water crane at the station, which stood on the up platform at the south end. Here we had to dig down to the main supply pipe, which was 12 inches in diameter and near to where it joined the crane's control valve. Between the valve and a flanged joint was a short section of pipe about two feet long. The joint had two flanges with a rubber seal in between and was bolted together by eight one-inch bolts, which by then were solid lumps of rust, having been buried in the ground over many years. There was no chance of undoing them with a spanner, so I had to resort to burning through them with an acetylene gas torch, the fitter's friend. I then had to try and part the joint, either by using a wedge, or smashing my way through the short pipe. In the end I chose the latter method, which seemed a bit crude but, after all, the pipe was going for scrap anyway. Smashing through a cast-iron pipe may sound difficult, but with the use of a seven-pound hammer and a bit of brute force it soon broke apart. As the pipe was still full of water, it immediately filled the hole, so we had to wait until it had soaked away before I could continue. Once the broken pipe had been removed from the hole, it then left me enough space to work in. I then set about making a blanking-off template for the end of the water supply pipe, out of a piece of wood. This I took with me to the workshop at Derby and fashioned a blanking-off plate, out of an inch-thick piece of steel. Next day I returned to site, fitted the plate and filled in the hole. All I had to do then was return to the garden, climb down the hole and turn on the water.

It may seem strange that I was blanking off the water supply pipes. Why didn't I leave them open? - after all everything they supplied was being taken out of service. Apparently when the line opened in the Victorian days, the railway company had agreed with a local farmer who lived near to the proposed site of Rowsley station, to supply water to his farm, in compensation for bringing the lines across his land. In 1967 that agreement was still in force and BR had no alterative but to comply with it, although at the time it was only feeding a cattle trough.

As I've mentioned before, sometimes the job may have been a bit difficult, but it did have its compensations. In this case it was the Express Dairy situated next to the up platform of Rowsley station. We were on site every day for a week and each morning we arrived, the ladies from the canteen came out and gave us all a breakfast; in fact they kept us supplied with food all week. They must have thought we were poor railwaymen who couldn't afford a meal and wanted fattening up.

It was not long after the Rowsley job that I was involved in water again. I walked into the workshop one morning, when suddenly Alf called me into his office. I don't know why because it was Derek who normally gave out the jobs each day; I think he had taken a liking to me. It was a very cold morning and we'd had a very sharp frost over night. 'I want you to go to the sheet stores for me; a pipe in the fire engine house has burst and I wondered if you could sort it out and repair it if possible'. The sheet stores were situated by the side of the main line to London just south of Sawley Junction station, today known as Long Eaton. Although they were no longer making sacks and sheets, they were still using the buildings as a store and had retained a small staff. It was an interesting site with the main buildings on the east side of the line, including the fire engine house and the former manager's house, then being used as an office. There was just one building on the west side and both sites were connected via a tunnel beneath the main line, through which ran a narrow gauge railway for transporting the sacks and sheets, the tub-like wagons being pushed by hand. A set of sidings joined the main line at the south end near Sheet Stores Junction, where the back line to Derby and Burton, via Castle Donington, left the main line. At the north end of the site ran the Erewash canal, at the point where it passed under the railway on its way to the River Trent. Here a small basin had been constructed for the loading and unloading of barges. Today it is used as a marina for pleasure craft.

John the mate and I arrived there around 09.00, after having travelled by train from Derby, to find the place deserted, and not a member of the staff could be found, let alone a key to unlock the fire engine house door. Eventually I found a group of them in one of the buildings, sitting amongst a pile of wagon sheets having a cup of tea. One of them condescended to unlock the door for me, but no one knew where to turn the water supply off, until someone came up with the bright idea that the shut-off cock was in the tank house near Trent station, half-a-mile walk away down the line. Arriving there I again found the door locked, but this time had to obtain the key from the station master's office on the platform. Opening the door and looking round I found no such shut-off cock for any kind of water supply to the sheet stores. It had been a wasted journey and by then the time was getting close to midday. When I eventually unlocked the door and got inside the engine house, I straightaway found the cracked pipe; it was on a sidewall about six inches above the ground. The concrete floor sloped towards the centre of the building, and running from the burst to a drain was a stream of water a foot wide. The water had been running for so long that the stream had grown green moss, about half an inch thick. The pipe had certainly burst in the night, but it must have been a good 10 years earlier! Alf was having me on. I think quite a few people had been sent to repair it, and like me, could not find the shut-off cock, so had walked away and left it to run. I was determined to carry out the repair and stop the leak. With no means of turning off the water, I cut out a length of rubber sheet and wrapped it round the pipe and sealed the leak by securing the rubber with a set of jubilee clips. The water stopped running and John cleaned away the moss. Within a short time the floor was dry.

When I got back to Derby I reported to Alf. 'How did you get on?' he said, and when I told him I'd repaired the leak he was a bit surprised, but had a laugh when I told him what I'd done. 'I've been trying to get that pipe repaired for years and you are the first one to do it!' As far as I know it stayed like that until the buildings were pulled down some years later. Whether the fire engine, a two-wheel trailer-type, would have worked if there had been a fire, I don't know. It had obviously been there since the war and never used and I guess that at the time I was doing the repair to the pipe, if there had been a fire, they would have found that the hoses had perished.

The electrical and eventually the chief foreman at the P&M depot at Derby was George Shackleford: here is George demonstrating his latest toy in the depot yard in Litchurch Lane, which he not only used for getting to work but for touring whilst on his holidays.
Malcolm Stevenson

The team which operated and maintained tamping machine No. TT51, the author on the left with John the fitters' mate and van driver, Dennis the inspector, Eric the lookout man and Tony the operator; the other operator Jim took the photograph.   *Author*

Chapter Eleven

A Few Characters

Unlike Hitchin which had a small staff where everyone knew one another, the P&M at Derby was on a much larger scale; there were at least a dozen fitters including two examiners, and the same number of electricians, with one of each based in a small workshop at the station. Most of these tradesmen had a mate, to help with the tools and to assist with the job when required. Other members of staff were the joiner, painter, van and lorry drivers, the storekeeper and his assistant and lampmen. It was the lampmen's duty to go round the district visiting offices and stations, etc., changing fused bulbs and cleaning shades. This was done on a regular basis working to a programme on which they would earn their bonus. In the office were Alf the chief foreman, his two assistants, Derek the mechanical foreman and George the electrical foreman, two general clerks, and Jack the bonus supervisor. Everyone kept on his side, just in case he favoured them with a bit of extra bonus, but it was really down to each foreman to make that decision. Last but not least there were the apprentices, usually numbering from six to eight, depending on the number sent to the P&M each year from the training school in the locomotive works. After their first six months' training, they were given a choice of either staying in the works or taking a post at one of the out-stations.

Most of the staff had their own style of character, some quiet, some outspoken and, like all places of work, the practical jokers. Alf the chief foreman was a quiet man, but very good at his job. Whenever I saw him in the office he always looked worried, often with his head in his hands, but that was his way of taking a rest. If he wanted you to do a job, he would always call you 'Dad'. I don't think he could remember names very well, and this was his way of getting over it. Derek the mechanical foreman had been brought up in the P&M and knew the job inside out. His only fault was not being very good at knowing where places were, and he had no conception of time and distance, especially if we were working on a tamping machine and having to travel to site. He would say to you, 'I see you are working at Kettering today', and give us half an hour on our work sheet to get there from Derby, or an hour to go somewhere that was only two miles away. I often wondered if he'd ever studied geography at school! It was a good job we were all honest. Mind you, at times it did work in our favour. George the electrical foreman was a different kettle of fish, good at his job and an excellent electrician. If any of his men were having difficulty in carrying out a job, he would soon show them what to do. His big problem was that he was too out-spoken and shouted a lot, and many arguments took place in the office.

On the shop floor we certainly had a few larger-than-life characters. One was Sid, the joiner. During lunch hour he would hold discussion groups in his workshop, and get several men to join in. When he got them wound up and it became a little heated, he would sit back and enjoy watching the reaction on their faces when tempers got the better of them. They never realized he was having them on, and the clever ones kept away. There would from time to time be demonstrations of strength, sometimes he would get them to lie on the floor, face down with arms outstretched, and then try and see how many bricks they could raise; there were always plenty of fools around. Sid was also an excellent domino player; after everyone had laid down their first domino, he could almost tell them the rest of the cards that each were holding in their hands.

I've already mentioned Joe the van and lorry driver. He was very quick-witted and had an answer for almost everything, but very pleasant with it and got on well with the rest of the staff. He and I became good friends and spent many happy hours together, especially in later years when I became the on-track supervisor. Joe was also the depot union representative and had many long arguments with the management, especially Alf and George the foremen and the area manager Harry Potts, and he always came out on top. After these exchanges he would leave the office with a smile on his face and a glint in his eye; no one was safe at union meetings when Joe was around. Just to show how quick he was when it came to making a decision, I will relate the following story, one of many. He was on his way back to Derby in the lorry, after having delivered material to Hasland locomotive shed near Chesterfield, and with him in the cab was the storekeeper. He was passing through Belper doing 45 mph in a 30 mph limit when he caught sight of a police car following him with its lights flashing. The car drew in front and pulled him over. He quickly said to the storekeeper, 'Sit there bent over and make out that you are feeling sick and keep groaning, we might get away with it'. The policeman came to the window and said, 'Do you realise, sir, that you were doing 45 mph in a 30 mph limit?' to which Joe replied, 'Of course I am, can't you see that my mate here is ill and I'm trying to get him to the Derby Royal Infirmary as quickly as possible'. 'In that case, sir, don't worry, just follow us and we will escort you through the traffic'. They drew into the Infirmary grounds and halted at the main entrance, but much to Joe's relief only stopped for a few seconds before drawing out again. He waited until they were out of sight and then made his way back to the depot. 'I will have to try that one again sometime', he said, 'at least you don't have the job of picking your way through the traffic when those lads are around'.

One of the most unusual characters I've ever met in my life was the messroom attendant, lamp-cleaner and, at times, acting fitter's mate. In his spare time he was an inventor and studied law, and against all regulations had built in his shed a whisky still and began to brew his own special brand of firewater. It was whilst acting as fitter's mate one day that he came unstuck with his brewing invention and found himself on the wrong side of the law. He and the fitter were sitting on the train on their way back to Derby, after having completed a job at Matlock. It was a bitterly cold day and he had brought to work with him a drop of his firewater: it would help keep the cold out and be good for the brain. Whilst sitting on the train he thought to himself, I will have a drink of my special brew, and pulled the bottle from his pocket and took a swig. He was just about to put it back, when a gentleman sitting opposite enquired of him what the contents of the bottle were. 'A drop of home-made whisky', he said, 'Would you like a drop?' To his shock and amazement he'd handed the bottle to a customs and excise officer on his way to work at the bonded warehouse in

Burton-on-Trent. He was duly summoned to appear before the court and was handed out a two weeks' jail sentence, and the police confiscated the still. It was agreed with the chief foreman that whilst he was serving his time in Lincoln prison, the two weeks' enforced holiday would have to count as his annual leave. He returned to the P&M refreshed from his experience and immediately set about building a new whisky still. He was working with me one day at Derby '4' shed and, during the lunch break, tried to encourage me into constructing a still, even supplying the drawings from his pocket. Needless to say, I didn't take up his offer!

On another occasion he bought a shed from a local firm and started paying for it on a weekly basis. Within a few weeks the firm folded and were taken over by a new dealer, who wrote to him instructing him to continue the weekly payments to them. He wrote back to them and refused to pay any further instalments, stating that his agreement was with the first firm and not with them, and if that firm had gone bust, then that was their bad luck. He received several threatening letters but, owing to his legal knowledge, had them over a barrel and there was no way they could catch him out. If they had taken him to court, it would have cost them more than the shed was worth, so in the end they gave up and he had a new shed for very little payment.

He was the only person I knew who, on his way to work, would buy or bring from home half a pound of bacon. At lunchtime he would fry it until it was almost black, but instead of using it to make a sandwich, he threw it out of the window for the birds and then ate the fat in the pan by dipping his bread into it.

My mate John Cooke was a good lad and very helpful, but a little naïve and small in stature and at times came in for quite a bit of leg-pulling, as he would always rise to the bait. He loved travelling and if we had a job a long distance away from the depot, he revelled in it. One afternoon I was in the workshop working at the bench and John was cleaning the tools, when in walked Joe and thought he'd have a bit of fun with him. 'I'm going round the Peak, would anyone like a ride with me?' Straightaway John took the bait and jumped in the van and off they went. Ten minutes later they were back, 'That was quick', I said, winking at Joe, 'What went wrong?' 'He only drove me round the Peak Bakery,' said John. The bakery was about half a mile away up the road. He thought he was going on a grand tour of the Derbyshire Peak District, which in any case would have taken them all day, so he should have had more sense than to believe Joe.

Malcolm Stevenson, one of the fitters, like Joe was a great leg-puller and when he was around you knew there was going to be a bit of fun. He joined the P&M after serving his apprenticeship in the locomotive works and I was the first person he worked with for his two weeks' introductory training. At the time I was working on tamping machine No. TT52, overhauling the diesel engine. Malcolm and I became very good friends and still remain so to this day and meet from time to time. When I left the P&M in 1978 to become an engineering Inspector in the CMEE office at Derby, Malcolm took over from me as the on-track supervisor.

In 1967, Nottingham Forest were doing very well in the Football League, and finished the season runners-up in Division One, and qualified for a place in the

European Fairs Cup, drawn against the German side, Eintract Frankfurt. During a conversation in the messroom, Malcolm asked me if I was thinking of going over to Germany to watch them play. 'If you are, I wouldn't mind travelling with you and we will make a few days' holiday out of it'. I thought about it and we decided to go. In the end there were three in the party, when the relief van driver and fitter's mate, John Diggles, asked if he could join us, as he too was very keen on football. We all agreed, and set about organizing the reservations and purchasing the tickets for the match, which was not difficult as I was a season ticket holder at the time. It would be my second visit overseas, and as the steam locomotives were disappearing off the rails of BR, it would give me a chance to see them still working on the railways of Germany, especially around the Cologne area, where most of the freight trains were being hauled by the class '50' and '44' 2-10-0s. Forest were playing on a Wednesday evening, so we travelled out overnight on the Monday from Harwich Parkeston Quay to the Hook of Holland. Arriving on Tuesday morning we joined the Frankfurt express and arrived there at 14.14. What impressed me was the wonderful sense of timekeeping. As the train pulled up in the terminus station at Frankfurt, the large hand on the giant clock on the station wall ticked over to 14.14: we were spot on time! And that was after a seven hours' journey. I saw my first steam locomotive as we crossed the border from Holland into Germany, a class '50' 2-10-0 waiting to follow our train, hauling a lengthy freight train made up of box wagons. More steam was seen at Cologne and Koblenz, where a class '01' 4-6-2 was waiting to take an express down the Moselle valley to Trier.

We had booked ourselves into a smart hotel near the station and on arrival took a shower. Malcolm being a joker decided to sample all the various shampoos and body lotions that were available and came out smelling like a walking perfume factory. We sent him back for another shower before we dared walk through the streets with him. On the Wednesday, Forest managed to win 1-0, in a heavy thunderstorm. At half-time we thought they might abandon the match and our journey was going to be for nothing, but the referee allowed it to continue to the final whistle. At breakfast next morning we found on our table a plate full of various types of cheese, one was very hard and dark brown, and looked almost like pipe tobacco, 'I will take it back with me [said Malcolm] and give it to your mate Johnny Cooke as a present and tell him that it's a very special type of German pipe tobacco'. One of John's faults whilst he worked with me was that he was always puffing away on his pipe. We thought that maybe this special tobacco might get him to stop smoking!

Back at work on the following Monday morning, John was in straightaway and wanted to know how we'd got on. 'We've brought you back a present', says Malcolm, 'It's a very special type of pipe tobacco, I'm sure you will enjoy it'. 'I've never seen anything like this before, but I guess it will be fine', says John and duly cleaned out his pipe and filled it with the cheese. He never cottoned on until he tried to light it and it wouldn't burn, but by then the pipe was clogged up with a brown sticky paste. Malcolm beat a hasty retreat before John could catch him. It didn't stop him from smoking though, as he still went on puffing the pipe, certainly for the rest of the time he worked with me.

Chapter Twelve

Relief Work at Toton

From time to time I was sent to carry out relief duties at Toton, usually when one of the fitters or the chargehand was on holiday or off sick. As I mentioned at the beginning, I should have taken a fitter's position at Toton, when I transferred from Hitchin, and was only sent to Derby on a temporary basis. One of the fitters was hoping to transfer back into the diesel depot, but decided against it, if I was willing to stay at Derby. I agreed as I had settled in and liked the job, especially the variety of work we carried out and the places we visited. I don't think I would have settled at Toton in the same way, after having had the freedom.

The P&M set-up was more or less the same as that at Hitchin; there was a working chargehand, three fitters, two electricians, mates and lamp attendants. By the time I went to work there, the steam locomotive shed had closed and everyone had been transferred into the new diesel depot, which at the time was the largest in Europe. The P&M staff were still based in their old workshop, which stood next to the steam shed and the water softening plant, which was still in use but not for its original purpose of softening water for the steam locomotives. The staff were employed to maintain the plant in the diesel depot and around the marshalling yard. In the depot they maintained the fuel pumps, central heating boilers (steam), overhead hoists and cranes, Matterson lifting jacks, the wheel profiling lathe and many other small items of machinery. Of special interest to me were the three steam cranes that the P&M also maintained, two Cowans, Sheldon breakdown cranes, one being the ex-Colwick 36 ton, having transferred there in 1966, and the small 3-ton one, mostly used in the yard for transhipping loads – this had also been transferred from Colwick, where it had been used for emptying the wet ash-pits.

In the marshalling yard the major items of maintenance were the north and south wagon retarders, four at each end. They were used to retard the wagons as they were shunted in to each road and were controlled from an enclosed room, situated above the pump house, by a number of signalmen on shift work. They also controlled the points, directing the wagons into the correct siding. The retarders were in constant use day and night, and thousands of wagons would pass over them in the course of 24 hours. They replaced the old 'chaser', who ran alongside each wagon and by the use of a wooden pole applied the hand brake, slowing the wagons down before they buffered up to those already in the siding. The ones at the south end were water-operated, but those at the north, being a little more modern, used oil. They were looked after by one fitter on a full-time basis and he had his workshop in the pump and accumulator house at the north end. I acted as relief, when he took his holidays, and hated working on them, as everything you touched was heavy and dirty, especially in the winter when it was cold and wet. There was always a spare retarder, at each end, both standing on baulks of timber, on a spare strip of land next to those in operation. Throughout the year they were overhauled, and every August Bank Holiday weekend the depot breakdown crane would be brought in to lift out a

Right: The ex-Colwick 36 ton breakdown crane, with its extra long jib, is seen here in the 1970s after transfer to Toton and it is about to lift a '06' Duomatic tamping machine for a new set of wheels to be fitted.
Author

Below: Toton water softening plant in 1966 no longer being used to soften locomotive boiler water but for neutralizing waste oil, etc. from the drains of the diesel depot. The large tank was used for storing the neutralized waste which had been mixed with lime. At the rear of the tank is the old steam shed, the water tanks still in use, the little building on the right was the plant and machinery workshop and office where at times I acted as chargehand fitter.
Frank Berridge Collection

worn retarder and replace it with an overhauled one. The operation sounds simple, but it took two days of hard work, and it ensured that each one was renewed every eight years.

As mentioned, the water softening plant had been retained and was used for purifying the waste from the drains in the diesel depot, before it entered the River Erewash. If it did get into the river in its un-purified state, the railway company were in for a hefty fine. Outside the depot a large lagoon had been dug in the form of a tank into which the waste liquid was pumped and stored before being purified. The softening plant worked almost the same as in the old days, when it removed lime from the water, but in this case it mixed lime with the waste from the drains and filtered it in such a way that it was pure enough to be pumped into the river without causing contamination. The lime and waste were mixed together in two large vats, about four feet high and 10 feet in diameter, and stirred by a set of rotating blades. The clean waste was then drained to the river and the lime, etc, pumped into a vast storage tank, 60 feet high and 20 feet in diameter, which stood outside, close by the P&M workshop.

The tank had not been emptied since being put back into service for its present role, and the lime was beginning to build up. In 1967 it had almost reached the top and required emptying. In the old days redundant steam locomotive tenders would be brought along and shunted into a siding next to the tank, and the lime would be pumped out into the tenders and taken away and dumped at some convenient site further up the line. But in 1967 this facility was no longer provided, so the only alternative was to empty it into road tankers. Before the lime could be sucked out of the tank through a valve at the base, the surplus water and waste floating on the top of the lime had to be removed. The only way to do this was to take a portable electric pump and a couple of lengths of hose to the top of the tank. John Brown, the electrician, and I climbed to the top, via the iron staircase, and hauled both the pump and the hoses up on the end of a rope and placed them on the platform by the rim of the tank. I don't know what would have happened if we had both fallen in, but we didn't think of that at the time! After connecting up the hoses, one into the tank and one down to the road tanker, we coupled up the electric supply and switched on and hoped that it would work. It took two days and several tanker trips before the water and waste was drained off.

At last Sam Boffey, the chargehand fitter, declared that it was now ready for the lime to be drawn off, but before the road tanker could be connected up to the drain valve he would have to carry out a test to make sure that the valve was clear of any obstructions. Sam opened the drain valve but nothing came out, and he assumed that there must be a blockage. Pushing a metal rod through the valve made no difference; everything seemed to be clear, so he came to the conclusion that the lime remaining in the tank was below the drain valve and that most of it had been drawn off with the waste water, and that's why it had taken two days. John and I climbed to the top of the tank, to have a look and see if we could determine where the level of the lime came, and to us it appeared to be around half-way, but no way could we convince Sam. He then instructed me to remove the inspection cover, which was 12 feet above the ground and required a ladder to reach it. Whilst I unscrewed the nuts, holding the cover,

Above: We had to tackle all kinds of jobs in the plant and machinery department anything from the humble potato peeling machine to the civil engineer's on-track plant. In this picture we are at Toton wagon repair shops about to unload and erect a new hoist for unloading wheel sets; the author is on the back of the lorry with fitter David Dolman and fitters mates Michael Alsop and David Simpson.
Author's Collection

Right: Fitter David Dolman and the author fitting the new hoist to the travelling beam at Toton wagon shops.
Author's Collection

Sam stood at the bottom guarding the ladder. I had just unscrewed the last nut, when suddenly the joint gave way and the cover burst off and the lime flowed out full bore. Thankfully I had propped the ladder at the side of the cover and not in front of it, but poor old Sam got the lot, and in a few seconds was covered from head to foot in white lime. Everyone present fell about laughing as he looked like a ghost. Within minutes the surrounding area was 2 ft deep in lime. Even I was isolated at the top of the ladder and had to be rescued by a couple of the lads wearing protective footwear. It took almost a week to clean up the area, before the road tanker could get anywhere near to finish off the job. The reason the drain valve appeared to be blocked was due to the build up of lime, which had formed behind it into a solid wall about a foot thick, and poking with the metal rod didn't even disturb it.

One of the nastiest jobs I got involved with whilst working for the P&M was at Toton, when Sam sent me to carry out a repair on the depot sewage pump. The sewage was collected into an underground tank before being pumped into the normal drainage system. Above the tank was a small building housing the pump. At first I was not sure if I really wanted to do the job, but then somebody had to do it, and Sam had reassured me that everything was okay, as the system was treated with disinfectant. The repair turned out to be a broken pipe, which had become disconnected. It was not a difficult repair and I soon had the pump running again. Being the summer it was a very hot day and whilst I was carrying out the repair the mate and I were being attacked by droves of flies - the disinfectant was having no effect on them. Next day at work I broke out in a rash around my neck and face. The depot ambulance man suggested that I should get it treated and I ended up in Nottingham General hospital for the rest of the day. I had a slight poisoning of the skin, they gave me a tube of cream and within a day or two the rash disappeared and I felt no ill effects. So much for Sam's 'it will be okay, don't worry'. As I said, in the P&M you were expected to tackle anything, and I think this job proved the point.

On a number of occasions during 1966 and 1967 I was sent to Toton to act as chargehand whilst Sam was away on holiday. Being a junior member of the staff, I could not understand why they chose me as they had tradesmen there who had had years of experience in the P&M. But I got on well with everyone, and there were no objections to my appointment, so maybe no one wanted to take it on. I became friendly with two of the staff, John Brown the electrician, who in later years, when the department was reorganized, became the supervisor after the retirement of Sam Boffey, and Eric Riley who had also served his apprenticeship in the locomotive department at Westhouses. When the shed closed he joined the P&M staff at Toton. His main interest was steam and at Toton spent most of his time looking after the three steam cranes. When the Midland Railway Preservation Centre opened at Butterley, Eric became a volunteer and worked on the steam locomotives in his spare time. Eventually he was appointed as its chief engineer and was instrumental in the rebuilding of several locomotives to main line standards, especially ex-LMS Pacifics Nos. 6203 *Princess Margaret Rose* and 6233 *Duchess of Sutherland*. Both have brought a good deal of pleasure to many enthusiasts when out on their main line runs, either tackling the Settle & Carlisle route, or climbing over the summit of Shap.

One of the many tasks we carried out at Toton was the repair and maintenance of the wagon retarders in the up and down hump yards, here a wagon is passing over the up yard retarder.
Frank Berridge Collection

Ex-LMS 'Princess Coronation' class 4-6-2 No. 6233 *Duchess of Sutherland* approaching Aslockton station on the Nottingham to Grantham line on Saturday 16th October, 2010. It was through the efforts and hard work of one of my former fitters, Eric Riley, of the P&M department at Toton, that she is running today. Eric eventually became the volunteer chief engineer at Butterley. *Author*

RELIEF WORK AT TOTON

On the domestic front we were on the move again, when in April 1967 June and I received the keys to a three-bedroom semi-detached council house at 42 Straws Lane, East Bridgford. I had been on the Bingham Council list for a number of years, having been a former resident in the area when I lived at Radcliffe-on-Trent. East Bridgford was 10 miles east of Nottingham, which now meant I had further to travel to work in Derby. But the village station at Lowdham, situated on the Lincoln to Derby line, was just two miles down the road and within easy cycling distance, and had a suitable train service to get me to work on time and home again in the evening; even if the journey did take almost an hour the newspaper or a good book soon passed the time away.

By then our two sons were growing up, so the extra rooms were most welcome and we also had a rather nice garden for them to play in. Once again we joined the local bell-ringing team at St Peter's church, which had a fine ring of six bells. Being brought up in Radcliffe, the next village down the road, meant that I knew quite a few residents of East Bridgford, so we soon made friends with the neighbours. I often visited one of the local pubs, the Reindeer, and got to know most of the Nottinghamshire County Cricket team, including Gary Sobers of West Indies' fame, who was playing for Nottinghamshire at the time. The landlord of the pub was a member of the Trent Bridge Board of Directors.

Lowdham station on the Nottingham to Lincoln line in the 1960s. It's from here that I travelled each day to my work at the P&M in Derby whilst we lived in East Bridgford.
Frank Berridge Collection

Not only did I carry out all kinds of tasks at the P&M at Derby, but after I went to live at East Bridgford in 1967 I was called on to repair the parish church weather vanes. There were four, one on each pinnacle on the corners of the tower and they are still working today as can be seen in this photograph taken in January 2011. It's the only church I know locally that has four vanes. *Author*

The highlight of my 2½ years living in East Bridgford, was helping in the repair of the weather vanes on the church tower. The top of the tower was capped off with four pinnacles, one at each corner, on top of which were fixed the vanes. Over the years they had seized up and stopped rotating and were pointing in different directions. The Vicar suddenly decided that he would like to see them working again and had asked Les Johnson, the sexton, if he could do something about it. Les, knowing that I was working in the engineering trade on the railway, asked me if I would help him. We dragged a ladder to the top of the tower on the end of a length of rope, and I then had the job of climbing to free each of the weather vanes in turn, whilst Les stood at the bottom and stopped the ladder from sliding. Afterwards he confessed to me that he was frightened of climbing ladders and I had helped him out of a mess. It took all day; first I had to treat them all with penetrating oil before I could get them to move, then the bearings had to be cleaned and finally packed with grease, in order to keep the weather out and hopefully keep them turning freely for the next few years. A few weeks later the architect came to see the Vicar and wanted to know who had done the work on the weather vanes. He was pleased with the work, but when told how we had achieved it nearly had a fright; apparently the pinnacles needed re-pointing and were thought to be a little unsafe at the time. It's a wonder we'd not ended up in the churchyard below, but we lived to tell the tale and it was another job well done.

Chapter Thirteen

Working on the CCE On-Track Plant

In the summer of 1966 a new divisional plant engineer was appointed to the head office at Furlong House in Nottingham and he brought with him from Carlisle a few new ideas about the maintenance of the CCE on-track plant, especially the tamping and lining machines. Derby P&M was still to maintain them on a divisional basis, but a new standby scheme was to be put into operation. Each of the P&M departments was to carry on as before regarding maintenance and standby duties with the large plant, such as the ballast cleaners and tracklayers. But instead of Derby P&M sending just a fitter and mate to do the casual standby duties with the tamping machines, either at weekends or on a weekday, especially when they were working on important sections of track and there was a fear that they might break down, a new method of working was to be put into operation. Whenever machines were working in groups, there was to be a fitter, electrician and a mate present at all times, whether they were working at weekends, on nights, or in the daytime. A team of six fitters, electricians and mates was selected and I was chosen to be one of the team. We worked on a rota system, which meant that we would be on standby with the tampers on average about once a month. But when we were not on these duties, we carried on with our normal everyday P&M duties of maintaining the static plant around the area. Hence my time working on the C&HPR and other such places.

Before I proceed it might be worth explaining what the CCE on-track plant really did and how they worked. I think it is fairly straightforward as to how the tracklayers and cranes functioned. They were simply there to lay down new lengths of track panels when the old sections had worn out. Track panels were made up in 60 ft lengths, the rails already fixed to the sleepers. These were conveyed to site, stacked in groups of around half a dozen sections on flat bogie bolster wagons, especially designed for the job. The tracklayer or a crane lifted out the worn sections of track and placed them on spare wagons and replaced them with the newly fabricated ones until the job had been completed. Using this type of machine meant that every time a section of track needed relaying, two roads had to be occupied which caused problems with the running of trains, especially if it was a busy two-track section. Most of the work was carried out at weekends, usually overnight between Saturday evening and Sunday morning, when traffic was light. For the odd passenger trains that did run, a supplementary bus service would be provided to get the passengers round the obstruction or trains would be diverted via another route. The French designed a tracklayer that would occupy the use of one track, but was only useful when the route was being relaid with long welded rails. I will talk more about that later.

Ballast cleaners were a different kind of beast altogether; they were large cumbersome machines, sometimes difficult to operate and everything you touched on them was either heavy or dirty. They were not my favourite machines, and when I had a standby duty, I hoped and prayed that one would

A two-arm compressed air-operated track-layer is seen here lifting out sections of track on the closed ex-GNR line, which ran between Derby Friargate and Egginton Junction. When using this type of machine two tracks had to be occupied at all times. *Sid Craddock*

A Plasser & Theurer track laying machine in the sidings at Derby Research Centre waiting to be tested before being accepted to work on BR. I was to get to know this type of machine very well in my later years at the P&M. *Author*

This pair of photographs show the 'Secmaffa' single line gantry track-layers in operation on the test track between Melton Junction and Edwalton near Nottingham. The relaying was taking place at the end of the line and what appears to be a plastic-sheeted train on the left-hand side is a runaway protection barrier for high speed trains when on test and is filled with polystyrene. The view above shows the tracklayers being prepared for work after being unloaded from their travelling wagons, they are running on a seven feet gauge track of long welded sections which will, at a later date, replace the existing rails once the sleepers have settled. They are diesel-hydraulic-operated, the engine and pump being situated inside one of the legs. Several of the control valves are beneath a metal panel at the top of the machine, fancy being up there on a dark winter's night in a sleet storm when one of the valves has gone wrong or a pipe has burst! In the view below, both the tracklayers are seen here at their fullest extent and ready to take out the next panel of old track and deposit it on a wagon, which is just out of the photograph to the right, they will then travel down to the train in the distance and collect a new replacement panel. *(Both) Sid Craddock*

Another type of two-arm track-layers were those constructed by Cowans & Sheldon, but these were controlled by diesel hydraulic power. This particular one is in the permanent way yard at Lenton Nottingham; although it appears to be in use on a relaying job, it is actually being examined and serviced by the fitters based at the P&M department in Nottingham.

Sid Craddock

Two 'Secmaffa' track-layers on their travelling well wagons in the permanent way yard at Lenton Nottingham, these are later models with their diesel engines and pumps now situated on the top of the machines.

Sid Craddock

WORKING ON THE CCE ON-TRACK PLANT 177

A Matisa ballast cleaner No. BC35 hard at work on the Derby to Birmingham line in the early 1960s; note that it's putting the waste ballast over the fence on the far side of the track instead of in wagons, this then kept the other line open to traffic. *Sid Craddock*

Plasser & Theurer RM62 ballast cleaner No. BC38 working on the research test track at Upper Broughton, situated between Melton Junction and Edwalton. The line had originally been part of the old MR main line from Nottingham to London until it closed in the late 1960s, with it now being a single track the ballast cleaner is having to deposit the waste spoil onto the bank side. It was always, in my time, the best-maintained section of track in the division, especially as it had to withstand high speed running. *Sid Craddock*

One of the later designed Plasser & Theurer 'RM74' ballast cleaners being serviced at the civil engineer's permanent way yard at Lenton Nottingham, unlike the tampers and liners, etc., the ballast cleaners and tracklayers were allocated on a regional basis. *Sid Craddock*

A Matisa tamping machine stabled in the sidings at Clay Cross station with the two operators, Dick Schumacher and Ivan Barnet about to make their way home after a hard day's work. In my early days at the P&M I was sent to Bakewell station sidings to replace a tamping bank bearing on one these machines, it was a glorious day and when I finished the repair the apprentice and I rode on the machine to Miller's Dale station. *Sid Craddock Collection*

not break down. But nine times out of ten my prayers were never answered! I could almost guarantee that the biggest breakdowns would occur during a cold, wet or snowy winter's night. Over a long period of years the ballast beneath the sleepers would get dirty, due to the constant vibrations of the many trains that passed over it. Soil from the base would filter up through the stones and, in the old days, mix with ash and coal dropped from the steam locomotives or the many mineral trains. This caused the track to become unstable and no amount of tamping made any difference - the first train over it, and it would be back to square one. So to overcome this problem the ballast cleaner was sent in to rectify the fault. The machine could be worked on a single-track occupation, but this meant that the waste spoil had to be deposited at the side of the track, and made an unsightly mess, until such time as the grass and bushes on the banks and cuttings had grown enough to cover it up. However, this method was used a lot because it saved on the use of wagons to carry the spoil away, and cut out the need to occupy a second track for stabling the wagons.

Although the ballast cleaner could propel itself, it would be towed to site by a locomotive, and attached to it was a coach, used as the operators' living quarters and a store for the spare parts and tools, etc., which were required to keep the machine in operation. Before the machine could work it had to be set up. First a trench was dug beneath the track, to accommodate the large claw-like chain, which scooped out the ballast and waste spoil and conveyed it to a hopper, situated at the top of the machine, where it was riddled and cleaned. The chain ran inside an endless trough situated down each side of the machine and below the track. It was the section of trough and chain which ran below the track that had to be lifted into the dug trench and connected up, before work could begin. The waste spoil was deposited into wagons or on the trackside, via a moving conveyer belt, and the cleaned ballast was deposited at the rear between the rails, to be reused again for supporting the track. When the job had been completed, the chain and trough beneath the track had to be disconnected and removed and stored on the machine and the side troughs raised clear of the ballast, before the ballast cleaner could be towed to its next assignment. If all went well, the machine would clean about a quarter of a mile of track in a 12-hour shift, as it slowly propelled itself forward. It was when it hit hidden obstructions below the ballast that the fun started. Sometimes a chain link pin would break or a hydraulic pipe would burst. But no matter what it was, it always seemed to be heavy or dirty work and after you had completed the repair, your overalls were covered in oil and grease.

Now we come to the tamping and lining machines, etc. Before these machines were invented all levelling and lining of the track had to be done by hand. With constant use by the many types of train which passed over it, the track would alter, maybe on the level one rail would be slightly lower than the other or the cant on a curve was not sufficient, so it had to be rectified. The ganger in charge of the platelayers would use a sight board to obtain the correct level or cant, then the men would jack up the rail and ballast was packed beneath the sleepers by using shovels until the correct level was reached. As power tools came into use, pneumatic hammers (known as Kango hammers) were used instead of shovels, which made life a little easier. Then the Swiss firm of Matisa invented

Standing in the siding at Thurgarton station on Friday 5th August, 1967, on the Nottingham to Lincoln line, is a Plasser '04' tamping machine stabled ready for weekend work on the Sunday. The crew are making their way to the station to travel home by van; the dock by the side of the siding was used by the Hoveringham Sand & Gravel Co. to load sand into railway wagons to be transported to BR Southern Region depots that were still using steam. *Frank Berridge*

In the early days the Plasser & Theurer '04' tamping machines did not have a fixed levelling trolley, the trolley was run out quite a long distance in front of the machine and then clamped to the rails, the machine would then work towards the trolley, with the levelly wires under hydraulic tension, unfortunately if there was a dip in the track the tamper would try and lift the track out of the ballast, so later fixed trolleys were used. This machine is one before the trolley became fixed, note in the centre the pendulum and above the levelling wires and contact boards.
Sid Craddock Collection

a machine to take over from the Kango hammers, and sections of track could be tamped and packed more quickly, but the track still had to be sighted and jacked in front of the machine. Eventually the Austrian firm of Plasser & Theurer arrived on the scene with their much improved class '03' machine and cornered the market. Unlike the Matisa tamper, which was operated by chains and hydraulic power, the '03' was totally hydraulic-powered, except when it was to be driven, then a conventional gearbox and clutch was used. But the track in front of the machine still had to be jacked by hand, until Plassers brought out their upgraded class '03' and called it an '04'. It was these machines that we worked on at Derby. The '04' did away with the need to have the track sighted and jacked by doing it automatically. At first, when setting up the machine a four-wheel trolley was run out in front to a distance of two or three hundred feet, and clamped to the rails in a fixed position. From the top of the machine to the top of the trolley ran two wires above each rail, both under hydraulic tension. As the machine moved slowly forward from sleeper to sleeper a pair of hydraulic-operated clamps would grip the rails and lift them. Above the clamps were two sight boards with metal strips on top, and as soon as these touched the wire, the lift would cut out and the track held until the ballast had been tamped under the sleeper, and when the track was released it would be level. On the curved sections each sight board would be adjusted by the operator, according to the height of the cant required, which had previously been marked out in chalk on the sleepers by the inspector in charge. This method was fine until the civil engineer found that as well as levelling, the tamping machine was straightening out the slight dips in the track as well, and in places the sleepers were being lifted out of the ballast. As long as the track was level the dips didn't matter, so another method had to be put in place. In the end it was decided that the four-wheeled trolley would be fixed to the machine, by means of a set of rods and mini trolley wheels, at a distance of about 30 feet, and each time it moved forward the trolley moved with it. This solved the problem and each machine worked this way until they were scrapped in favour of new updated machines. Even they continued using the same method, but instead of a wire, used an electronic beam.

The ballast was tamped under the sleepers by a set of tines attached to two hydraulically-controlled tamping units (or banks as they were known) fitted inside the main frames at the front of the machine. There were eight tines to each unit, four placed either side of the rail. The operator would lower the units by the means of a hydraulic cylinder on a vertically-fixed piston rod and two guide rods, which he operated by placing his feet on a set of pedals, and the units forced the tines into the ballast. To allow the tines to penetrate the ballast beneath the sleeper, they had to be vibrating at high speed; this was done through a revolving shaft driven by a hydraulic motor and a set of leather belts to a pulley wheel fixed to the end of the shaft. The top of the arms holding the tines was linked to the shaft on a set of eccentric roller bearings, which caused them to vibrate. The tine arms were attached in the centre to a hydraulic cylinder, one each side on a pivoted stub bearing. The squeeze cylinder, as it was known, operated on a fixed horizontal piston rod and once the tines were in the ballast the operator moved hand-held levers, attached to two hydraulic control valves, and the cylinders

The Plasser & Theurer '05' tamping machines were almost identical to the '04s' except they had an electronic beam for the levelling instead of a wire and a closed-in engine area and better cab facilities for the operators. I never got the chance to work on one as we had none allocated to the Nottingham Division. This machine is working on the West Coast main line, note that the levelling trolley is driven forward by hydraulic motor and not connected to the machine.
Sid Craddock Collection

Plasser & Theurer '06' 'Duomatic' tamping machine No. DTM12 working in the Leicester area, the pipes hanging on the cable in front of the machine are for the hydraulic drive to the levelling trolley.
Malcolm Stevenson

WORKING ON THE CCE ON-TRACK PLANT

Two Plasser & Theurer machines working in tandem on the ex-MR up main line north of Leicester between Syston and Cossington as the '06' tamper levels the track the liner follows on and the job is completed in one visit.
Malcolm Stevenson

This time the Plasser & Theurer '06' is working on the MR down main line south of Trent tunnels, the two slow lines are on the right and beyond them is the branch leading into Ratcliffe-on-Soar power station, the base of the cooling towers can just be seen at the top of the picture. Just beyond the bridge on the left is the present day site of the new East Midlands Parkway station.
Malcolm Stevenson

Above: In the siding at Market Harborough in October 1972 are stabled Plasser & Theurer track lining machine No. PLM15 and Plasser & Theurer '06' 'Duomatic' tamping machine No. DTM15; both had been working during the night between Kilby bridge and Market Harborough on the MR main line.

Frank Berridge

Right: The operator's seat on a Plasser & Theurer '06' 'Duomatic' tamping machine. At the top can be seen the lamps on the levelling trolley for the electronic beams and the contact boards on the machine which cut off the beam when the track was at the correct level. In front of the seat are the operating levers for the tamping banks, etc.

Sid Craddock

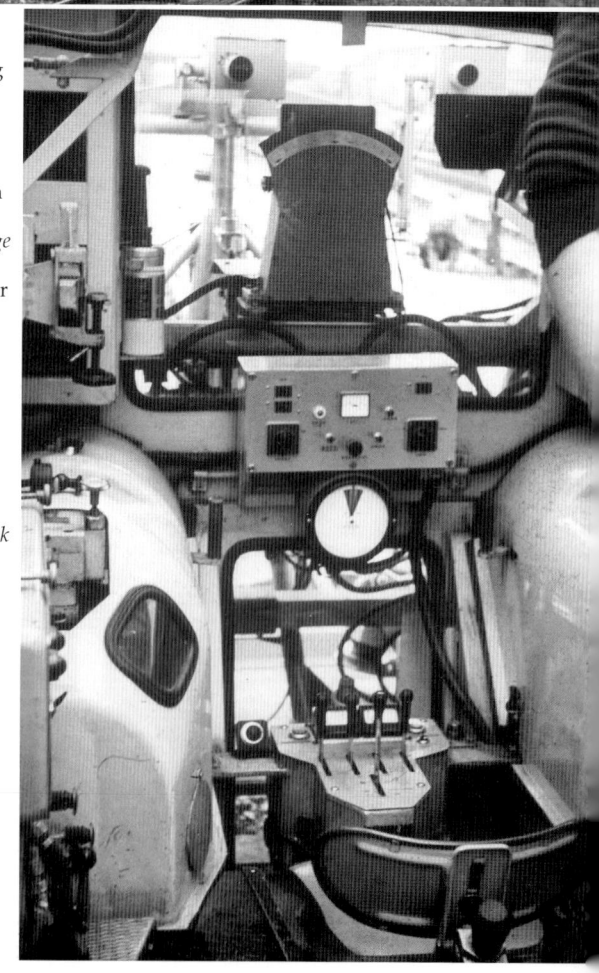

WORKING ON THE CCE ON-TRACK PLANT 185

Standing outside the old goods shed at Northampton Bridge Street is a Plasser & Theurer points and crossing '07' class tamping and lining machine. Not only could the tamping banks be raised and lowered but also moved laterally across the machine to line up with the rails when working over a set of points or a crossover. The trolley on the left was for carrying the tools and oil cans.
Sid Craddock

A Nottingham Division-allocated Plasser & Theurer '07' tamper/liner working on a relaying job between Kettering and Wellingborough on the Midland main line. The electronic levelling beams were incorporated within the machine so it didn't require a trolley to be in front, the small trolleys are for the lining wires which ran beneath the tamper. *Sid Craddock*

Plasser & Theurer track lining machine No. PLM15 stabled in the yard sidings near Trent station. We had two of these machines allocated to us in the Nottingham Division. *Malcolm Stevenson*

The other odd machine we had allocated to the Nottingham Division was a Plasser & Theurer ballast consolidator and it is seen here stabled in the sidings near to Leicester Midland shed. It consolidated the ballast between the sleepers and the shoulders by hydraulic controlled vibrating steel pads, which can be clearly seen attached to the side of the machine.

Sid Craddock

closed, tamping the required ballast beneath the sleeper. When the operation was completed the levers were released and the cylinder opened the tine arms; the operator then took his feet off the pedals and the units rose and the machine was ready to move to the next sleeper. Each unit could work independently of the other. When moving to another site, the four-wheel sighting trolley would be fixed to the front of the machine and raised clear of the rails, and the connecting rods and mini trolley wheels were stored on the machine.

The machine could be driven in two different ways. When travelling from site to site it would be driven in the conventional way through a five-speed gearbox and clutch. The operator sat in the cab on a sideways-facing seat, which enabled him to see the track in both directions, regardless of whether the machine was travelling forwards or backwards, and gave him a clear view of the road ahead when looking out for signals and other dangers. It was like driving a lorry, except that it had a forward and reverse lever, so that the five gears could be used in either direction. The clutch was operated by a foot pedal, via a mechanical linkage, but the accelerator was operated by hand, the lever being attached to a frame at the side of the driver's seat. When working in the tamping mode the operator sat in a facing seat between the two tamping units and operated the clutch by the use of a pneumatic control valve, worked from a foot pedal. First gear was selected and the accelerator lever locked in the maximum engine speed position. What with the noise from the vibrating tines and the engine, the sound was almost deafening, so anyone working on the machine had to wear ear protectors, especially the operator.

As well as the six tamping machines, we also looked after two Plasser track liners, a Matisa ballast regulator and a Plasser ballast consolidator. Compared with the tampers these machines were fairly simple and easy to work on. The lining machines cut out a lot of hard work for the platelayers. In the old days the track had to be lined by hand with gangs of men using crowbars and levering the track into line. The liner worked in a similar way to the tamper by using wires to line up the track, but the wires ran beneath the machine and were connected at either end to outriggers and were under hydraulic tension. As the machine moved along, an indicator in the cab would tell the operator which way the track needed to be moved to bring it into line, and by how much. A hydraulically-controlled pair of arms on the end of a horizontal piston rod would swing down and engage the side of the rail and push the track until it was in line with the wires; the cylinder which worked the piston was also controlled by the operator, which allowed him to apply as much hydraulic pressure as required.

The ballast regulator, or 'Basil Brush' as it was known, simply tidied up the track after it had been relaid, ballast-cleaned or tamped. Large plates on each side of the machine regulated the shoulders of the ballast by ploughing away the surplus stone; this also applied to the stone left loose on top of the sleepers between the rails. At the back of the regulator was a revolving brush, which completed the job and left the track looking tidy, hence the name 'Basil Brush'! The machine also had the facility for picking up loose stone and storing it in a hopper. In my time on the railway, it was considered bad practice to have loose ballast lying about on top of the sleepers.

The Nottingham Division had a super Plasser & Theurer tamper/liner allocated to it, which not only tamped and lined the track, but also consolidated the ballast on the shoulders. No. SLC3 is seen here standing on the down slow line at Loughborough Midland waiting for the road to Derby, in the background is part of the Brush works. *Malcolm Stevenson*

This picture shows the difficulties we had in repairing and servicing the machines when they were out on the road and no pits were available. No. SLC3 appears to be standing on a running road, but fitter Keith Wheeldon, of Derby P&M, is squeezing himself beneath the machine between the frame and the rail to carry out some kind of repair. Mind you, he looks quite happy about it, and his mate electrician Michael Bethel and the lookout man also seem to be enjoying the moment, it's amazing what a camera will do! *Malcolm Stevenson*

WORKING ON THE CCE ON-TRACK PLANT

No. SLC3 is having a wheel set change outside the diesel shed at Toton, this time their 75 ton Cowans & Sheldon diesel-powered breakdown crane is being used instead of the steam crane. Standing admiring the work is, on the right, Alan Cowx the area plant engineer and next to him is Neville Smith, the plant section STO from the CM&EE office at Derby. *Sid Craddock*

The Neptune track recording trolley working on the MR main line somewhere between Derby and Leicester. It was the Chevrolet engine fitted to this machine that I overhauled at the P&M workshop at Derby in the late 1960s. *Sid Craddock Collection*

In the Nottingham Division we only had one 'Basil Brush' Matisa ballast regulator allocated to us and it's seen here standing on the goods road at Derby station. In the background on the right are the CM&EE offices in Nelson Street. *Sid Craddock*

Some Matisa ballast regulators had hoppers attached to them to collect any spare ballast or to reuse it as required when there was a shortage between the tracks. Seen here is one such machine at the Matisa works at Lausanne in Switzerland. *Sid Craddock*

The consolidator was a strange looking machine, and in my opinion it did not serve any kind of purpose. It was an expensive piece of machinery to have running around on the railway system. After the tamper, liner and regulator had done their work, this machine was sent in to consolidate the ballast on the shoulders and between the sleepers. On each side of the machine it had a kind of long vibrating steel pad which, when operated, came down and packed the ballast tight into the shoulder. Under the machine and each side of the rails were a set of vertical steel pads which operated in the same way as the outside ones, but packed the ballast tight between the sleepers.

The new plant engineer decreed that the staff involved in the standby of the on-track machinery should have some training, so a few of us were sent on a course. I don't know why, because most of the fitters had been working on the tamping machines for a number of years. When the class '04' tampers were sent for their general overhaul, they went to the old Lancashire & Yorkshire Railway locomotive works at Horwich in Lancashire, and were overhauled in the old locomotive erecting shop which had been adapted for the purpose. My turn came in the autumn of 1966, and I was sent to Horwich for a week. All I did was work with one of the fitters in a similar way to an apprentice. I'm not sure if I learnt very much, and in the end taught the fitters there a few tricks that we'd learnt when working on tampers out on the running lines. Those that went on the course felt that it was a waste of time and money. I lodged with a lady who lived in a terraced house across the road from the works entrance. All this brought back memories of my time spent in Doncaster works way back in the 1950s. I shared a room with another fitter from Carlisle, who was also on the same course. He was around my age and had also served his apprenticeship in the locomotive department. We both had an enjoyable week, especially in the evenings when we went and had a pint and a chat in the local railwaymen's club. On the Tuesday we managed to win the full house first prize on the bingo, so the next evening caught a train from Bolton to Blackpool and spent the money on a few pints, a meal and several rides on the trams. To my delight when returning home on the Friday afternoon the train from Manchester to Nottingham was hauled by one of the very last steam locomotives still working in the Manchester area, a 'Black Five' '5MT' class 4-6-0, probably standing in for a failed diesel.

When I first joined the P&M at Derby there were still a few of the old grey-painted Matisa tampers working in the area, and I can remember Derek the foreman sending me to one stabled in the sidings at Bakewell station to renew a set of roller bearings on the right-side tamping bank vibration shaft. I took with me one of the new apprentices that had just joined us from the loco works training school. Geoff Brown was a bright lad and soon got used to working in the P&M. After finishing his apprenticeship, he went on to greater things and became a supervisor and in later years a chief engineer. He spent a lot of time working with me and I would like to think that the training I gave to him helped him towards achieving his goal in life. When the repair was completed, the machine moved up the line to Millers Dale station, ready to start a new job the following day, and the operator was keen for Geoff and me to travel with him. The Matisa tampers were a little cramped for space in the cab, so whenever they moved from site to site towed or propelled a four-wheel trolley containing the various tools and cans of oil and grease. It was a lovely sunny day so Geoff and I chose to ride on the trolley, especially as it was being propelled. We both sat on a couple of grease drums, and left the limited space in the cab to the operator and pilotman. Whenever the on-track machines travelled to another site of work, a member of the locomotive footplate staff, who had signed to say that he had route knowledge of that particular stretch of track, had to be present to point out the signals, etc. A number of years later the operators were trained into learning the various routes around the Division and, when confident enough, signed for the route themselves, thus obviating the need for a pilotman. Geoff was over the moon about the trip, sitting there on the old drum like some grand noble in his stately carriage, and at the same time taking in the wonderful Peak District scenery, as we passed through Monsal Dale, Cressbrook tunnel and over the high viaduct south of Millers Dale station. It would have been a different story if it had been raining. Who said working on the railway was boring?

My first standby duty under the new scheme took me back to the Peak District and the very same stretch of track, but this time I was working on nights, during a cold winter's week in January. One other fitter and a couple of mates kept me company. We were looking after three tampers and a lining machine working on the down main line between Bakewell and Millers Dale. Our base was in a platelayers' cabin near Monsal Dale station. Whilst the machines were working satisfactorily, the inspector in charge preferred to have us clear of the running lines and at a point where he knew he could contact us in case of a breakdown - we didn't have the use of a mobile telephone in those days. Besides, the cabin was comfortable and we sat in front of a roaring fire. What more could we have wished for! It was not long before a knock came on the door to say that one of the tampers had broken down. Unfortunately it was a mile down the line on the other side of Cressbrook tunnel, on an embankment high above the little hamlet of Lytton Mill. The only way to reach the machine was to either walk the mile through the tunnel, or go by van on a five-mile detour via the villages of Tideswell and Millers Dale to Lytton Mill, which would be much quicker and be a big help in carrying the tools. The only trouble was, Lytton Mill was on the opposite side of the River Wye from the railway, but we were reliably informed by the local platelayer, who had come to collect us, that a footbridge crossed the river and a narrow path led up the bank side to the railway tracks and that someone would be there to meet us, carrying a storm lantern. As we left the cabin it started to rain, and by the time we were at the top of the hill at Tideswell it was snowing a blizzard. Arriving at Lytton Mill, in the snowstorm, we drew up alongside a high wall where the platelayer with his lantern was waiting to escort us across the river. As we got out of the van I heard a strange noise; shining my torch towards the top of the wall I realised where it was coming from: sitting in a row were about a dozen chickens, all with their backs to the storm; no doubt the wall was their regular roosting place. If we'd had enough time we could have had one for the pot, I don't think anyone would have missed it. The platelayer led us down a narrow path between two cottages and on to the footbridge, crossing the river. We could see nothing, although we had a light, and all we could hear was the water rushing past beneath the bridge. Climbing a narrow path brought us to the top of the embankment and the railway tracks, where the broken down tamper, No. TT44, was just a few yards down the line. On close inspection I noticed that the right-hand side tamping bank was smothered in hydraulic oil, and realised that one of the squeeze-cylinder oil seals had burst, which was quite a common fault on those machines. When a seal or a pipe burst, oil was sprayed everywhere, due to the high pressure in the hydraulic system, 100 atmospheres, which works out at 1,470 psi. Luckily enough it was a small seal and not the large one, but even then it took a couple of hours to carry out the repair. I was having to work under hazardous conditions on the six-foot side of the machine, next to the up main line, so had to keep an eye out for passing trains, which were difficult to see approaching owing to the inclement weather. I asked the inspector why he'd not run the tamper down the line to the cabin, but learnt that there was another machine working in Cressbrook tunnel, so it had not been possible without disturbing them. Instead of returning to the cabin I stayed with the machine until it had completed its shift and it was time to return the track back to normal running. By then it was almost daylight, and as we descended the path to the footbridge I realized how close it was to the edge of the river; one slip and we'd have fallen down a 60 ft sheer drop into the flood-swollen river, which was a raging torrent as it passed beneath the bridge, and the bridge didn't look too safe either. I broke out into a sweat thinking about what might have happened, especially if I had had to report to the P&M and tell them that I'd lost my mate to the fish. Once again it shows what kind of conditions we had to work under to keep the railway running. It's doubtful if it would take place today, as Health & Safety would not allow it to happen!

Again I was working nights, but this time in the Leicester area, near Syston on the line to Melton Mowbray. I was doing standby with No. TT40, which was completing a section of track on the down line between Syston East Junction and Queniborough, which had been left over from a weekend possession. By 01.00. the job was complete and No. TT40 was ready to move to its next site of work, near Derby. I was riding on the machine in the operator's seat. We came off the Melton line onto the north curve, where we picked up the pilotman. After a few minutes the signalman in the North Junction signal box gave us a green light from the box window, but forgot that we were running on the wrong road. The pilotman instructed the operator to proceed, but within a few yards there was a crash and a bang as No. TT40 ran off the road, all wheels off, at the catch points, ending up a few feet from the end of the rails, well and truly sunk in the ballast.

There was nothing I could do straightaway but send for the breakdown train. Whilst the pilotman protected the machine by placing detonators on the rails, I walked to the box to make arrangements to call out the breakdown gang from Leicester locomotive department. Within half an hour a traffic inspector arrived on the scene, no doubt called by the signalman, and together we contacted the loco shed foreman at Leicester. All he could offer me was a tool and packing van and a couple of fitter's mates to help with the lifting, but suggested that we might call out the breakdown gang from Toton. As I'd had previous experience working on derailments at Colwick and Hitchin, I took the bull by the horns and said, 'Send me the tool and packing van and I will sort it out myself'. Forty minutes later a class '20' diesel locomotive arrived towing the van. We shunted the van on to the down road and stood it next to the tamper; the locomotive then came to the rear of the machine, ready for when I required it for re-railing purposes. With help from the mates, I cleared the ballast away from the ends of the rails at the catch points to the rear wheels of the machine, we then laid down wooden packing and on top of that, two short lengths of rail lying on their sides. Breakdown trains usually carried different lengths of old rail for this purpose and it was a trick I'd learnt when working at Hitchin. We then jacked up No. TT40, put more packing down and slid the rails under the rear wheels and lowered the machine. The locomotive was then coupled to the towing point on the rear of TT40, by the use of a seven-link chain. These towing chains were also part of the breakdown trains' equipment and were very useful when it was difficult to get close to a derailed vehicle. The driver on the locomotive slowly eased away from the tamper and took up the slack in the chain, and then, under my instructions, started to pull TT40 along the temporary rails, the wheels running inside the groves on the side. As soon as the rear wheels were back on the road, we jacked up the front of the machine and put down more packing and gradually eased the front wheels on to the temporary track. Everything went well and within a short time TT40 was back on the road. Whilst everyone cleared up the mess and packed the tools, etc., back into the breakdown van, I examined the machine and found that it had sustained no serious damage and declared it fit to travel; by 05.00 it was on its way to Derby. It had only taken us about four hours and we'd not delayed any traffic. In those days very few trains used the Syston north curve, especially at night. I had tried it on and once again got away with it. If things had gone wrong I would have been on the carpet, but I didn't think about things like that at the time, all I was interested in was keeping the job running.

Arriving back at the office in the morning, I was met by the divisional plant engineer and Derek the foreman; they had found out about the derailment through a message passed on by the traffic inspector. Their first words were, 'Why did you not call us out?' To which I replied, tongue in cheek, 'If I'd called you out, we would still have been there now, and besides I have breakdown experience, having worked in the locomotive department, and I got the job done quicker myself without any bosses interfering'. I don't think they knew what to make of me and, in the end, agreed that I was right. Before I left for home, the plant engineer actually thanked me for my efforts and quick thinking. It would have been a different story if things had gone wrong. Derek even got a call from the chief civil engineer also thanking me for my efforts and hard work in getting them out of a mess.

At the subsequent enquiry, the signalman and the pilotman got the blame: the signalman for thinking the machine was standing on the other road behind the signal, and if it had been, why had he not pulled the signal off instead of giving a green light out of the box? - and the pilotman for allowing the machine to move on the wrong road, knowing that there was a set of catch points just a few yards ahead of the machine.

One cold Saturday night I was given a standby duty with a set of single line gantry tracklaying machines, working on the Derby to Birmingham main line, near to the then-closed station at Barton and Walton, south of Burton-on-Trent. Instead of having a mate with me I was paired up with electrician Sid Craddock.

WORKING ON THE CCE ON-TRACK PLANT

We were to be paired together some years later, but under different circumstances, when we were both promoted to the supervisory staff, he as an inspector and myself as staff supervisor, but more of that later. The single line tracklayers were unusual looking machines and only used when the track was going to be relaid with long welded rails, and they only operated in pairs. Designed in France, they were constructed by the French firm of Secmaffa. They were arch-shaped, with two vertical legs eight feet apart. At the base of each leg were two double-flanged wheels, and inside the legs were the hydraulic rams which raised them up and down. A small diesel engine, which drove the hydraulic pump, was also enclosed inside one of the legs and accessible through a small metal door. Most of the hydraulic control gear and pipes were at the top of the machine inside a container covered with metal sheets, which were fastened down with rows of screws. The tracklayer was operated from a control panel on the side of the machine, the operator sitting on a seat which swung out from the side of the leg.

When a section of track was going to be relaid with long welded rails, it would first be ballast-cleaned and have new ballast added to compensate for that wasted during cleaning, and would then be tamped and left for a number of weeks to settle down and consolidate. During this time new lengths of long welded rails would be laid on wooden blocks, down each side of the track and gauged to eight feet, making a road for the tracklayers to run on. When the civil engineer decided that it was ready for re-laying, a possession order of the track would be booked for a weekend and the tracklayers sent in, plus a re-laying train loaded with 60 ft lengths of new track panels. The two tracklayers would arrive on site mounted on turntables, on specially constructed well wagons. In this position they would be unlocked and turned through 45 degrees, ready for the wheels to be lowered onto the long welded rails. The hydraulic rams were operated and the top part of the machine rose, giving clearance for them to pass over the top of the wagons containing the track panels. There was always an empty wagon ready to receive the old panels as they were lifted out of the ballast. The tracklayers would lift out an old panel, by the use of bales which gripped the rails, and these were attached to the ends of hydraulic-controlled wire ropes. The tracklayers then travelled along the long welded rails, carrying the old panel above the loaded wagons, and placed it on an empty one. After lifting out several more panels they would then start to replace them with the new ones, which were normally made up of flat-bottom rails and concrete sleepers. This went on until all the panels had been replaced. The panels of track would be joined together, and when the tracklayers and re-laying train had been moved away, the tamping and lining machines were sent in to complete the job. For a few weeks the renewed section of track would have a speed restriction imposed on it, until it had settled down. Then the 60 ft lengths of rail were removed and the new long welded ones laid in their place. Again the tamping and lining machines would be sent in to iron out any faults. The speed restriction would be lifted and the track returned to normal use.

It all sounds very easy, but the tracklayers were always prone to breaking down and gave us endless trouble. When Sid and I set out from the workshop on the Saturday evening, it was an awful night, blowing a gale with heavy rain and sleet, just the kind of night when anything might break down. We had only just arrived on site when the first breakdown occurred. One of the diesel engines would not start, but we soon located the fault, a disconnected wire, rectified it and the machines were ready to start work. As usual we made for the nearest sleeper-constructed cabin, hopeful that there would be enough bits of wood and coal around to make a fire, and at least keep ourselves warm between calls and be able to brew a cup of tea to have with our snap (mid-shift meal). Arriving at the cabin we found it full of Irish labourers, contracted to the railway to help with the night's re-laying job. In the centre of the cabin was a stove in which someone had attempted to light a fire, but by then there were just a few red embers on the bottom of the grate, and the place was freezing. Now when it came to fires, Sid was renowned for being a bit of a hell-raiser; rubbing his hands to indicate that he was cold, he set about sorting out the fire, gradually putting on more and more coal until the stove was glowing red hot. One by one the Irishmen left until we had the place to ourselves. Sid settled himself down on a bench in the corner, still wearing two overcoats, and obviously feeling no ill effects. I on the other hand was beginning to strip off. Within the hour the tar on the sleeper walls began to melt. It came as a relief to me when the operator called us to a fault on one of the machines.

The weather was still awful and by then it had started to snow, but I was pleased to be cooling off. One of the machines had lost hydraulic pressure and it was obvious that a pipe or a seal had burst. It was vital that I find the fault and rectify it as quickly as possible, because the job was losing time and men were standing about waiting, and as in most breakdowns, the inspector kept saying, 'How long will you be? I've got to have this job completed by such and such a time in the morning'. So you were working under pressure all the time and many a time I have told an inspector, 'Go away and I will tell you when the fault has been repaired!' Oil was dripping from the top of the machine and I suspected a burst pipe, but the problem was finding it. Sid and I climbed up the side of one of the legs with great difficulty, because of the wind and snow. First we had to unscrew the hexagon bolts and remove the cover plates to reveal the hydraulic pipes and control valves, and found the area beneath the plates was swimming in oil and water. I asked the operator to open one of the control valves and luckily saw air bubbles rising from a pipe joint. As best we could, with the aid of an old tin can, we managed to drain off some of the oil and water until I could see the joint. I unscrewed the pipe and found that the olive connection had split in half; luckily enough I had a spare one the right size in my tool bag. I soon remade the joint, tested it under pressure and it worked alright, so all we had to do was refit the cover plates. It had taken me a good hour, and most of that time Sid held the torch so that I could see where I was working, and at the same time hung on to my coat, to stop me being blown off the top of the machine on to the up main line, which was still open to traffic. I was soaked to the skin, with my boots full of water.

Back at the cabin the heat from the fire was still intense and the tar was still running down the walls, but it was a welcome sight. It took me the rest of the night to dry out and I was pleased when morning arrived and we could go home. In the event the job was not delayed, so there had been no cause for the inspector to have a panic session.

Chapter Fourteen

Living with a Tamping Machine

At the beginning of 1968 it became obvious to both the management of the P&M and the civil engineer's department that the '04' tamping machines were nearing the end of their useful life and needed constant attention, as breakdowns were occurring almost daily. So between them they decided that, until the new upgraded class '06' machines arrived, the '04s' would have to be permanently manned on a full-time basis, by a fitter and mate. This decision was to be implemented as soon as possible, when the required fitting staff became available. Having six machines to look after meant that six fitters and six mates would not be available for other P&M duties, and if Derby were to take on these duties they would lose almost half their allocation of fitting staff. To overcome these problems, two new fitters were employed to help out with servicing and repair of the static plant, one of them taking on my relief duties at Toton. In the end it was decided that there would be four fitters and mates from Derby, plus one of each from the P&M depots at Leicester and Nottingham. I was selected to be one of the four Derby men, but I had to lose my mate John Cooke as he was unable to drive, and it was vital that the mate could drive the van, not only to get us to site each day, but mainly for the purpose of breakdowns. If the machine broke down and I required spares, I could send the mate back to the Stores at Derby to collect them, whilst I continued stripping down the defective parts. My new mate was the former relief van and lorry driver, John Diggles. He had wanted to work with me for a long time and this proved to be his opportunity. He even went and asked the foreman, before anyone else jumped in before him. We made a good team. John Cooke worked for the P&M for a few more months, but could not hide his disappointment at not being able to continue working with me, and in the end handed in his notice and went to work for Rolls-Royce as a store keeper; but before he left, he managed to be with me for two weeks, whilst the other John was on holiday. Thankfully we didn't have any major breakdowns that required spares.

I was allocated No. TT51, a machine that had not been in the division all that long and had come with a bit of a reputation for breaking down. But it was manned by a good team: Dennis, the inspector in charge, who lived in Alfreton, Tony and Jim, both excellent operators, and Eric the lookout-man, who had been a former rodent catcher. With John and myself, the machine had a crew of six. The next 18 months with No. TT51 were some of the most enjoyable in all my 26 years working on the railway, even if we did have to work a lot of the time during the night and at weekends, very often long hours, sometimes as much as 16. I think at times June thought I'd left home. Getting to and from work was sometimes a little difficult, but I managed it, very often travelling on the last train to Derby from Lowdham. If we were working east of Nottingham on the lines to Lincoln, Grantham or in the Mansfield area, I had permission to be picked up by van at home.

Each tamper worked to a monthly programme allocated by the divisional civil engineering inspector in charge of the on-track plant, and at the end of each

Plasser & Theurer '04' tamping machine No. TT51 working at Kirkby-in-Ashfield on the Nottingham-Worksop line in 1967. In front of the machine is the levelling trolley connected to TT51 by rods running on four small trolley wheels; between the top of the trolley and the machine were two wires under tension used for track levelling. *Author*

Tamping machine No. TT51 hard at work at Kirkby-in-Ashfield in 1967, the track has been lifted and the units are down and the ballast is being compacted beneath the sleeper. The two contact boards which control the level can be clearly seen at the front near the top, when the boards touch the levelling wires the lift is cut off. *Author*

LIVING WITH A TAMPING MACHINE

month their performance figures were published. In my 18 months with the machine, No. TT51 came out on top almost every month, except for one, when we had disappointing figures due to a major breakdown, more about that later. If necessary I would even have tied it together with string if it meant keeping it running.

Before we took up our new duties, it was decided that we should all have some training on operating and driving a machine and were sent to the sidings at East Leake station on the former GCR main line, where TT40 was waiting for us to practise on. We spent the morning tamping up and down a long siding, and in the afternoon had driving lessons. At the end of the day we each received a certificate to say that we were competent tamping machine operators. We all thought it was a waste of time, because we all knew what to do anyway, having had several goes in the past, but at least we'd now got a certificate to prove it.

As well as the repairs and breakdowns, we also had the servicing and examinations to do. The smaller weekly and monthly ones were done on site in a station siding, wherever we were working. Sometimes it meant having to book on early to do the exam before the operating crew arrived. The three- and six-monthly ones were carried out at either Derby, Colwick Loco erecting shop or Leicester Loco workshop, depending on where we were stabled at the time - it also helped cut down the travelling time. These places were used because they had pits available. It seemed strange working at Colwick, it was like returning home.

I had not been working with the No. TT51 for very long before troubles started. We'd been working all the week on the Leicester to Birmingham line between Narborough and Hinckley, and on the Friday afternoon set out to travel to the Nottingham area for our Sunday duty. Whenever the machine travelled from site to site I always rode with it, just in case there were any problems that might result in a breakdown; at least I would then be on hand to sort it out. Whilst this took place my mate drove the van to meet me at the destination, calling in at various locations en route to make sure everything was alright. Approaching Leicester I realised that things were not as they should be, as the operator was having difficulty changing gear; by the time we reached the station the machine was running in one gear only, as the clutch plate was burning out. The inspector got a message to the North box signalman and he diverted us into a siding behind Humberstone Road station down platform. My mate had been on Leicester station platform and I shouted to him, 'Meet us at Humberstone Road, the machine is in trouble and I need your help'. To renew a clutch plate you really required the machine over a pit, but there was no way that we could have got it in to Leicester Loco, without it being towed there. I decided that I would renew the plate where the machine stood, but unfortunately I didn't have a spare one in the van. From the signal box I got a message to Derek the foreman, and asked him to send me a new clutch plate down with Joe the depot van driver, it would be quicker than sending my mate, besides I needed John there to help me as it was a double-handed job. Derek was a bit concerned and said, 'You can't renew a clutch plate on the open road without a pit, I will arrange for it to be taken to the loco shed'. To which I replied, 'Don't bother, send the plate and I will do my best.'

Luckily enough I had a set of slings and a pull lift in the van. Whilst John removed the floor plates in the cab, I crawled beneath the machine, on my back, lying on the sleepers and in a limited space of about 18 inches. As soon as the plates were removed, John hung the pull lift from the main frame of the cab roof and I got a sling round the clutch housing and hooked it on to the pull lift, ready for John to work the ratchet and take the weight. Once the housing was supported, I disconnected the prop shaft, removed the bolts which held the housing to the gearbox and slid it back, but working in such a confined space made it very difficult. Joe arrived with the new clutch plate, and all I had to do was insert the plate and reconnect everything. Whilst I was finishing off underneath, John removed the pull lift and replaced the floor plates. Then I tested the machine to make sure the gears were working correctly. Thankfully it was a dry day and not too cold. About 12 months later I had to renew the clutch plate again, using the same method, this time at Ambergate, but the weather was freezing with six inches of snow on the ground. Before I could work beneath the machine, we had to clear the snow away and put down sacks for me to lie on, and my mate had to warm the tools by a fire before I could handle them. The Leicester job had taken us 1½ hours and as far as I know it was the first time a clutch plate had been changed without the machine being over a pit. I said I would do anything to keep TT51 running!

But our problems didn't finish there. We set off from Humberstone Road on the down goods road and, approaching Thurmaston, heard a strange noise coming from the left-hand side rear wheel. Suddenly the roller bearing supporting the wheel collapsed allowing the wheel to fall to one side and rest on the axle and the frame, whilst still on the rail. Under normal circumstances the breakdown gang from Toton would have been called and the machine lifted and placed on a low loader wagon and taken back to Leicester or Derby. The alternative would have been to jack the machine, remove the wheel and renew the bearings, which we didn't have with us. But that would take too long and block the goods road even longer. I had to make a quick decision. As the wheel was still turning and we were only a short distance from Syston station sidings, I decided to have it towed or propelled. It was not possible to drive it to Syston, so a locomotive had to be sent for from Leicester. Whilst all this was taking place the pilot driver protected the machine at the rear, by placing detonators on the rails and Dennis the inspector walked to the box and arranged for a locomotive. It was not long before a class '25' diesel locomotive arrived on the down main line, ran through to Syston, crossed over and reversed down towards us. The machine was running in reverse, so it was easy to couple on to the loco with the special towing bar provided, which all machines carried for these kind of emergencies. We set off at walking speed, with me walking by the side of the wheel to make sure it kept turning. It wobbled along like a drunken old man. Within 10 minutes we were running into the siding, after having reversed onto the up road to gain access. We were just clear of the running road when the wheel finally collapsed and seized; I poured oil on the rail and the wheel slid along until we were in a position to stable the machine. The locomotive uncoupled, ran round and returned to Leicester. I had taken a gamble and it had paid off, saved a lot of time and expense. Thankfully my mate

John had called in at Syston to monitor our progress, so was aware of what had happened. If he'd gone on to Nottingham I would have had difficulty getting a message to him, which in those days had to be done through the signal boxes or the control office.

As the following day was a Saturday, we were not booked on duty until the evening, when TT51 was to take up a possession in the Nottingham area, but without the machine the possession would have to be cancelled or allocated to another machine. With such short notice it meant a lot of hard work for the allocating inspector to reorganize the duties, so I agreed to come in to work in the morning and fit a new set of bearings which was fairly straightforward. All I had to do was jack up the machine, remove the wheel and damaged bearings, clean the axle and fit new ones. The operators helped by doing the labouring jobs and by lunchtime the job was completed and the machine was on its way to Nottingham ready for the night possession. By the time I got home, I had about six hours rest, then it was back to work. Oh, the joys of working on TT51!

Some weeks later, we were again working on a night shift at Wellingborough, tamping the up goods road between there and Bedford. Walking round TT51 I noticed oil running down the side of the left-hand tamping bank, and realised that there was a crack in the oil tank, attached to the top of the bank, no doubt caused by the excessive vibration the machine was undergoing when tamping was taking place. To keep TT51 working until the end of the shift, we kept topping up the oil. Next morning I drained the tank, cleaned off the paintwork round the crack and marked it with chalk. I then asked Derek to send someone down during the day and weld the crack. When booking on in the evening, he'd left me a note saying that the job had been done and the machine was ready for work. Two days later the crack reappeared, and once again I had it welded. The third time it happened, I gave up, and went to the nearest ironmonger's and bought a tube of plastic padding. That did the trick and we had no more trouble from it for several more months. It's amazing what you could do, if only you stopped and thought about it. I suppose in a way it was a form of tying it up with string!

The only time I've lived in fear of my life, when out working on the open road, was one summer night near Harringworth viaduct on the Manton Junction to Kettering line. The weather was close and humid and you could tell that at some point in the night we were in for a thunderstorm, and sure enough within a couple of hours we could hear distant rumbles of thunder. John and I were sheltering in a trackside cabin, whilst TT51 was working a short way down the line. It was not long before Dennis the inspector called us to attend to a minor fault on one of the tamping banks. As we left the cabin it started to rain and by then the thunderstorm was very close. We'd only walked a few yards down the side of the line, when suddenly there was a mighty crash, and a streak of lightning passed us, running along the top of the rail on the down road. John and I were walking in the cess of the up road about 15 ft away, but we felt the force of it, which left us with a tingling sensation and feeling sick. It took a couple of hours for us to settle down. I think it was the closest we've been to being cooked alive!

Talking of strange sensations, and in this case a little haunting, we had a possession one day working on the down main line inside Clay Cross tunnel.

Dennis had asked John and me to stay with the machine, just in case a breakdown occurred, as it would have been difficult to get a message to me, especially if they were working near the centre. The up road was open to normal traffic, so we had to keep a close lookout for approaching trains. TT51 was already making a strange noise as it echoed around the walls of the tunnel, when suddenly there was a bang and a lot of whining as a London-bound express passenger train burst in at the north and shot past us doing at least 70 mph. The noise was deafening and ghostly, and I can now understand how the many railway ghost stores came about in the past, especially the one written by Charles Dickens, *The Signalman.*

Whilst on the subject of tunnels, I have an amusing story to tell. One week we were booked on the day shift, which was a pleasant change, this time to work on the line which once ran between Mansfield and Southwell. Most of it by then had closed, except the section between Mansfield and Rainworth which was still being used as a branch line to Rufford Colliery. The only way to reach it from Derby or Nottingham was via what is known today as the 'Robin Hood Line', but in those days the line passed through the old Kirkby-in-Ashfield station, near to the centre of the town. From Linby and Newstead the line is on a rising gradient, especially inside Kirkby tunnel. Unfortunately we'd been stopped at a signal south of the tunnel, and it was difficult to get a run at the gradient. We set off slowly and made our way, but got slower until we came to a stop in the middle of the tunnel. The only thing we could do was set back and have another run at it, but the same thing happened again, and back we went for another try. Anyone watching must have thought we were playing the fool, or we'd seen a ghost and shot out frightened, it was all a bit of a laugh. Finally we made a third run and half-way through everyone aboard jumped off, except the operator, and gave it a push and to our surprise it worked. I don't think the signalman realized what had happened, except that he must have thought to himself, 'They are taking a long time to clear the possession!'

The only other tunnel I can think of that caused us trouble was the one north of Corby in Northamptonshire. It was the longest tunnel in the division. The machines always had difficulty tamping the track, because in certain places it was almost waterlogged. Water poured through the tunnel walls, and when working inside, you thought you were in a storm. Working outside the machine meant that you had to wear your topcoat, and I kept my fingers crossed and hoped that TT51 was not going to break down.

In all my time with TT51, there was only one occasion when it became derailed. Again it was while we were working nights, this time on the Nottingham to Lincoln line at Lowdham. Tony was the operator, and when he was in full swing he could work the machine at a faster rate than anyone else. They were tamping towards Burton Joyce and by 04.00 in the morning had covered a lot of ground. Suddenly the tamping banks came down and instead of the tines entering the ballast, they struck something hard beneath the surface, which turned out to be a buried fishplate. Straightaway the tamping banks lifted the machine and when the pressure was released, they came down and the front wheels slipped off the rails and ended up on the ballast. Weighing up the situation I came to the conclusion that if it came off the rails that way, then it was going back on that way. Luckily enough there were a few old sleepers lying around at the side of the track, left over from a relaying job. I got Tony to drop the banks and lift TT51 until the front wheels cleared the rails. We then quickly slid the sleepers underneath, resting them across the rails. Tony then lowered TT51 down onto the sleepers and, with the help of the screw jacks carried on the rear of the machine, we slowly jacked it over until the wheels were above the rails. Tony again dropped the banks, lifted the machine, and we removed the sleepers and the wheels were lowered onto the rails. I checked round for any damage and as there was none, TT51 went on to complete the night's work and as far as I know no one found out about it, certainly not the bosses at Nottingham and Derby.

I was enjoying my time with TT51, and the work was not always serious, it did have its lighter moments. One such moment occurred when we were working a day shift at Langley Mill, tamping the down goods road. We spent a lot of time in that area, because the lines were affected by colliery subsidence. It was a lovely warm day and John and I were sitting on the bank side, taking in the sun and watching the machine hard at work. It was being operated by one of the relief operators, Bill, who was standing in for our regular operator Jim, who was away on holiday. Suddenly the machine shut down and there was a loud hissing noise coming from the front end, the cab door flew open and out shot Bill, soaked from head to foot in hydraulic oil. He was just moving to the next sleeper, when the rubber hose leading from the foot pedal to the tamping bank control valve, burst and the full force of oil shot up his trouser leg. Within seconds he was smothered, both on the inside and out, and at 1,470 psi he didn't stand much of a chance. The rest of us fell about laughing, but I don't think Bill quite appreciated the joke. Luckily he lived only a short distance away from Langley Mill, so whilst I renewed the pipe, John ran him home for a bath and a change of clothes. I suppose in the end Bill had the last laugh on us, because he got a new set of clothes out of the railway company and all we got was a mess to clean up. Oil was running down the roof and cab walls and had got everywhere. It took weeks before we finally got rid of it, but then these were the perils of working with such high-pressure machines.

Knowing the distances we had to travel by road in order to reach many of the sites where the machines were stabled before starting work, it's a wonder we were not stopped more often by the police, especially when travelling during the night. The only county that seemed to be keen on pulling you over was Leicestershire and I can't remember ever being pulled up in any of the others. We were travelling to Market Harborough one dark night and making our way down the A6 road towards the village of Great Glen, when a car with a flashing blue light on the roof overtook us and jammed its brakes on, and a sign appeared in the rear window saying 'Stop, Police'. We managed to stop without crashing into the car. Unfortunately we were travelling in an unmarked van, specially hired for the purpose of carrying out the standby duties. Suddenly two burly policemen appeared at the window; whilst one asked the questions the other walked round to the back and shone his torch through the rear windows. When they saw that we were carrying tools, etc., they thought they had got a conquest on their hands, but they were to be disappointed. The first question was, 'Where are you going?' and we had great difficulty in convincing them that we were on our way to work, until we mentioned that we worked for British Railways. Then they noticed our overalls and the tools marked BR, and the spare parts for the tamping machine. They thought we were on our way to do a robbery in Market Harborough. Their parting shot was, 'Okay lads, on your way and have a good journey'. But one policeman made us laugh when he said, 'Most sensible people are usually in bed at this time of night, and the only fools out are policemen, railwaymen and prostitutes; we must be in the wrong job!'

One cold winter's night TT51 was working at Spondon station near Derby. My regular mate John Diggles was taking a few days off, so Derek had sent my old mate Johnny Cooke to work with me. As Spondon was close to the P&M workshop, it didn't matter about the mate being able to drive the van. If I required any spares from the stores, he could almost have walked there, and besides John C. was only going to be with me for a few days. By the time we arrived at Spondon it was 22.30, and everyone was ready for a cup of tea, so Dennis the inspector gave my mate instructions to go to the lineside cabin at the station, light the fire and the Tilly-lamp (storm lantern), whilst the rest of us went out to set up the machine. He'd been gone about an hour when we arrived at the cabin and found him sitting in the dark with a well burnt-through fire roaring up the chimney and the kettle boiling itself almost dry. 'Why are you sitting in the dark, what's happened to the lamp?' said Dennis, to which John replied, 'Oh that thing! I was just lighting it, after pumping up the pressure, when it flared up and flames shot out of the top and it nearly burnt me. I ran outside and dropped it in the water tub before it exploded, and it's still there'. Everyone fell about laughing and informed John that it very often happens before the mantle ignited, and there was nothing to worry about as it would soon have settled down. We all had to sit there and drink our tea in the dark, which was no bad thing, because if John had brewed we never knew where he'd got the water from, or what colour the tea would turn out to be. I do know that sometimes you could almost stand the spoon up in it, as it was so strong.

It was July 1968 and TT51 was stabled in the sidings next to Derby station, whilst I carried out a weekly examination. Suddenly I heard the sound of a steam locomotive. This was strange, because by July 1968 regular steam workings in the Derby area had finished. In fact what I was witnessing was the last steam-hauled passenger train to pass through Derby, before steam was finally eliminated from BR in August of the same year. It was an enthusiasts' special being worked by 'Britannia' class 4-6-2 No. 70013 *Oliver Cromwell*. Thankfully the locomotive was preserved for the nation and until recently resided at Bressingham. If I had read my monthly *Railway Magazine* at the time I would have known it was running, but in those days I was too busy looking after TT51. I had hoped to take a trip on one of the very last steam-hauled trains on BR, which took place on 11th August, but we were too busy with the tamping programme, and it was very difficult to get time off, especially at the weekend.

A good example of working exceptionally long hours, especially at weekends, occurred one weekend when TT51 was booked to work on the Derby to Sheffield main line at Wingfield, north of Ambergate. No. TT51 had been brought in to do the tamping, after a track-relaying possession that had also been deep-ballasted. Booking on in Derby at 22.00 on the Saturday evening, we arrived on site with TT51 just after midnight, to find that the track relaying had been delayed by quite a number of hours, owing to the breakdown of the tracklayer. There was nothing we could do but sit and wait until the re-laying inspector came and gave us the all clear. So it was 09.00 (Sunday morning) before we received the instructions to start tamping; by then we had already been on duty 11 hours. But at least there had been a cabin close by where we could sit and have a cup of tea and eat our sandwiches. Being summer it was quite warm and there was the lovely Derbyshire countryside to admire and wildlife to enjoy. We spent most of the time cleaning and polishing the machine, I don't know why because at the end of the shift it was just as dirty again. No. TT51 was soon into her stride, and by midday had covered a good distance, when suddenly there was a spray of hydraulic oil from the right-hand tamping bank. A squeeze-cylinder cover seal had burst, a common fault, but unfortunately it was the one on the large cover side of the cylinder. Thankfully it was on the outside of the machine and easy to work on. To renew the seal meant a long delay, as the cylinder and piston rod had to be removed, and if everything went well the job would take me about two hours to complete. The thought of another delay caused panic with the inspectors and there was even talk of sending for another machine. To put their minds at rest, I said I would try and carry out a temporary repair, which would take me about 30 minutes. If it failed then another machine would have to be sent for, to save time.

I quickly unscrewed the 12 cylinder cover screws and then drew back the cover, sliding it along the piston rod until clear of the cylinder. I cut through the damaged seal and removed it. The seal ring was made up of a thin layer of asbestos sandwiched between two metal plates, the inner circle round the piston rod being about six inches in diameter and the seal half an inch wide by about an eighth of an inch thick. After a period of time the hydraulic oil, owing to the high pressure in the system, would work its way between the metal plates and blow out the asbestos, and the seal burst. At the time we were changing the seals to more reliable ones, and I had a couple of the new spares in my tool bag. These were made of an asbestos material called Walkerite, but were much harder in consistency and didn't require tin plates to keep it together. To make the temporary repair I decided to cut through the seal, fit it round the piston rod and rejoin it. But instead of doing a straight cut, I cut it with the aid of a very sharp knife, into the shape of a letter 'W', which appeared to look like a set of teeth. Once it was round the piston rod I joined the two ends together and glued them, replaced the cover and screwed it up to the cylinder. It had taken me 25 minutes to complete the repair. Then came the testing time: would it hold under such high pressure! To my amazement it did, and I kept my fingers crossed that it would last to the end of the shift. Not only did the seal last out to the end of the shift, but went on for several more months before it was renewed.

No. TT51 finally completed its programmed work at 17.30, but the dramatic events of the day were not over by any means. When the possession had started on the Saturday evening both main lines had been closed, but without notifying us, the area traffic inspector had re-opened the down main line to normal traffic at 15.00. At around 17.00 we were all concentrating on TT51, making sure that it would complete the job, when round the corner came an express passenger train, and flashed past the machine. Thankfully no one was standing in the way or they might have been killed, but we did have a good lookout man, who had just a few moments to warn us that the train was approaching. As the train shot past, it sucked up the dust from the new ballast and created a fog, which nearly blinded us all. Dennis our inspector went to find the traffic inspector, and I guess when he found him he would have been quaking in his boots, with the roasting that Dennis would have given him. At 17.30 we packed the machine away, ready for travelling to Derby for the following day's work. By the time John and I booked off it was 20.00. We had been on duty for 22 hours, and I still had to get home to East Bridgford. During the afternoon, Dennis had given John money to go out and buy extra food to keep us all going. He returned with packets of sandwiches, meat pies and bars of chocolate, so at least we didn't go hungry, but I was ready for my meal when I arrived home.

Some of the distances we had to travel when moving from site to site seemed to me to be rather ridiculous, especially when over the week we'd been working in the Chesterfield area and then at the weekend the machine was programmed to work at Kettering or Wellingborough, when other machines had been working in those areas. It was during one such run that I had quite a frightening experience, but at the same time an enjoyable day out.

We'd been working all the week, on the day shift, in the Westhouses area and had been stabling TT51 in the old Westhouses locomotive shed, which by then had become roofless. On the following Sunday we were programmed to work at Corby, and had been diagrammed to move to Corby on the Friday. John and I arrived at Westhouses in time for the departure, to find Dennis, who had made his way there from his home in Alfreton, and the pilotman, an engine driver based at Toton, but no operators - their van had broken down on the way up from Derby. A quick decision had to be made or we would lose the path in the timetable, which meant having to wait for a number of hours for another one, or cancel the move altogether and cause disruption to the weekend's programme. After a discussion I agreed to drive TT51 to Corby. Technically it should have been one of the operators, but as I had been passed out to drive and operate Dennis decided to let me go, whilst he and John called in at various stations en route to monitor my progress. We departed on time and made our way down the goods road to Toton, the pilotman calling out the signals. At Toton the signalman routed us via the goods avoiding line, past Trent station and through Trent tunnel to Syston. There we took the north curve onto the Melton Mowbray line, and everything was going well until we were approaching Oakham, when suddenly the pilotman shouted 'Stop! The station signal's at danger, and the crossing gates are closed to the railway.' I did my best to slow down, but there was no way I was going to stop in time without passing the board and running into the gates which protected the main 'A' road. I arrived at the station platform in first gear with my foot hard down on the brake, and my hand on the horn, blowing a continuous note. The signalman realised that we were in trouble, so quickly closed the gates to the road and pulled the signal off. We shot past the box and crossing at 20 mph and breathed a sigh of relief that we'd made it without disaster. The road ahead was clear and we arrived at Corby without any further problems. No one ever found out about it, but Dennis and John were on Oakham station platform to witness what had happened. I never saw them as I was too busy with the brake and the horn to take much notice. I think they must have had their eyes shut at the time, or they were praying. It was the pilotman's fault as he'd forgotten to mention to me that the Oakham distant signal was at caution after we'd left Langham Crossing. If I'd known that, I would have slowed down to walking pace, knowing that the line through Oakham was on a falling gradient.

As time went on, the '04' machines were getting further run down and were becoming difficult to maintain, and several in other areas had been taken out of service. I was at Derby one day, working on TT51 in the old shed at the back of the P&M workshop, carrying out a three-monthly examination, when Derek called me into the office and asked me if I could get them out of trouble. No. TT45 had failed during the Sunday possession at Belper, with a seized left-hand tamping bank vibration shaft roller bearing, and there was no one to attend to it as the fitter who looked after it was on holiday. He couldn't spare anyone from the general pool as he had too much work on attending to the static plant. I agreed to go, provided I didn't lose too much time working on TT51; after all we'd got a set programme to work to, and we didn't want to lose out on our performance figures.

I arrived at Belper and found TT45 stabled in the goods yard sidings south of the station. It appeared as though someone had already had a go at carrying out the repair because the belt drive cover and pulley had been removed, and the tine arms disconnected. All I had to do was rig up the extractor to remove the damaged bearing from its housing, fit a new bearing and reassemble the arms and pulley. It sounded simple, but it's not always that easy, especially if the bearing is tight on the shaft. I fitted the extractor to the bearing and tightened the extracting screw onto the end of the shaft. After slowly turning the screw and applying pressure I realised there was something wrong when the bearing refused to move. We then set up the gas burning equipment, which we'd brought with us as a precaution, and I started to warm up the bearing and apply more pressure to the screw. Under normal circumstance this usually did the trick and the bearing would pop off the shaft, but not this time. In the end I put so much pressure on the extracting screw that it stripped the threads and the extractor fell to pieces. On closer examination I found that the bearing had run so hot that not only had it seized up, but the metal of the shaft and bearing had melted and fused together, creating one solid block of steel. This should never have been allowed to happen as you could always tell when a bearing was failing: it made a loud whining noise, even above the noise of the machine. So whoever was in charge should have heard it and stopped the machine, before it caused any further damage to the shaft.

I could now see why someone had had a go and given up the day before, and once again it was left to me to clear up the mess. An easy job had turned into a major one, because I now had to remove the entire vibration shaft and take it back to the workshop at Derby. It was the middle of the afternoon before I reached the

P&M stores, only to find that a new shaft was not available. It was such an expensive item, and was seldom asked for, and if one was required it had to be ordered from the Plasser works in West Ealing, who would then dispatch it to Derby by train within a few hours. We relied a lot on the express 'Red Parcels' service for the transporting of such expensive items, and they never let us down. Derek telephoned Plassers and found to his surprise that they had none in stock either. They had decided to run down their stock of class '04' parts, as the machines were slowly being taken out of service and scrapped. Panic then set in with the operators as they thought they were going lose TT45 to the scrapyard, but they'd not counted on me. I asked Derek to contact other P&M departments in the Midland Region, and we eventually located a second-hand one at Crewe. Joe the depot van driver was dispatched straightaway, and when I arrived for work the next morning it was waiting for me on the workbench. I fitted the new shaft and bearings, which delayed me further, and TT45 lived on to fight another day, much to the relief of the inspector and operators. With a bit of extra overtime, I had TT51's examination completed and we were back on schedule.

Before I completed my time on standby duties with TT51, and with a bit of quick thinking, I managed to save her from going to the scrapyard twice. No doubt by the early months of 1969 the '04' machines were coming to the end of their working lives, and were constantly giving trouble, but they had, if possible, to last a little longer in the Nottingham Division until the new class '06' Duomatic machines were brought into service. As I mentioned before, the oil tank above one of the tamping banks had cracked whilst we were working at Wellingborough. I'd had it welded several times and in the end patched it up with plastic padding. Once again it started to leak and the crack began to run along the length of the tank; this time there was no way we could repair or patch it, every time I tried it just simply opened up again, due to the excessive vibration caused by the machine. The tank was an integral part of the tamping bank and the only way it could be renewed was by changing the whole unit. After a meeting with the civil engineers it was decided that TT51 would be withdrawn from service. But I didn't give up that easily, and set about seeing what I could do to solve the problem. I suggested to Derek that we locate a scrap machine, remove the tamping bank unit and use it to replace the one on TT51. 'Not possible', said Derek, 'because it's never been done before outside the main works, without the use of a crane'. 'There's always a first time for everything.' I said, 'and if we can borrow a forklift truck, with a three-tons lifting capacity, I could easily do the job'. To my surprise the civil engineer and the P&M decided to let me have a go. First a tamping bank had to be located and again the P&M department at Crewe came to the rescue. A redundant machine was standing in the sidings at the electric traction depot, next to the Chester and North Wales line, and they had a three-ton forklift truck available.

Next day John and I set out for Crewe followed by the P&M lorry, driven by Jim the relief driver, and we arrived on site just before lunch. The P&M foreman and a forklift driver were waiting for us. The first thing I did was have the machine brought down to the depot entrance and had it standing on the level, on the concrete apron. The forklift then took the weight of the tamping bank unit and I removed the locking pin, and set about disconnecting it from within the main frame. This didn't take too long, as all I had to do was remove the vibration shaft drive belts, disconnect the various hydraulic pipes and the two main guide shafts which held the unit in place. We then loaded it onto the lorry and fastened it down with ropes, ready for the journey back to Derby, arriving there late in the evening.

The following morning when Derek turned up for duty, I think he was surprised to see the tamping bank sitting on the lorry. Deep down he thought it was impossible to do. We now had to find a location with a flat area, where we could access the machine and where a three-tons forklift truck was available. On enquiry, the Technical Centre on London Road in Derby came to our rescue. We ran TT51 into their workshop and they gave us full use of their forklift truck and driver for the day. First I removed the damaged unit from TT51 and then fitted the new one. It turned out to be a full day's job, but in the end the new unit, after test, worked satisfactorily and TT51 was back in business. I went home that evening with a smile on my face, as I'd beaten the system. As far as we know it was the only time a tamping bank unit had been changed outside the main works. The old unit was taken back to the P&M, and after off-loading with the crane, stood in the yards for months. I never did find out what happened to it in the end.

No. TT51 only carried on for a few more weeks before disaster struck again - this time it was the diesel engine. I'd noticed over several days that the operators kept topping up the engine radiator. On checking the oil sump level I found that it was well above the maximum level, and the oil contained a large amount of water. My heart sank; after all the effort with the tamping bank, we were in trouble again. I was keeping my fingers crossed and hoping that it was nothing too serious. With a bit of luck it might only be a cylinder head gasket or a liner seal!

As we were working in the Nottingham area at the time, I had the machine taken to Colwick Loco Shed. If we required a lift, then I could have the use of their overhead crane. You never know, we might have to change the engine! I removed the cylinder head and to my dismay found that the main cylinder block casting was cracked. Would this now be the end of TT51? It was doubtful if the civil engineer would go to the expense of paying for a new block. But as I said previously, 'I don't give up that easily', so I made it known to all concerned that we should look around for a spare engine from another machine. Surely there must be one standing redundant somewhere in a siding. As it turned out we had one in our own Division. No. TT40 stood in a siding at Heanor, after having been involved in an accident rendering it beyond economical repair. There was no damage to the engine and it was a sound unit, so would be ideal to fit into TT51. No. TT40 was towed to Colwick and both machines were placed in the erecting shop side by side. With the use of the overhead crane I set about removing the roofs to gain excess to the engines, after first calling in the electrician to disconnect the various items of wiring beneath the roof and those attached to the engine. I could have done it myself, but it was every man to his trade in those days, and you had to be careful not to over-step the mark, in case you caused a strike. Once I'd disconnected the prop-shaft, fuel pipes, etc., and unbolted the engines from their beds, I was ready to do the swap. No. TT40's

We covered a large area in the Nottingham Division from just north of Bedford to Chesterfield and worked in some beautiful parts of the country, especially Derbyshire and Rutland. This view of Manton Junction station was taken from the top of the tunnel, in the centre is the signal box with the main line platforms on the right and the Stamford/Peterborough line on the left.
Author

In September 1967 I was at Nottingham Victoria station to witness the very last passenger train depart for Rugby Central before the station closed and was demolished. The dmu for Rugby is departing from a bay platform at the south end. *Author's Collection*

engine fitted like a glove and I had no difficulty in connecting it up to TT51. I replaced the roofs on both machines and Sid the electrician returned and reconnected the wiring on TT51 only. No. TT40 was eventually towed away for scrap. It had taken me a week to complete the work and no doubt had saved the railway company quite an expense. Like the tamping bank change earlier, as far as I know this too had been the only time that an engine unit had been exchanged outside the main works, but I couldn't vouch for that, as it was a fairly easy job to do if you had access to a crane. It just took a long time.

It was the last time I had the chance to work in Colwick erecting shop, before the engine shed was closed in 1970, and eventually pulled down. It was ironic that I should finish some of my latter days working as a fitter for the P&M at Colwick, the place where I started my railway career, way back in December 1954.

The changing of the engine on TT51 was one of the last things I did for the machine. In May 1969 I was transferred to one of the new '06' Duomatic tampers and another fitter was assigned to TT51. Roy Orton, who had just completed his apprenticeship, took over from me. He and I became good friends in later years when he worked for me, and eventually followed me on to the supervisory staff when I left the railway in 1980.

No. TT51 continued for a few more years, doing light work, and as far as I know never experienced any further major breakdowns. It ended its days working for the Research Department at Derby as a test machine.

I had enjoyed my time working on the on-track plant and it had taken me to all corners of the Division and at times beyond. We had spent several weeks working on lines that are now closed, especially the old GCR main line between Nottingham and Rugby, closed in May 1969, the same month that I finished with TT51 - the line between Ambergate and Pye Bridge, now owned by the Midland Railway Preservation Trust, the Wirksworth and Little Eaton branches, plus the old main line through Darley Dale to Buxton. One line we were always called back to, which is still open today, was that between Leicester and Burton-on-Trent via Coalville and Ashby-de-la-Zouch. It was always prone to colliery subsidence owing to the many coalmines in the area, with their tunnels and passageways being so close to the surface. No matter how many times the line was tamped, within a week it was just as bad again. One section near Bagworth had to be raised so much that the line ended up on an embankment, where previously it had been level with the surrounding countryside.

During the course of my time working for the P&M I had done standby duties or worked on all types of on-track plant, including in my early days carrying out an engine overhaul on a track recording trolley. It was a petrol engine constructed in the USA by the Chevrolet Company. I must also have frequented almost every line-side cabin in the division. If one was not available, we could always brew a cup of tea, because each machine carried a gas bottle and a gas ring, contained inside a disused five-gallon oil drum for safety. At times we camped out on the line side like gypsies, in all kinds of weather. Very often during the winter period we would start tamping, and then have to stop because there was too much frost in the ground; then it was a case of either going home or retiring to the nearest cabin for the rest of the shift. I remember that happening on the Mansfield line at Linby. We stabled up the machine and made for the cabin. The local platelayer had lit a fire and by the time we arrived it was feeling very cosy. With every member of the team inside it soon turned into a furnace, but no one would move in case they lost their place. There was an old varnished kitchen table in the centre of the cabin, and by the end of the shift the varnish was running down the legs, it was so hot.

These were happy days and, when the time came for me to move from No. TT51, it was a sad day because I'd got used to living with the machine and had done so much to keep it running that it had become part of my life. I spent more time with TT51 than I did at home, because of the long hours we had to work. The same applied to the other fitters on standby with the other machines. It's doubtful if anyone would do the same today!

No. TT51 is packed up and ready to travel, the levelling trolley attached to the front of the machine and lifted clear of the rails, the connecting rods and small trolley wheels being stowed away on the side by the engine. *Author*

Chapter Fifteen

A Pioneer for Freightliners

My move to work on a class '06' tamping machine was to be temporary, as the civil engineer only needed a fitter to act as standby with them until they got over their early teething troubles, then it was back to the normal call-out duties and standby at weekends.

I had now been out of my apprenticeship for almost 10 years, and it was about time I started looking for a step up the ladder to a supervisor's position, if possible. It would be better pay and being on the salaried staff meant a better pension on retirement. And I'd attended college for six years and had obtained my engineering qualifications, so in my opinion I stood a fair chance of eventually finding a supervisory post.

During May 1969, at the time of my leaving TT51, I noticed on the staff vacancy list that they required three new engineering shift supervisors at the soon-to-be-opened BR Freightliner terminal at Beeston near Nottingham. As I had already done relief chargehand duties at Hitchin and Toton, and a two-weeks' stint as foreman at the P&M, I thought I might stand a bit of a chance. If successful it would also mean that I would be nearer to home and have less distance to travel to work. So I filled in the appropriate forms and applied. One of my colleagues, the relief foreman Keith Barber, also applied for one of the other positions at the same time.

We both received a letter to say that our applications had been successful and we were to go to the Freightliner HQ at Leeds for an interview on Monday 2nd June, in the morning. As our interview times followed each other, we both travelled on the train together. When we arrived at the office the secretary told us that there had been 95 applications, and we were two out of a total of 20 that had been selected for an interview. When we saw a number of the other applicants, we didn't think we stood a chance. There they were all dressed up in their smart suits, carrying their briefcases, and looking every inch the businessman. Most of them were former management trainees, hoping for a quick step to promotion.

I was the first to enter the Lions Den, and the interview was a disaster from start to finish as far as I was concerned. The three men behind the desk asked the most awkward questions, which went on for half an hour. I did my best and gave them as many clear answers as I could; one man even had a bit of an argument with me over an engineering technicality regarding the tamping machine, a subject I knew well so I stood my ground. I came out of the room convinced that that was the last I would hear about any supervisor's position at Freightliners. Keith fared no better and we both travelled back to Derby, prepared to continue as fitters with the P&M.

The following day I was off duty taking a two-weeks' holiday. On the Thursday I was busy in the garden at East Bridgford, when June called me and said, 'A telegram has just arrived from the P&M at Derby, with the message "Please telephone the P&M office, important"'. I had to make the call from the box down the road, as we had no telephone in the house in those days. When I got through to the office, it was Derek who spoke to me, 'Well done!' he said. 'You and Keith have both landed the Shift Supervisor's positions at Beeston Freightliner terminal, and they want you to start on Monday, so can you please come in to work tomorrow'. The third position had gone to a fitter from the diesel depot at Toton. Apparently we were the only practical men they had interviewed, and they liked the answers we'd given them, even after my argument over the tamper.

I went to Derby on the Friday and had just eight hours to clear the locker and remove my personal items from the P&M. Derek allowed Joe to take me and my tools, etc., home in the van. Needless to say the rest of my holiday had to be cancelled. It was a good job we'd not booked to go away.

On Monday morning 9th June, 1969, I reported to the main office at Beeston and met my new boss, the chief engineer Harold Cross, along with Keith and Ian, the ex-fitter from Toton. For the first week we were all on the day shift together, until we'd familiarized ourselves with the layout of the terminal and what we were expected to do. The terminal was to open for work on the following Monday.

The layout was quite a simple affair. The main office was situated at the road entrance, and in the centre of the terminal were the engineering department's offices, stores and workshop. Down the side of the Nottingham to Derby and London main line were two long sidings to house the container trains, whilst they were waiting to be loaded or unloaded. The sidings were spanned by two enormous Morris cranes, running on their own tracks, which were used for transferring the containers from road to rail or rail to road. At the back of the terminal was a lorry park. The drivers had their own rest room near the main office, and were responsible to the traffic controller.

The engineering staff required on duty for working the three shifts was quite small. The chief engineer, who had his own office, was on a permanent day shift, working Monday to Friday. The three supervisors worked the day, night and afternoon turns on a rota basis, also Monday to Friday, with an extra Saturday morning when working days. Each supervisor had working for him a fitter and an electrician, and if he or any of the tradesmen were off duty at any time, the others were expected to cover the job by working two 12-hour shifts. As well as supervising the staff and planning the maintenance programme, I was responsible for controlling the stores, and also expected to help with any failures and breakdowns that occurred on the lorries, cranes and rail wagons. So I had not quite finished using the tools and getting my hands dirty. The men did the examinations and repairs, including any damaged containers, which often arrived with holes in their sides. The road vehicles and rail wagons were a new experience for me, but I was quite at home when it came to the static plant and cranes.

Most of the breakdowns occurred on the cranes or the rail wagons. In the case of the cranes it was nearly always electrical problems to do with the complicated container-lifting bales. Each bale was fitted with around two-dozen small limit switches, which controlled the lifting of the containers. Steel pins located the top corners of each container and then turned, enabling the container to be lifted on or off the rail wagons and lorry trailers. If it was one of the flat type containers, then four arms swung down and located into sockets on each side, near the base. Sometimes we spent half a shift tracing the faults that often occurred in the complicated wiring system. In the winter we had quite a job keeping our fingers from freezing, but as time went on we got used to the problems and soon had them sorted out.

Class '45' No. 45019 waiting to depart the Nottingham (Beeston) Freightliner terminal with the 19.33 hrs train to Coatbridge. Note in the background the crane for loading the containers onto either the train or a road vehicle. *Sid Hancock*

As far as the rail wagons were concerned, most of the faults were to do with the braking system. It was usually the control valve at the end of each wagon that stopped functioning. As we had plenty in stock, it was just a matter of changing a faulty one for a new one.

The lorry units were most reliable and I can't ever remember one failing with a major breakdown. The only time I went out with the fitter to help with a breakdown was to Melton Mowbray, when one of the units had failed at the pet food factory, but then it was only a minor fault with the ignition and was soon put right. I had a very good fitter working on my shift, who had served his apprenticeship in a garage, not only dealing with cars, but also heavy plant and lorries. He was also a very good panel-beater, so was useful when it came to repairing the damaged containers.

After having had the freedom of the countryside when working on the tamping machine, it now seemed strange being based in one place and it took a bit of getting used to. In the short time I worked at Beeston I only went off the depot twice to attend to an incident, the one just mentioned and another on the Nottingham Ring Road. I was on afternoon shift and had not been long on duty, when I had a call from the police, 'One of your lorries has had an accident at the Crown Island on the Ring Road, the load has fallen from the lorry and is blocking the island. No one has been injured, but can you please come and clean up the mess'. Fearing the worst I set out in the depot van. Although not very far away it took me quite a time to reach the scene, as the accident was blocking part of the ring road and the police were controlling the traffic. The lorry unit and trailer were not damaged, and had been parked by the side of the road on the pavement, but the container lay on its side across one lane of the highway. Before leaving the terminal, the driver had forgotten to clamp the container to the trailer, which was okay whilst travelling slowly or on the straight, but when turning a sharp curve, such as the one at the Crown Island, the whole thing tipped over on its side. It was a wonder that no one was killed. The container was packed full of bottles of liquid Camp coffee and powdered coffee in cardboard cartons. It was being taken to a storage depot in Arnold for distribution to the catering trade. Quickly, through the help of the police, I managed to contact the terminal engineer, who arranged for a crane to come and lift the container back on to the trailer. Then the driver and myself set about trying to salvage as much of the load as possible. A good many of the bottles had broken and the packets split open and strewn over the

A general view of Beeston Freightliner terminal with class '31' No. 31167 departing with the 4G50 to Birmingham (Lawley Street) on 27th July, 1984. The maintenance workshop, office and stores building can just be seen to the left of the Morris crane. *Paul Shannon*

road. Liquid coffee was running down the gutter like a brown river, and the local children and dogs were paddling in it, much to the dismay of their mothers and owners as it had happened during the school holidays. It took us most of the afternoon to sweep it up and fill dustbins with broken glass, etc., the bins being loaned to us by the locals provided they got a free packet of coffee in return; I imagine they had had enough to last them for the rest of the year, I know we did. We managed to salvage about half the load and took it to Arnold, but the firm didn't really want to know, as they would be making a claim on the insurance. I expect they dumped it, and it was wasted.

The second such incident I dealt with concerning a container involved the train. It was a hot summer's day in 1970, and during the day lorries had been arriving with a variety of containers for the evening departure to London. By late afternoon most of the train had been made up and was ready. Walking along the train checking the wagons I noticed that one container had thousands of flies hovering round the end doors. Looking at the label I realized that it was full of fruit and contained a consignment of grapefruit and oranges bound for a warehouse in London, and owing to the warm weather the contents must have gone rotten, hence the army of flies. Both doors were sealed, so we had to call in the customs inspector and a representative from the Citrus Fruit Board. The Inspector broke the seal and when the doors were opened, we found that the fruit in the first few layers of boxes had certainly gone rotten, and the smell was appalling. The Citrus Fruit representative refused to accept the consignment, as he assumed that the rest of the boxes were in the same condition. The customs inspector instructed us remove the container from the wagon, take it on to the waste land at the back of the terminal, empty it and burn the contents as quickly as possible. I borrowed a couple of the terminal labourers and watched them, as requested, whilst they unloaded the boxes. After the first few layers, we realised that the rest of the load was in perfect condition, boxes full of beautiful grapefruit that could be peeled and eaten straightaway, they were so sweet. The word soon got out and before we knew it, half the railway staff in the Beeston area were turning up and trying to help themselves. Even the locals tried to get in on the act, turning up at the main office and asking where the free boxes of grapefruit were. Some of them even tried to sneak in through the perimeter fence. We had to call back the customs inspector to re-seal the doors before things got out of hand. But in the end they didn't seem to mind and even allowed the staff to help themselves to a box or two before the rest were burnt, which to my mind seemed a shame. I suppose they were frightened that someone might get hold of them and try and make a quick sale, especially as the Citrus Fruit Corporation were claiming insurance.

Like all jobs, you often have an amusing incident. One of mine occurred one Saturday morning, although it was not amusing at the time because it caused us quite a lot of hard work. But afterwards we all sat back and had a jolly good laugh. A new fitter had started a few weeks earlier, and was working on the day shift with me. I had sent him out to examine the wagons on the train that had arrived in the night from Leeds and had already been unloaded. It was waiting to be shunted onto the sidings for stabling over the weekend. All he had to do was look for worn brake blocks and replace them if necessary, and check the 'Ferodo' pads on top of each bogie, which the wagon rode on. Owing to the many curves on BR

After we moved to live in Southwell in 1969 I had to travel to work from Fiskerton station on the Nottingham to Lincoln line. This is a view of the station looking towards Lincoln in May 1973: on the left is the leaning MR signal box and on the right the old station buildings incorporating the station master's house, now private, in the goods yard the office and iron lamp-cabin, where I kept my bike whilst at work. *Frank Berridge*

Something I always looked out for in my younger days when passing through Southwell was the 'Paddy' train which ran from there to Rolleston Junction. Ex-'MR '1P' class 0-4-4T No. 58065 is about to depart Southwell with its one coach to Rolleston; on the right is Caudwell's mill, the main industry in the town at that time. *Charles Bayes/Author's Collection*

the pads soon wore out and often required changing. He was doing well until he found a pair of pads on one wagon almost worn away and down to bare metal. They were not difficult to renew, but required a bit of hard work. The pads, about a foot square and a quarter of an inch thick, sat on top of two steel blocks above the bogie, inside a shallow metal recess. Above the pads were two corresponding steel blocks attached to the underside of the wagon and those resting on the pads took the weight and moved freely as the wagon negotiated the many curves. You had to either jack up the wagon or lift it with a sling, by using one of the Morris cranes, until there was just enough room to carry out the repair. The pads were attached to the bogie by the use of a strong type of glue. So the first thing to do was chip away the worn pads until you had attained a clean and smooth surface. Then mix the glue and apply very quickly, before it went off. All you had to do then was stick the pads on to the bogie, lower the wagon and the job was completed.

The fitter returned to the workshop and signed to say he had carried out the examination and the repair to the pads. A little later a locomotive arrived to shunt the train into the siding, but as the repaired wagon entered the curve at the end of the terminal, the bogie tried to climb on to the top of the rail. The train returned and I went to investigate the problem. Everything looked okay, but I was a bit worried about the new pads: were they too tight, or the wrong thickness? I called in the crane driver to give a lift to see if I could solve the mystery. As the crane started to lift the wagon, to my amazement I noticed that the bogie was following it, and the wheels were leaving the rail. Jokingly I said to the fitter, 'What have you done - screwed the wagon down to the bogie?' Then he admitted that he'd applied the glue to both sides of the pads, which must have bonded the bogie and wagon together. The glue had held the two so tight, it had managed to take the weight of the bogie. What a good advertisement it was for the glue manufacturers.

It took us hours to saw through the pads, using several hacksaw blades in the process, and then chip away the 'Ferodo', afterwards fitting new pads, and making sure that the glue was applied to one side only. I was booked to be off duty at lunchtime, and had arranged to have a meal in Nottingham, before going to see Forest play at the City Ground; in the end I just made it in time to see the kick off at 3 o'clock, missing out on the meal.

I was mad with the fitter at the time, for doing such a stupid thing. But on the Monday when the chief engineer read out my report to the staff, they all fell about laughing, and we wondered what would have been said if we had had to report that the train had been derailed by glue. I don't think anyone would have believed us; they would have thought we were cracking a joke!

Just after joining Freightliners, June and I decided that it was about time we started to think about buying our own property, especially as I was now earning a salary and had a little more security for the future. In the January David would be starting school, so it was essential we found the right type of school for him to settle in. We looked around and eventually found a three-bedroom bungalow in the Minster town of Southwell, a place I knew quite well previously when in the early 1950s I sang in the Minster during choir festivals which were held annually. On several occasions I sang evensong with my local village choir, at the Minster, whilst the Minster choir were away on holiday. After my voice broke in 1953 I learnt to ring the bells, and on Tuesday evenings each week cycled over to the Minster to join in with the weekly practice. Mind you, I did have an ulterior motive as I was friendly with the sister of one of the ringers. I will say no more! I also cycled through Southwell on many occasions, to reach one of my favourite trainspotting locations beside the East Coast main line at Muskham, and on the way would call in at the station to watch the Southwell 'Paddy' depart on its way to Rolleston Junction, or wait and see one of the coal trains pass through on the way to Beeston Sidings from Bilsthorpe or Blidworth Collieries. I never did ride the 'Paddy', but then I had very little money to spare and couldn't afford the fare, which was a pity really, because by the time we moved to Southwell in 1969, the line had been closed for five years. Although most of the buildings still stood, including the station, goods shed and the station master's house, the track had been lifted in 1967. Today it is the site of a new housing estate, constructed in the late 1970s: the only things remaining to remind everyone that a railway once ran though the town are the station master's house and the trackbed nature trail to Farnsfield.

We moved from our council house in East Bridgford to 5 Springfield Road, Southwell during December 1969. The weather was cold and at the same time I had a dose of the flu. It was a move that would have a dramatic effect on our lives at a later date, but we didn't realize it at the time. David started his school days at the National School in Nottingham Road in the first week of January 1970. It now meant I had further to travel to work, but it didn't make a lot of difference, because I could easily cycle the few miles to Fiskerton station to catch the train. I just had to start out a little earlier. June and I joined the Minster congregation and the local bell-ringing team. Within a short time I became ringing master, a post I held for the next 10 years. I became an altar server and sidesman, and soon found myself elected to serve on the parochial church council.

I quite enjoyed working at the Freightliner terminal, but within a year realised that trade was not picking up, and unless it did so in the next few months, there would have to be some changes, and several of the staff might become redundant. I was alright, as I'd been made senior shift supervisor, due to my length of service working for the railway, so I would be one of the last to go.

Scanning the staff vacancy list I noticed two new supervisory posts advertised for the P&M at Derby, and they were a grade higher than my present position. During my time at Freightliners the P&M depot had moved from Litchurch Lane, near the carriage and wagon works, to the diesel depot at Etches Park, situated on the opposite side of the London main line to the technical centre, just off London Road. By then the London Midland Region Divisional P&M departments had expanded and taken on more work looking after the civil engineer's on-track plant. The fleet had grown and the machines had become more sophisticated and difficult to maintain, and it was now becoming too much for one man to supervise. So between them the divisional P&M and civil engineers had decided to create a new section to supervise the maintenance of all the on-track plant. There were to be two positions in each division, titled on-track maintenance supervisor and an on-track inspector. These were the vacancies I'd noticed on the list. The rule was that you were to apply for both vacancies, and if you were successful after an interview, the management appointed you to the post they thought most suited your particular talents.

Class '31' No. 31407 is approaching Beeston station on its way into the Freightliner terminal with a train of containers from Birmingham (Lawley Street). *Sid Hancock*

I put pen to paper and sent off my application, as did my colleague Keith Barber, who, when he found out that I'd applied, said I stood no chance, as he'd previously worked in the P&M longer than me. 'We will see', I said, and left it at that. Two weeks later a letter arrived on my desk. I had been granted a date for an interview at the area manager's office in Derby, much to the disappointment of Keith who was not given one. He stayed working at the Freightliner terminal for a few more months, then left and went back to the locomotive works in Derby as a fitter.

This time the interview went well and I had no problems answering the questions posed by the area manager, the divisional plant engineer and the senior technical assistant. I went home happy, in the thought that I may stand a chance, but I was up against several clever lads from the other P&M depots, plus a few from Derby. A week later a letter arrived to say that I'd been successful and had been appointed to the position of Nottingham divisional on-track supervisor grade 'C', with my office based at the P&M depot, Derby. I was to share an office with my old foreman Derek Skidmore and George Shackleford, the electrical foreman. By then the chief foreman, Alf Etchells, had retired and no one had been appointed in his place - we were all answerable to the area manager and the divisional plant engineer. Sid Craddock, who I had worked with in the past on standby duties, had been appointed to the position of on-track inspector. He and I had a close working relationship, but he spent most of his time travelling round the Division, carrying out the routine inspections and I only saw him in the office on odd days in the week, when he came to fill out the forms and report to me on any faults he had found.

I had worked for Freightliners for 21 months, and on the day I left to return to Derby, the maintenance department was cut down to two-shift working. I moved just at the right time, as it saved one of the supervisors from being made redundant. The terminal carried on operating for a few more years and was then closed. Today the sidings are still extant, but the Morris cranes were dismantled and taken away, and the offices and workshops are now used as a base for one of the contractors who carry out track maintenance on behalf of Network Rail.

By the time I moved back to the Plant & Machinery Department in Derby in 1971, as the new on-track supervisor, they had moved the office and workshops to the diesel depot at Etches Park. This is the three-road depot in 1966 when first opened, and the P&M had the use of No. 3 road on the right for the maintenance of the on-track machines. The centre road was where in July 1973 I brought in *Flying Scotsman* to change the heating pipe between the engine and tender.

Frank Berridge Collection

In the early 1970s some of the older tamping machines were being replaced by the new Plasser & Theurer '07' class tamper/liners, although we still had the '06' 'Duomatics'. Standing in the sidings at the Research Centre in Derby is one of the new '07' machines No. 73253, under test before entering service.

Author

Chapter Sixteen

Back to Happy Days at Derby

It was exactly five years to the day since I first went to work for the P&M at Derby as a fitter, but this time I was returning as the supervisor. It made a change to be working on a regular day shift again. This time I was responsible for a much larger staff, having six fitters, six electricians and three apprentices under my control. The fitters and electricians worked in pairs. I also had to take my turn on call-out duties with Derek and George, so once again had to acquaint myself with the static plant as well as the on-track plant. I was no longer allowed to use the tools; if I had picked up so much as a spanner, the tradesmen would have walked out on strike. For the first time in my life, and after handling the tools for the last 16 years and four months, I was now a white-collar worker. This at times was a bit frustrating, especially when we had a fault on a machine and the fitter was having difficulty in tracing it or carrying out the repair. Often I felt I could have done the job much quicker myself, but I had to bite my tongue and let him get on with it. The only thing I could do was offer advice.

Again I was responsible for programming the examinations and repairs and controlling the stock in the stores, but for this I did make use of the 'Red Star' parcels service, because it was so fast and efficient and saved me carrying many of the little-used items on the shelves. Plassers were very helpful and would have a part sent to Derby in a matter of a few hours. As there was a lot of weekend and night work, especially with the standby duties, I had to run a strict staff rota, making sure that every tradesman had his fair share of the overtime. It was essential that you had everyone on your side otherwise they would make the job difficult. In the seven years that I was on-track supervisor, I can't remember having any problems with any of my staff. Every morning I had the task of working out the daily bonus for each tradesman. As they were not on timed work, owing to the nature of the job and distances travelled, it made life a little difficult, and I could only give them an estimated percentage, which varied between 100 and 125 per cent. I tried to get out of the office at least once a week, to visit the staff on site. It showed that I was taking an interest in what they were doing, and hopefully gave them a boost. And once a month I had a meeting with my opposite numbers in the civil engineer's department at Nottingham, very often with the plant engineer present. This enabled us to monitor progress and iron out any problems within the two departments.

Having moved back to Derby, it now meant that I had even further to travel to work, but thankfully an early morning train from Fiskerton got me to Derby in plenty of time to reach the office. There was a time when they spoke about removing this train from the timetable between Lincoln and Nottingham, but in the seven years that I travelled the departure time never varied more than two or three minutes either way. The journey time took almost an hour, and over the years I think I read more newspapers than I'd ever read before or since. I'm not a keen reader of newspapers, because I think they often give out wrong

'07' class No. 73202 at work on the old GCR main line between Loughborough and Quorn, the trolley on the left is used for the lining of the track and not lifting as in the case of the '04', '05' and '06' machines.
Author

Both supervisory staff and fitting staff were sent to the training school at the Grove in Watford for training on the new machines. The civil engineer's school was housed in a set of wooden buildings in the grounds, seen here is the main house. I did attend a course in the main house on work study. The Grove had been the HQ of the LMS during World War II and the wooden buildings were offices for the control organization.
Author's Collection

information and are the cause of many of the present-day problems. That's only my opinion, but other people may think differently. The week I was on call I was allowed to have the use of a van just in case I was called out in the night, which often happened, especially with the tamping machines. Even when the other two were on call, if there happened to be a problem with one of the tampers, then I would be called out and collected from home.

In the 1970s new tamping machines were being introduced into service. We also had the class '06' Duomatic tampers, which were an up-dated version of a class '04', but with a more sophisticated electrical system and powered by a more powerful Rolls-Royce six-cylinder diesel engine, of which we had six allocated to the division. In addition, several brand new combined tamper and lining machines appeared on the scene and were classified as '07'. These were an altogether different type of machine and were much longer than the others and ran on a set of bogies. Instead of having a trolley out in front to measure the level of the track, the levelling device was an integral part of the machine and operated by an electronic beam. The lining was similar to that used on the standard lining machines. Tensioned wires ran beneath the machine and were attached to small trolleys at either end. When travelling, the trolleys were raised from the rails by a hydraulic cylinder and locked to the machine. The one unusual thing about the '07s' when set up was that they could be operated manually or on their own, by the use of a track sensor without an operator being present, provided the sleepers were evenly spaced and there was nothing lying on the ballast. If there was, the machine just stopped and the operator took over. It was rarely used because it was too much trouble having to keep correcting the mechanism, so most of the time they were worked in the manual mode.

With all this new equipment coming into operation, it was decided to send the fitting staff on training courses, as well as the inspector and myself. The Civil Engineers had set up a training school at The Grove in Watford. The Grove was a large country house on the edge of Watford set in its own grounds and surrounded by fields, and was approached via a long drive off the A411 main road. It had been taken over by the LMS at the beginning of the World War II, and used as their HQ, keeping it away from the bombing in London. After the war it was converted into a management training school, and the temporary buildings in the grounds at the rear had become the civil engineer's department. Because it was difficult to reach, a regular bus service had been set up to run between there and Watford station, to meet and take students arriving off or departing on the trains. Over the years that I was supervisor, I attended the training school on several occasions, usually staying for two weeks and occasionally a month. I was even sent for a month to the management school in the main house on a work study appreciation course. Whether it did me any good I'm not sure, because I thought it was all a waste of time. Other courses I attended were to do with the different make of diesel engines which powered the various types of machine. A one-week residential course was spent at the Deutz engine works in South London to learn about their diesel engines, which were fitted in most of the machines constructed by the Swiss firm of Matisa. Another one-week course took place at the Rolls-Royce diesel engine works training school at Shrewsbury. At the end of this course all students sat an examination and, if we reached an 80 per

The author, *third from the right*, on an '07' tamping machine course at Watford, out on location at Watford Junction station. The rest of the training group were either fitters or supervisors and the gentleman in the centre in a white overall is Willy Hamilton who had played football for Kilmarnock in the Scottish League. *Author's Collection*

In 1972 I was invited to visit the Plasser & Theurer Works at Linz in Austria and during the visit was not only shown around the works but was taken out to the main line to observe one of their latest '08' class tamper/liners under test. The fitter is lying beneath the machine making adjustments to the lining apparatus. *Author*

cent pass rate, qualified as Rolls-Royce diesel engineers. We also received a certificate and were told that this would enable us to obtain a Rolls-Royce engineer's job anywhere in the world. I was proud to have achieved a 93 per cent pass. I was even sent on a one-week course to learn how to operate the class '06' Duomatic tampers. The course was held at Northampton on the line between Northampton Bridge Street station and Blisworth.

Early in 1972 I was invited to visit the Plasser Works at Linz in Austria, so in the spring of that year I booked a week's holiday, took out a free pass, and June and I travelled to Linz. We were well looked after by the works manager, and whilst I was being shown round the works and the training school, even being taken out on to the main line to watch one of their new class '08' tampers at work, June was escorted round the city on a shopping spree. Having not been to Austria before, we took advantage of our pass and enjoyed a visit to Vienna. In Linz I was lucky enough to witness some of the last steam locomotives working on the main lines of Austria, as most of the freight trains to the Czechoslovakian border were being hauled by the class '52' 2-10-0s. There was even the occasional branch line passenger train, being worked by a class '93' 2-8-2T, or a class '77' 4-6-2T. Passenger trains on the Steyrtalbahn narrow gauge line, near Linz, were in the hands of the class '98' 0-6-2Ts, and the odd freight train, worked by a class '99' 0-8-0T.

June and I had enjoyed our first holiday in Austria, and our last evening was spent in Linz, enjoying a delightful meal, hosted by Plassers. During the meal the works manager offered me a position working for Plassers on contract work. The Austrian railways do not own their own track machines, but contract Plassers to do the maintenance for them, and the works manager was looking for supervisors to be responsible for this type of work. It sounded very inviting but I'm sure there would have been a language barrier, and I think the staff would have resented being supervised by a foreigner. But working in the Alpine regions in the summer months would have been a little different from working in the Peak District of Derbyshire, or the coalfields of Nottinghamshire.

The following year I arranged with Plassers to take a group of six on-track plant fitters and electricians, not all from Derby, to Austria to visit the works and spend a day in their training school. Again we did it at our own expense, using up a week of our annual leave and free passes, but once again we were well looked after. As it was a holiday we spent quite a bit of our free time travelling round the railways of Austria, visiting Vienna and other interesting towns and cities, and this time spending a full day travelling the length of the Steyrtalbahn, before the line closed. It did close some years later, but not before I'd made a further visit. A section of it is now preserved, with a few of the original steam locomotives hauling the trains.

Passing through Germany on the way to Austria and seeing the steam locomotives aroused my interest in foreign steam, and I spent the next few years using up my European rail passes, seeking out the last pockets of working steam, especially in Germany. With my fellow enthusiasts I visited the last of the narrow gauge workings in Austria, a steam-worked colliery branch at Ponferrada in northern Spain, the narrow gauge lines leading off from the Douro valley in Portugal, especially the one near Ammerante, and several areas

In the Plasser & Theurer works at Linz where a new ballast cleaner is under construction.
Author

In the Plasser works yards a ballast cleaner is being put through a test before being sold on to whichever railway company had purchased it. The conveyor on the right is for the return of the clean ballast to the track whilst the one on the left is for the disposal of the waste spoil either into wagons or onto the banks and the sides of cuttings.
Author

BACK TO HAPPY DAYS AT DERBY 229

A new ballast cleaner has gone through its tests and is now ready to be dispatched from the Plasser works.   *Author*

in Germany, including the Black Forest, the lines bordering East Germany, the Ruhr valley and the main line between Emden and Rheine in the north. The latter at the time was almost totally worked by steam. The passenger trains were being hauled by the oil-fired, three-cylinder class '012' 4-6-2s, and freight was in the hands of the class '042' 2-8-2s, and '043' and '044' 2-10-0s. These were mostly hauling the 4,000 ton iron ore trains from Emden docks to the steel works of the Ruhr. The final steam workings in Germany were in this area in September 1977, and I travelled over to Rheine with the Locomotive Club of Great Britain for the special events happening over the final weekend. Every timetabled train working between Rheine and Emden was turned over to steam haulage, and many specials ran in between. At Rheine shed there was an exhibition of rolling stock, including several classes of locomotive that had worked in the area in earlier years. It was a sad occasion, but one to remember. Like Britain, we all thought that was to be the end of steam working on the main lines. But since then many steam-hauled special trains have run, and on occasions special weekends have been arranged in certain areas, where steam locomotives have replaced diesels on normal timetabled trains, especially for the delight of the enthusiasts. It raises a lot of revenue for the German railways, as every train is packed to the doors and at times it is difficult to board a train. All the locals turn out and join in with the fun. In recent years, since the Berlin Wall came down, I have visited the steam-worked narrow gauge railways of East Germany and Poland, and the standard gauge lines round Wolsztyn in the Poznan region.

In the early 1970s I was also taking an interest in European railways, especially those still using steam locomotives. One of my favourite countries was Germany especially the line between Rheine and Emden in the north. Departing Rheine and hauling a Cologne to Norddeich Mole express is one of the '012' class oil-burning 3-cylinder Pacifics No. 012-066. *Author*

As well as travelling round Europe to see the railways, I took the opportunity, whilst I had free passes, to pursue one of my other interests, looking at cathedral architecture. Before I left the railway service in 1980, I had visited most of the major cathedrals in Europe, including France, Spain, Portugal, Italy, Germany, Austria, Belgium, Holland, Switzerland, Denmark and Britain. But there are still many more to visit and one day I hope to complete my list.

During my time as on-track supervisor, as well as being responsible for the fitting staff I helped out with the training of management trainees. In the winter months they studied at university, but during the summer vacation were sent out to the various maintenance depots around the region for a period of practical training, and the maintenance of the on-track plant was high on the list. I usually had them with me for 12 weeks and during that time they were expected to do practical work as well as watching me in the office. Several of them didn't like getting their hands dirty, and when I suggested that they should wear a pair of overalls, they often looked down their nose at me. But it made no difference as far as I was concerned, for the only way to learn was to have a go themselves. A boss who never got his hands dirty, in my opinion, is not much good, and half the time does not know what he's talking about if he has not had his hands on the tools. It was no good the fitting staff trying to pull the wool over my eyes, because I'd done it all before and learnt from experience. I am proud to say that one of the trainees I had working with me is now the head of Chiltern Rail, and a very good job he's making of it in introducing new stock and expanding the network.

BACK TO HAPPY DAYS AT DERBY

Surprisingly I had not quite finished working on the steam locomotives, but it had been a long time since I'd had dealings with one, almost 10 years. In early 1974 the *Flying Scotsman* was in Derby and had been stabled overnight in the Etches Park sidings, before travelling down to the Paignton and Dartmouth Railway the following day, which was a Sunday. Attached to it was the old Caledonian Railway observation car, ready to convey Sir William McAlpine, who had recently purchased *Flying Scotsman* from Alan Pegler, after the disastrous tour of the USA.

It was my turn on the Sunday to be the plant supervisor on duty, which meant being in the office from 07.30 to 17.00. From 13.00 there was no supervisor on duty in the traction department, only a fitter for any emergency callouts. If anything went wrong they relied on the P&M to help them out, and if necessary call one of their supervisors. Sir William was due to arrive in the middle of the afternoon by helicopter, landing in a cleared area in the locomotive works. He had just arrived and was boarding the Caledonian coach, when suddenly a heating pipe between the engine and tender on *Flying Scotsman* burst and there was steam everywhere. Panic set in, as they were ready to depart and required heat in the coach for the long journey ahead. Unfortunately the resident engineer, Bill Harvey the former shed master from Norwich, was not present. A member of the staff came rushing into my office, and asked if I could help them out, as the traction fitter didn't know anything about steam locomotives. I borrowed a pair of overalls and went to see what I could do to keep them happy. The heating pipe was a standard fitting, the same as those used on the passenger carriages, and there was plenty in stock

The author on the footplate of *Flying Scotsman* at Derby Etches Park, the photograph was taken by the ex-Norwich shed master Bill Harvey using the author's camera; at the time Bill was the engineer in charge of the maintenance on No. 4472. *Author*

in the stores. I needed the locomotive over a pit, so had a word with the driver and told him to keep the fire low, so that it didn't create too much smoke, and then bring *Flying Scotsman* on to the raised pit just inside the railcar depot. Everyone present was worried because, under normal circumstances, steam locomotives were not allowed inside diesel depots. But when you have an emergency and you want to help someone out you do anything, and I didn't want to turn out to be a bit of a 'job's-worth'. With the help of one of the P&M fitters, I soon had the new pipe fitted, whilst being filmed by Sir William's personal film unit. I never did see the results of the film, but no doubt it is now locked away in an archive and forgotten, until someone unearths it at a later date, and wonders what it's all about, and who those strange men are, performing some kind of ritual on the *Flying Scotsman*. We were both thanked personally by Sir William, and the train then set off on the long journey to Devon, a little later than scheduled, but no doubt happy that someone had helped them out of a mess. I got it the neck next morning for not calling the traction supervisor, but the depot boss thanked me for using my initiative. Nothing was said about bringing the locomotive inside the depot. That was the last time I worked on a steam locomotive, but not the last time I had anything to do with steam.

Working in the office was not exactly exciting and at times I missed working on the machines, but then you can't have everything and have to sacrifice something for promotion and a better pension. I enjoyed the call-outs, especially to supervise the major breakdowns or derailments, and two or three I remembered quite well because I had a few conflicts with the senior management, and I loved it when I was right and they were wrong.

One afternoon I was called to a derailment at Leicester station. A class '06' Duomatic tamper had left the road just south of the station on the up goods road. I took with me a fitter and an electrician, and when we arrived the Leicester Loco depot breakdown train was already on site, trying to re-rail the machine. In charge was the newly appointed depot manager, who two years previously had spent a 12-weeks' stint following me around as a management trainee. I regarded him as a bit of a know-all. On seeing the machine, I suspected that something had gone drastically wrong, because it was standing on a straight section of track, and was hardly likely to have jumped off the road. Just as we arrived on the scene they were lowering a jack, but the right-hand side front wheel would not lower onto the track and stopped about three inches above it. Straightaway I knew that one of the stub axles was broken and checked to see which one it was. Feeling under the machine I found that the left-hand rear axle had sheared, allowing the machine to drop. This was why the front wheel would not lower onto the rail. I went back to the depot manager and asked him if he'd checked for a broken axle, to which he replied, 'I have looked round this machine and it has no broken axle,' so I let him struggle on for a bit longer. The truth was he didn't know what he was looking for. After about 15 minutes, I led him by the arm and pointed out the broken axle. He didn't even apologize and admit he was wrong. 'What do I do now?' he said, to which I replied, 'It's up to you, mate, you are in charge, but I know what I would do, call for the breakdown crane from Toton'. He didn't even believe me then, and said, 'What good would that do?' until I said, 'Okay then, are you going to lift it by hand?' At that point he rushed off to the nearest telephone, and I shouted after him, 'Tell them not to forget to attach a well wagon to the train, to put the tamper on when lifted'. Two hours later the breakdown crane arrived, the tamper was loaded and towed back to Toton, ready for a new wheel set to be fitted the following week.

Only a few months later the same thing happened again, this time on the down goods road at Sileby, north of Leicester. The main back axle broke and let the rear end of the machine collapse onto the track. By the time I got there, the machine and traffic inspectors, between them, had had the sense to send for the breakdown crane. I had only been on site for a few minutes when one of the plant engineer's assistants turned up and tried to take control. The breakdown train duly arrived, but to my surprise they had brought with them a flat top wagon, instead of a well wagon. Some thought had to go into this, because we might be involved in a few problems at a later stage in the proceedings. The crane lifted the tamper, the fitters removed both wheel sets and the machine was ready to be loaded onto the wagon. In the tool van, the breakdown gang had brought with them a set of old sleepers to act as packing for the tamper to sit on, when on the wagon. The supervisor in charge of the gang, who I knew very well, then approached me and asked how many sleepers I required beneath the machine. Thinking about the problems that might occur, I said, 'Just one at each end'. Then an argument broke out between the assistant plant engineer and myself. He said he wanted more sleepers under the machine to raise it at least three sleepers high, to keep it well clear of the wagon. I didn't tell him what I was thinking about, but just said, 'Be it upon your head when we have problems later'. In the end the breakdown supervisor settled the argument by saying, 'It is up to what John wants - as far as I'm concerned, he's in charge'. I had my way and we lowered the machine onto one sleeper, secured it to the wagon, packed the crane away and set off at walking pace to the sidings at Syston station. It was not long before we approached the first road over the bridge at Cossington. Would the top of the machine clear the underside of the bridge? This is what I'd thought about when I first saw the flat wagon. There was just six inches to spare. On arrival at Syston, my first words to the assistant plant engineer were: 'Now you know why I only wanted the machine to stand one sleeper high. If you had had your way we would have been unloading and reloading again'. He thanked me for pointing this out to him, and I replied, 'Put it down to experience'. Like the previous Leicester derailment, again both the up and down goods roads had been blocked to traffic whilst the loading of the machine took place. The breakdown train, on its way back to Toton, dropped the assistant plant engineer and myself off at Sileby and we returned to our respective offices.

On another occasion where I had interference from a member of staff, this time a traffic inspector, was at Desford on the line between Leicester and Burton-on-Trent ('the Alps'). One of the new class '07' tampers running down the little-used goods road to the rear of the signal box had passed the signal and one bogie had run off the end of the catch points and landed on the ballast. The inspector in charge of the machine telephoned to say they were off the road, but were not causing a hold-up to traffic. I grabbed two of the fitters, who were working on a machine in the shed, loaded the van with wooden packing and a couple of lifting jacks and set out for Desford. On arrival I was approached by the traffic inspector, a young man who had obviously just come out of training school and was feeling his feet, 'I've ordered the breakdown train from Toton,' he said, to which I replied, 'Whatever for?' 'There's no way you're going to re-rail that machine without a crane,' was his answer. 'We had better see what we can do then,' I replied. With the help of the operators we jacked up the machine and packed the wood beneath the wheels of the bogie, until they were well above the level of the rails. After lowering them onto the timber packing, I got the operator to ease the machine gently forward until the bogie wheels ran onto the rails. The whole operation had taken about an hour. We were just checking over the machine to make sure it was safe for travelling, when the breakdown train arrived on the scene. Leaning out of the window was the supervisor, who turned out to be Chris, a former apprentice from Colwick, who I knew very well. 'What's your problem?,' he asked. 'Nothing, if I were you I would make my way back to Toton', I replied. Then the air turned blue, 'What idiot ordered the breakdown train?' 'I think you'd better speak to the traffic inspector in the box.' Chris stormed into the box and gave the inspector a lecture on how to run a railway, and said, 'Next time, let the on-track supervisor make the decision, he knows more about tamping machines than you do'. I guess he would never make the same mistake again.

Although I was enjoying my time back at Derby, and I was working with a good set of colleagues, I still had a long way to travel to get to the office each day, so I was always checking the staff vacancy list to see if anything was advertised in or around the Nottingham area. In 1976 I noticed that there was a vacancy for an assistant area manager (engineering) at Grantham, to look after the mechanical engineering facilities in and around the Grantham and Newark areas on the East Coast main line. I put pen to paper and applied, and to my surprise was put on the short list for the vacancy. I had my interview at Gresley House in Doncaster, but this time was unsuccessful. It was the only time I'd been turned down for a staff position. I received a letter from the area manager, explaining why I'd not been successful; apparently several people had applied, but only two of us had been selected for the interview, and the man who got the position was already in the post acting as relief, so it was only fair that he should have it on a permanent basis. He said that I'd had a good interview, and wished me all the best for the future.

It was 1978 before I saw anything on the list to my liking. This time it was a vacancy for a statutory engineering inspector in the chief mechanical and electrical engineer's (CM&EE) department at Nelson Street in Derby, but out-based at Nottingham - just what I was looking for, and it was promotion. The CM&EE had decided to create a new section to deal with all statutory inspections in the London Midland Region of BR. In the past they had been done on an ad hoc basis, calling in outside Insurance Inspectors when required, and it was becoming expensive, so they decided it would be cheaper to do the inspection in house. There were to be nine inspectors spread around the Region, based in the following places: Preston, Manchester, Liverpool, Crewe, Rugby,

BACK TO HAPPY DAYS AT DERBY

London and Nottingham, and two in Birmingham. I applied and had my interview at Nelson Street, which turned out to be a bit of a formality, as they had decided to give the position to me as soon as they'd seen my application. I was given a starting date in June, and to report first to Nelson Street where I was to meet my new boss and the rest of the inspectors.

After 7¼ years in the P&M department as on-track supervisor, I was once again on the move. I was a bit sorry to leave, because in that time I'd made a lot of new friends, especially in other P&M depots. When I first started at the P&M, we formed a P&M Foremans' Association, meeting each other from time to time on a social basis, and once a year spending a few days away on a long weekend break, usually travelling by train and ferry to visit a European city, where we would have a coach tour and on the Saturday evening enjoy our annual dinner. I went several times and enjoyed trips to Holland, staying in Rotterdam and Amsterdam, and to France, where we toured the northern coast around Le Touquet, and on another occasion visited Strasbourg, with a coach tour along the French/German border.

The last thing I did before leaving Derby P&M was to make a recommendation that Malcolm Stevenson should take over from me as on-track supervisor. He had acted as my relief over the years and had done an excellent job. I am pleased to say that he was successful and stayed in the post until he took early redundancy in the 1990s.

The Plant & Machinery supervisors at play, it was not all work! At the time we were all members of the London Midland Region Plant & Machinery Foreman's Association and having a weekend visit in 1973 to northern France, after lunch and a few drinks we were enjoying the sun on the seafront in Le Touquet, it appears as two of us may have had one too many! *Left to right*, Sid Craddock (P&M on-track plant inspector), David Dolman (assistant P&M mechanical foreman), the author (P&M on-track plant supervisor) and Derek Skidmore (P&M mechanical foreman). *Author's Collection*

Chapter Seventeen

Working for the CM&EE

In Nottingham I had to share an office with three other inspectors and their clerks. One of the clerks was George Cooke, who lived in Radcliffe-on-Trent, and had been booking clerk at the local station when I used to visit as a boy in my trainspotting days. It was George who often invited me to join him in the ticket office, when Mr Headland the station master was off duty.

Room 'F' in the area manager's department, was located in a large building across the road from the station entrance in Carrington Street, and had formerly been the main offices for the goods department. It was constructed in 1875 on the site of the old Midland Counties Railway station, which had opened in 1839. It was a large room, so there was plenty of space for me to have my desk and filing cabinet. But it did not really matter as I would be spending a lot of my time out on the road, and only came into the office once a week to make up and file the records.

We had difficulty setting up a programme for the Nottingham Division, owing to problems with the unions sorting out the lines of demarcation. All the other areas had been completed before the posts were advertised. So the boss at Nelson Street, Derby used me for the first year as relief to the other Inspectors, when on holiday or off work sick, which was fine with me as I got to travel the length and breadth of the London Midland Region, and worked anywhere between London and Carlisle and West Wales. I spent a lot of time helping the inspector at Crewe, who had too much to do owing to the distances he had to travel. The district should really have been split in two, and two inspectors employed. When there I worked from an office in the centre of Crewe station, so it was handy for catching the trains.

The inspections varied from loose lifting tackle, such as slings and chains, to passenger lifts and escalators, all types of cranes, including road, rail and overhead cranes, tracklayers, road motor vehicle lifts, hotel food hoists and locomotive lifting jacks. Lifts, escalators and loose lifting tackle, etc., had to be inspected every six months, and cranes and hoists between 12 and 14 months, but to keep the records straight we did them 12-monthly. The inspector had the final word and if anything was found to be faulty, it was taken out of service until it had been repaired. Very often with the cranes and lifts it would be a worn or damaged wire lifting rope that required replacing. I remember condemning a rope on one of the lifts on Crewe station and placed the lift out of service, which caused all sorts of problems for the station staff. The station manager tried to talk me into letting it go, but it made no difference and the rope had to be changed, which took the P&M fitters about two hours. If he had overruled me, and some one had got hurt, then it would have resulted in a court case and he would have been dismissed.

During my time as inspector I travelled to most major places on the London Midland Region, some of the more interesting places I visited being Carnforth, Ullswater and Barrow-in-Furness in the Lake District, and Carlisle. Travelling there I had my one and only ride on the footplate of a main line electric locomotive, No. 87011 *The Black Prince* between Preston and Carlisle. Hauling 11 coaches, she topped Shap Summit at 70 mph. In Wales I inspected the loose lifting tackle at Llandudno Junction and Holyhead, the road motor vehicle lifts at Llandudno station and the food hoist in the refreshment room at Aberystwyth. But some of the more interesting jobs were the inspections of the steam breakdown cranes at Manchester Trafford Park, Chester and Toton (the ex-Colwick 36-ton crane). It's good to know that at least two of them have been preserved. I even got sent on a one-week training course, to the Cowan, Sheldon crane works in Carlisle, where I spent most of the time in Kingmoor marshalling yard learning how to operate and carry out inspections on their new 75-ton diesel breakdown cranes.

At the beginning of 1979, I fell on my way to the office in Nottingham and dislocated my right shoulder and was off work for the next three months. It was the first time I'd spent such a long time away from work in all my 26 years in railway service; before it just been an odd day here and there.

By mid-1979 I was finally allowed to take up my post carrying out the inspections in the Nottingham Division, which limited my travelling to a smaller area, but meant that I would be back home each evening at a more reasonable hour of the day.

In March 1980 I was walking through the Minster at Southwell when the then Provost offered me the post of head verger, which was becoming vacant at the end of September. I said I would think about it, but I was quite happy working for the railway, and as far as I was concerned would be staying with them until I retired. Besides I could not see the Minster paying me a salary equivalent to what I received from the railway. Whilst I was giving it some thought the shock news came from Nelson Street that in a few months' time they would be moving me from Nottingham to Stanier House in Birmingham. Most of the offices in Derby were closing down with the staff being moved to Birmingham as it was a more central location.

This made my mind up for me, as neither June nor I wanted to move to Birmingham. We had done enough moving about in my time working for the railway. The Minster matched my salary in a roundabout way, by offering June part-time work, and for us to have one of their houses to live in. This was a big help, because father-in-law, who by then was a widower, could now give up his home and live in our bungalow.

I gave the railway six weeks' notice, so that they could advertise the position and appoint someone, and I could then give my successor at least a week's training before I left. To my delight they appointed one of my former apprentices.

I finished my railway service on 3rd October, 1980, but not before my colleagues had given me a big send-off. I was taken to the chief mechanical engineer's office in Nelson Street, Derby, for a presentation, and to my surprise many of the men I had worked with in earlier days had turned up to say farewell. June and I were then taken out for a five-course meal, all paid for by my friends and colleagues. I still meet a lot of them, and on occasions we have reunions in Derby.

The presentation on my leaving the railway in October 1980. The event took place in the chief mechanical engineer's office at Nelson Street in Derby and was performed by Bill Taylor the then CME, and to my surprise many of my former colleagues from around the area were present as this photograph portrays. My wife, June, holds a bouquet which was presented to her.

Author's Collection

The modern day image of the civil engineers on-track plant is a far cry from my time in the 1960s and 1970s. This photograph taken in January 2011 is of a Volker-rail ballast regulator in the sidings at Leicester station, not quite like the old Matisa 'Basil Brush'! *Author*

After leaving the railway in October 1980 I took up employment at Southwell Minster in Nottinghamshire as head verger, still supervisory but very different from railway work. This view of the Minster is looking towards the west facade showing its very distinctive 'pepper pot' towers, and on the left the famous chapter house, noted for its carved 'Leaves of Southwell'.
Author

So on the 4th October, 1980, after 25 years, nine months and seven days, I was no longer a railwayman but had become an employee of the Church of England.

I often think back to those days, and think of the times I sat on the platform at Radcliffe-on-Trent station, noting down the numbers and making records of the various classes that passed through. I thought too about the time I was employed in the locomotive depot, when during the lunch break I would wander round the shed, taking stock of the many different classes that had worked in from other areas. I only wish those days could return; what a time I would have with my notebook and the trusty Ian Allan ABC!

Postscript

After I ceased to work for the railway company and lost the use of free passes and privilege tickets, my interest in the railways has never waned, in fact I have become even more enthusiastic and over the years have travelled the length and breadth of the British Isles and most countries in Europe, visiting many preserved lines and seeking out and photographing the last of the remaining steam locomotives. Amongst my favourite countries are those of Ireland, the Isle of Man, Poland and Germany, especially the narrow gauge lines in the old East Germany. And in 2002 I fulfilled a life-long dream, when my son and I visited India to travel on the Darjeeling Himalayan Railway, a line I regard as being one of the most spectacular in the world.

240   STEAM, DIESELS AND ON-TRACK MACHINES

Although I left BR in 1980 I have never lost my love of all things railway, especially chasing the last of the working steam locomotives. And in 2002 I fulfilled a lifelong dream of visiting the Darjeeling Himalayan Railway in India, and here we see one of the Glasgow-built 0-4-0STs, No. 779, taking water at Tung hauling our special train to Darjeeling. *Author*

I have also continued to pursue my many other interests, especially that of church architecture, and on my railway travels have managed to visit many more of the major cathedrals of Europe. And when possible I still manage to climb the steps of many churches and practise the art of campanology (bell-ringing). Long may my journeys and visits continue!

Acknowledgements

First of all I must dedicate this book and also say thank you to all my former railway colleagues past and present, without them it would never have been written.

I would also like to thank my two proof readers Penny Young and David Jager for all their help and encouragement when at times I felt like giving in, and especially to Christopher James of the Southwell Railway Club for writing the Foreword.

And to the many friends and societies who have allowed me the use of photographs, including former railway colleagues Malcolm Stevenson, Sid Craddock and Frank Berridge, also Robin Sharman of the Southwell Railway Club, photographic friends and fellow line-siders Syd Hancock and John Clarke, Paul Shannon, Allan Sibley of the GNRS, Midland Railway Trust and Graham Stacey of RAS for the use of the former Photomatic photographs.

A special thanks to Jane and Ian Kennedy of Oakwood Press for their help and assistance.

Last, but certainly not least, a big thank you must go to my wife June, who has put up with all my endless questions and computer problems and has given me support and encouragement in completing the book.